BEYOND THE PROTECTIVE STATE

BEYOND THE PROTECTIVE STATE

The political economy of Australia's manufacturing industry policy

ANN CAPLING

Department of History, University of Calgary

and

BRIAN GALLIGAN

Federalism Research Centre, Australian National University

CAMBRIDGE
UNIVERSITY PRESS

Published by the Press Syndicate of the University of Cambridge
The Pitt Building, Trumpington Street, Cambridge CB2 1RP, UK
40 West 20th Street, New York, NY 10011-4211, USA
10 Stamford Road, Oakleigh, Melbourne, Victoria 3166, Australia

First published 1992

Printed in Australia by Australian Print Group

National Library of Australia cataloguing in publication data
Capling, M. Ann (Margaret Ann), 1959–
Beyond the protective state: the political economy of Australia's manufacturing industry policy.
Includes index.
ISBN 0 521 41626 4
ISBN 0 521 42629 4 (pbk.).
1. Protectionism – Australia. 2. Australia – Industries. 3. Australia – Manufactures. 4. Industry and state – Australia. 5. Australia – Commercial policy. I. Galligan, Brian, 1945– . II. Title.
382.45670994

Library of Congress cataloguing in publication data
Capling, M. Ann, 1959–
Beyond the protective state: the political economy of Australia's manufacturing industry policy / M. Ann Capling and Brian Galligan.
Includes index.
ISBN 0-521-41626-4. – ISBN 0-521-42629-4 (pbk.)
1. Australia – Manufactures – Government policy. 2. Australia – Commercial policy. I. Galligan, Brian, 1945– . II. Title.
HD9738.A82C36 1993
338.4'767'0994 – dc20 92-17349 CIP

A catalogue record for this book is available from the British Library

ISBN 0 521 41626 4 hardback
ISBN 0 521 42629 4 paperback

To our beloved spouses
Roslyn and Shane

Contents

Figures and Tables

Figures

Tables

Preface

Since the 1980s, Australia has been undergoing a quiet revolution in manufacturing industry policy. Protection, which was its core and a settled part of Australian politics and public policy during nearly a century of federation, has been abolished. The federal Labor government, under Prime Minister Bob Hawke from 1983 until late 1991 and continuing under his successor Paul Keating, switched national policy from tariff protection to corrective policies of phasing out tariffs and facilitating structural adjustment through quasi-corporatist plans for troubled sectors such as steel, motor vehicles and textiles, clothing and footwear. The implementation of corrective policies entailed a reassertion of state action comparable in significance to that used in forging Australia's protective state in the early decades of federation.

Our book is a historical and theoretical account of this transition from a protective to a corrective state. It provides a comprehensive account of the corrective policies of the Hawke government and the special industry plans devised by its industry minister, Senator John Button. These are contrasted with the protective policies that typified Australia's traditional political economy in order to highlight the extent of the transformation that has occurred. For this purpose we have developed a statist approach, in preference to using alternative pluralist, Marxist or corporatist paradigms, which blends the insights of pre-war Australian political economy with those of modern institutional analysis.

In the book we have tried to show just how fundamental the transformation from a protective to a corrective state has been and, indeed, needed to be. Our historical and political economy perspectives should, we hope, give an appropriate focus and context for scholarly evaluation of the current changes and assist in the reorientation of public attitudes. The book should also help to highlight the internal compensation gap that is emerging in the new national policy of deregulation and exposure of Australia's economy to international market forces. Generations of Australians forged and consolidated a protective state to ensure a stable and prosperous life in a domestic economy protected from the volatile world market. The current challenge is to devise alternative ways of coping which, inevitably, will entail a different role for the state in Australian political economy but one that has not yet been fully developed. Nor is Australia's national deregulatory policy without risk as the major trading countries of North America and Europe retreat into giant trading blocs from which Australia is excluded or, like Japan, persist with protective practices.

In a sense, this book is a by-product of a larger comparative project on the role of the state in managing national economic policies in Australia and Canada. These two 'most similar' countries have gone in quite different directions in recent years. Canada has opted to join the United States in a Free Trade Agreement which has created a major world trading bloc, soon to encompass all of North America with the inclusion of Mexico. In contrast, Australia has nowhere to go and, since protection is no longer viable, must become more competitive and live by its wits. This book tells part of that story – the jettisoning of protection and implementation of corrective policies to force greater competition and industry restructuring in manufacturing. The story told here is incomplete in ways we plan to remedy in the larger comparative study which will include agriculture and trade policy.

The ending of this story is uncertain and not necessarily a happy one because only time will tell whether the brave Australian experiment of unilaterally dismantling protection has been beneficial or disastrous. With some trepidation, we assume the former. We also argue that there was no real alternative to this dismantling process since Australia's great primary exporting industries such as wool and, more recently, coal could no longer support the massive costs of protecting manufacturers. In any case, we are convinced that Australia's move beyond the protective state in manufacturing industry policy is of such far reaching significance and complexity to merit a separate book.

Joint authorship requires intensive working together, with a certain meeting of minds and marrying of prose styles as well as a flexible division of labour. Up to a point, you can blame the other guy but finally both authors have to work through it all together. Our collaboration was made possible in the first instance by support towards the larger comparative project from the Canadian government's first Canada–Australia Bicentennial Research Award which rescued Capling from the exclusive demands of motherhood and writing her doctoral thesis in the suburbs of Canberra. Subsequent support for research and writing was provided by the Australian National University's Federalism Research Centre (FRC) and Monash University's Public Sector Management Institute (PSMI). We should like to acknowledge the generous support of these illustrious institutions, and the personal enthusiasm of Cliff Walsh, FRC's Director, Alan Fels, PSMI's Director, and Owen Hughes, our good friend, colleague and fixer.

In writing the book, we have been assisted by personal interviews and written feedback on draft chapters from a number of key people. Senator John Button took time out from his busy schedule of making industry policy and leading the government in the Senate to read various draft chapters and talk at length about manufacturing industry policy from his vantage point. He also allowed us to use an important source document in which he had formulated his early views on industry policy. Others who offered valuable insights or comments on drafts included the following: Cliff Dolan, previously President of the ACTU and a key member of the Steel Advisory Authority; David McCarthy, formerly of the TCF Development Authority; Brian Broomhall of AFTWUA; Peter Krietals of the TCF Council of Australia; Paul Sexton of the Automotive Industry Authority; Jeff Borland of the Economics Department of Melbourne University; Ian Cox of the Carpet Institute of Australia; Richard Curtain of the National Key Centre for Industrial Relations, Monash University; David Nelson of AUSTRADE; and Andrew Webster, formerly of the Confederation of Australian Industries (CAI) as well as John Sullivan and other officials from BHP who combed the steel chapter and provided us with the tables on the steel industry. In addition, two anonymous readers for Cambridge University Press provided useful critical comments on the manuscript. We should like to acknowledge the helpful assistance of all these people.

We have also taken advantage of the usual academic forums to try out our ideas. Papers on 'Tariff policy in Australia and Canada: From the Protective to the Corrective State' and 'The Hawke Government and Corporatism' were presented respectively at the

Biennial Conference of the Association for Canadian Studies in Australia and New Zealand at the University of New England in July 1990 and the Annual Conference of the Australasian Political Studies Association in Hobart in September 1990. Parts of these have been incorporated into the earlier chapters of the book. Chapter 2 has also drawn fairly extensively on an earlier article by Galligan, 'The state in Australian political thought' in *Politics* (now the *Australian Journal of Political Science*), Vol. 19, No. 2, 1984, pp. 82–92. An earlier version of Chapter 7 was also published by the authors as 'Sectoral corporatism with a difference: the Textiles, Clothing and Footwear Plan' in *Australian Journal of Public Administration*, Vol. 50, No. 1, 1991, pp. 47–60.

Throughout this project we have relied heavily on the cheerful assistance of a number of special people at the Federalism Research Centre. David Mardiste has been the ideal research assistant throughout and has played a major role in the collection and compilation of seemingly endless government reports, press clippings and background materials. He and we relied extensively on the comprehensive newspaper clipping archive of the Political Science Program maintained so professionally by Gill Evans. Stephanie Hancock, assisted by Megan Wells, has helped to type and format numerous drafts and the final manuscript. Linda Gosnell has assisted with a multitude of arrangements in keeping the project on course as Capling moved first to Melbourne and then to Calgary. Bridget Brooklyn read the final manuscript. We should like to thank all of these, and finally Cambridge University Press for publishing the book. Any errors or omissions remain, of course, our joint responsibility.

ANN CAPLING AND BRIAN GALLIGAN
Calgary and Canberra

Abbreviations

ACI	Australian Consolidated Industries Limited
ACPI	Advisory Council on Prices and Incomes
ACTU	Australian Council of Trade Unions
AFTWUA	Amalgamated Footwear and Textile Workers Union of Australia
AIA	Automotive Industry Authority
AIDC	Australian Industry Development Corporation
AIS	Australian Iron and Steel Company
ALP	Australian Labor Party
AMC	Australian Manufacturing Council
AUSTRADE	Australian Trade Commission
BHP	Broken Hill Proprietary Company Limited
BIE	Bureau of Industry Economics
CBU	completely built-up
CDB	Commonwealth Development Bank
CER	Closer Economic Relations (with New Zealand)
CES	Commonwealth Employment Service
CRA	Conzinc Riotinto of Australia
DEET	Department of Employment, Education and Training
DITAC	Department of Industry, Technology and Commerce
DPIE	Department of Primary Industries and Energy
DPM&C	Department of the Prime Minister and Cabinet
EEC	European Economic Community
EFS	Export Facilitation Scheme
EMDG	Export Market Development Grants Scheme
EPAC	Economic Planning Advisory Council
FIA	Federated Ironworkers Association
FVIU	Federation of Vehicle Industry Unions
GATT	General Agreement on Tariffs and Trade
GBE	government business enterprise
GDP	gross domestic product
GM	General Motors
GMH	General Motors-Holden's Automotive Limited
HEC	Holden Engine Company

IAC	Industries Assistance Commission
IC	Industry Commission
IEP	Industry Efficiencies Program
ILO	International Labour Organisation
IRC	Industrial Relations Commission
MFA	Multi-Fibre Arrangement
MIT	Massachusetts Institute of Technology
NPA	National Preference Agreement
NSW	New South Wales
OECD	Organisation for Economic Cooperation and Development
PBS	Pharmaceutical Benefits Scheme
R&D	research and development
SAA	Special Advisory Authority
SIA	Steel Industry Authority
SIAC	Steel Industry Advisory Council
SIDCAI	Standing Interdepartmental Committee on Assistance to Industry
TAA	Temporary Assistance Authority
TCF	textiles, clothing and footwear
TCFCA	Textiles, Clothing and Footwear Council of Australia
TCFDA	Textiles, Clothing and Footwear Development Authority
TDC	Trade Development Council
UNCTAD	United Nations Conference on Trade and Development

CHAPTER 1
Introduction

Protective statism has been the dominant mode of Australian political economy for most of its history since federation, but this has been challenged in recent years by liberal economic ideas and greater reliance on market forces. The ability of Australia to maintain its positions of protected privilege and relative affluence has finally been undermined by the impact of dynamic changes in the international order that have eroded the profitability of traditional commodity markets and threatened protected and inefficient industries. In order to appreciate the transformation that has occurred in Australian industry policy, it is necessary to set the present transition towards a corrective state within the context of the past established order of national protection.

THE ROLE OF THE STATE

The state has always played a central role in Australian political economy and has been especially prominent in the country's industry policy. After the constitutional framework had been put in place at federation in 1901, Australian nationhood was achieved through the implementation and manipulation by the new Commonwealth government of grand national policies: land settlement, immigration, and the provision of transport and commercial infrastructure in opening up vast and relatively inhospitable lands; the provision of public utilities and support schemes to assist production and stabilise the marketing of primary commodities in volatile world markets; the nurturing and protection of manufacturing industry to diversify the national economy into import-replacing manufacturing industries; and the operation of a comprehensive system of arbitration that set national wages, partly redistributed the benefits of protection to labour and generally mediated in industrial relations so as to ensure fair rates of pay and reasonable conditions of work. This statist political economy of the Commonwealth government was derived from the earlier 'state socialism' of colonial governments during the nineteenth century which persisted among state governments after federation.

Perhaps at the very beginning, we should indicate how and why we use the term 'state' which pervades the entire book. As should be clear from the context, the terms 'state', 'statism' and 'statist' refer to the system of government or the government as authoritative actor and formative policy-maker, as in 'the protective state'. With a federal system such as that of Australia, usage is complicated somewhat because 'the state' can mean the total system of Commonwealth and state governments as in 'the state in Australia', or either the Commonwealth government or state governments separately. And there is of course the further complication that regional government entities are called states in Australia rather than provinces as in Canada. Since our subject is national manufacturing industry policy after federation, state usually refers to the Commonwealth level of government which has prime responsibility for such policy. That is not always the case, however, but the meaning should be clear from the context.

We have preferred to use the term 'state', rather than 'government' which is more usual among pluralist political writers, because it encapsulates both the enduring institutional framework of government and established public policies which persist as governments and elections come and go. Such usage is standard for political economy, both in the earlier Australian literature and in contemporary writing, as Chapter 2 makes clear. In that chapter, we review the main conceptual paradigms which have been used in analysing Australian industry policy and business–government relations. We work towards a broad definition of the state in terms of what it is, what it does, and how that varies over time. We view the state as a distinct but complex organisation capable of formulating and implementing purposive national policies which influence groups and individuals in society as well as economic development.

To study national policy-making, policy implementation and policy maintenance, we need to focus both on the state as a unified organisation and on the activities and interrelationships of the relevant parts that have primary influence over the policies at issue. Furthermore, since political economy and public policy are historically contingent, the role of the state has to be articulated on the basis of historical research rather than from *a priori* theorising. This we do broadly in Chapters 3 and 4, and for specific industry sectors in Chapters 5, 6 and 7.

POLITICAL ECONOMY, PROTECTION AND INDUSTRY POLICY

Our purpose throughout is to describe and interpret the central role of the state in national manufacturing industry policy and to show how this has been changing in fundamental ways. The book is about 'bringing the state back in'[1] to focus by explaining its key role in the formation and consolidation of Australian manufacturing industry through developmental, protective and redistributive national policies. We argue that, in fact, the state has never been 'out' in its primary role of anchoring the formative national policies of Australia, but rather ignored or overlooked by post-war political scientists who focused on the fine details of party politics and took for granted the larger, established national policies that structured such politics. To an extent, the state began to be brought back into political analysis in the 1980s when Australian scholars took stock of changing roles of the Commonwealth government and state governments in coping with new challenges arising in a range of policy areas (including mineral resource development[2] and economic management generally[3]). This changed focus is nicely illustrated in Martin Painter's recent study of the restructuring of central agencies in three states, a book appropriately entitled *Steering the Modern State.*[4]

The state has always been the main steering agent in Australia's political economy. Only by recognising its real, albeit constrained, autonomy for coordinating policy and keeping in place major national policies which shape political and economic activity can we properly appreciate the overall character of Australia's political economy and especially the changes that have been taking place since the early 1980s. Moreover, unless we appreciate the strength and pervasiveness of protectionism as Australia's national industry policy, we are unlikely to appreciate the full extent of the transformation that has been taking place. The state has been reducing its protective role in industry policy by winding down tariffs in order to expose Australian manufacturing industry to international market competition. At the same time, to help compensate the weaker sectors such as the automotive industry and textiles, clothing and footwear, it has improved structural change by means of specific industry plans.

Chapter 2 argues the case for fully reinstating the state and reviving the earlier political economy perspective that was strong in Australia before the Second World War. This statist perspective received its classic formulation in W. K. Hancock's depiction of the state as a 'vast public utility' which was at the core of the 'system of political economy' developed by Australians in their national attempt to soften, exclude or overcome international market forces.[5] The chapter reviews critically the pluralist perspective that was predominant in Australian political science through the 1960s, and the alternative Marxist and corporatist paradigms that were shaped in the 1970s and 1980s in a bid to explain Australia's post-war policies and its political economy. It proposes instead a statist approach that focuses on the primary role of the state: in other words, a synthesis of Hancock's earlier political economy and a renewed focus on state institutions and their officials.

According to this approach, national policy is influenced but not set by the interplay of social groups or classes, nor is it determined by economic forces (although they obviously shape and constrain the options and opportunities for policy development). Rather, national policy depends primarily upon governments, ministers and public officials organised in, and operating through, the institutions of the state. Of course policy-making and implementation is only partly voluntaristic and instrumental since it is the product of the action and reaction of state organisations and officials among themselves and with a complex and changing array of factors. These include individuals, corporations, interest groups and industry sectors, major events, technological innovation and structural changes due to economic and social forces, with all of these interacting in a national system open to both the direct impact and indirect influences of international political and economic affairs. Obviously, given the domestic complexity and international permeability of such a system, the state apparatus of a single nation state cannot be the sole or autonomous determinant of national policy. But, we contend it is the primary one – and since it synthesises all the others (to an extent) in the process of national policy initiatives and responses, it is the appropriate place at which to focus this analysis.

In summary then, Chapter 2 argues that the state has a real capacity for independent policy development that is both purposive in its effects and enduring over time. Such capacity for autonomous policy action is essentially contingent and variable because it is realised through an interactive process with other variables over time. Actual state power and effectiveness wax and wane, so must be studied not by *a priori* reasoning but through political and historical analysis. We therefore develop and defend this statist approach through a process of critical reflection on alternative conceptual frameworks.

In Chapter 3 we characterise the established role that the national state performed until the 1980s as essentially a protective one. We trace the history of Australia's protective statism from 'New Protection', which first legitimated the national tariff during the decade of federation, to the more persuasive 'Protection All Round' which extended state support to areas of agricultural production as well as to manufacturing. This national synthesis reached its high point in McEwenism during the 1950s and 1960s, but its main features and rationale were all in place thirty years earlier with the 'Scullin tariff' which had pushed Australian protection to record levels. McEwen was not the father of protection but only its most prominent post-war exponent.

New Protection enabled some of the benefits of tariff protection to be redistributed from manufacturing capital to labour. Importantly, this was done by an independent state arbitration system which mediated between corporate owners and wage labourers in a way that was acceptable to both sides and only partly reflective of market considerations. New Protection was in turn part of the wider political economy of White Australia in which national policies of racial exclusivity were fused with concerns for high standards of living and fair and reasonable wages and conditions of work. The protective state kept out both cheap non-white labourers and cheap foreign products, and through state arbitration of national wage levels passed on a proportion of the benefits from protection to the labour force - benefits which would otherwise have accrued to manufacturers. In fact New Protection for manufacturing industry had its origins in an earlier scheme for the sugar industry that entailed compensating sugar growers for the termination of cheap Kanaka labour through ensuring higher domestic prices in a protected national market. The growers were paid additional bounties for employing white labourers, with payment of these bounties being made dependent on their paying reasonable wages. Thus New Protection was far more extensive than the particular Lib–Lab compromise that Prime Minister Deakin had stitched together to support a precarious political alliance in the early Parliament and which was embodied in the Excise Tariff Act of 1906. While that initiative was defeated by a conservative High Court,[6] the larger battle for comprehensive protectionism with benefits shared between capital and labour was well and truly won[7] – and a whole continent was thereby secured for protective nation building.

'Protection All Round' entailed the extension of state assistance to agricultural industries through price subsidies, bounties, marketing schemes and protected domestic markets. As summed up by the eminent economic historian, Edward Shann:

> The national policy of protection, having taken Labour under one wing, could surely find room under the other for its older allies the farmers. It had already befriended the sugar growers, and war-time expedients had shown how 'orderly marketing' might proceed. Out of such beginnings rose the ideal of protection all round.[8]

Of course, protection all round is a nonsense for a modern economy that is highly dependent on trade because someone eventually has to pay the cost. In Australia this fell on the strong agricultural export industries – wheat, meat and especially wool – and increasingly on bulk mineral commodities such as coal and iron ore from the 1960s. Through this national system of cross-subsidisation, the costs of 'both protected manufacturer and privileged labour' were 'passed back to the exporting industries by all and sundry in the sheltered industries'.[9] The popular aphorism of 'Australia riding on the sheep's back' was an apt metaphor for the economic basis of protectionism, but for prophetic economists like L. F. Giblin this was something of a nightmare:

> The cost to the consumer must be paid for out of production, and in the last resort out of production for exports. The sheltered industries and occupations . . . as well as the protected industries, are all supported by the exporting industries, and as these one by one themselves demand and receive protection, it looks as if the day were not far off when the whole burden would fall on wool. The vision that comes is of Australia as one enormous sheep bestriding a bottomless pit, with statesman, lawyer, miner, landlord, farmer and factory hand all hanging on desperately to the locks of its abundant fleece.[10]

While the sheep's back remained strong and the international wool market buoyant, Australia's protective statism had a secure economic base. But it was anchored in much more than an economic base, as Hancock explained: 'Protection in Australia has been more than a policy: it has been a faith and a dogma' that had become 'interwoven with almost every strand of Australia's domestic nationalism'.[11] In this way, Australia's protective statism was thoroughly grounded, as Britain's post-war statism was not,[12] in its national political culture as well as its political economy.

With the demise of the Free Trade Party shortly after federation, protectionism was supported by all Australian political parties until the 1970s. The two major parties that have dominated Australian politics since 1910, Liberal (under its various guises) and Labor, found common cause in protecting the mutual interests of both industrial capital and labour. The partisan differences of these two great parties were accommodated within the established national policies of protective statism. Indeed, it was the Lib–Lab political coalition which, having ousted the free-traders after federation began to set in place the policies for protectionism. Nor was this consensus disturbed by the Country Party which entered the political scene in the 1920s, because it fought for the extension of protection to agriculture rather than its overall abolition. In fact protection all round reached its apogee in McEwenism during the 1950s and 1960s when Country Party leader, John McEwen, who dominated the trade and industry portfolio in the Menzies government, forged a powerful coalition of primary producers and manufacturers that sustained both protectionism and the Country Party's political influence. Both were unduly prolonged into the 1970s because of lucrative minerals and energy booms that were accompanied by exaggerated expectations about Australia's future prosperity from such sources.

Protection all round was not sustainable, however; Australia's overall trading position declined considerably in relative terms during the post-war decades. Australia's inefficient manufacturing industries became less competitive against imports from more technologically advanced economies and newly industrialised Asian countries. At the same time, the world became less dependent on the primary commodities that traditionally powered Australia's export economy. Added to this was the power of critical ideas that finally took their toll on protectionism. Despite the early demise of the Free Trade Party, protectionism had always had its critics; in the early years these were a handful of dissenting economists such as Giblin and Shann. Nevertheless, and this is one of the ironies of Australia's protective state, there has always been a quasi-independent institution - first the Interstate Commission, then the Tariff Board and its more recent mutants, the Industries Assistance Commission and the Industry Commission - charged with a public watchdog function. Although often captive of the dominant protectionist ideology and interests, these bodies provided some corrective to rampant protectionism and, more recently, trenchant rebuttals of its whole basis.

Chapter 3 shows how the critique of protectionism was kept alive as a countervailing, if minor, theme during the decades when protectionism was paramount until, in the 1980s, it became the new orthodoxy. This painful learning process occurred gradually through the reports of the Tariff Board and special commissions of inquiry during the 1960s and 1970s. Changing the public mind was assisted by a spread of ideas from neo-classical economics which had become pervasive among the senior bureaucrats in Canberra's central agency departments during the 1980s and which provided the intellectual ammunition for the final assault on protectionism. With greater appreciation of the costs and inefficiencies of protection came increasing public acceptance of corrective ideas favouring free trade and industry restructuring. Partly through the power of economic ideas, partly because of the new coalition of interests that were penalised by high tariffs, but largely because of the impact of international forces and the growing perception of Australia's deteriorating economic standing relative to other countries, the political parties, and in particular the Labor Party, backed away from outright protectionism.

For the Labor Party and the Hawke government, such a switch from protectionism was possible only because of a quiet revolution in trade union thinking that has also been taking place. As Ewer, Higgins and Stevens have documented, unions in the Australian manufacturing sector were involved in 'a fundamental change of orientation, from being opponents of modernisation and rationalisation in industry, to becoming leading proponents of industrial renewal and expansion'.[13] Long regarded as the 'retarded adult' of the Australian political and economic system where, as Max Walsh described it in 1979,[14] mental development had lagged far behind its physical strength, the union movement broke with its traditional commitment to blanket protection and *ad hoc* assistance to industry during the 1980s. Instead, unions have become major advocates of industry restructuring, public sector reform and improved management and work practices. Although uneven across unions, as we shall see in examining particular industry sectors in later chapters, and as yet only partly realised in streamlined union organisation and more efficient work practices, the changes in union thinking and culture have been quite profound. But it is fanciful to attribute the structural irrationality and technical backwardness of Australian manufacturing industry to some past 'absence of a union input into the direction of industrial development', as Ewer, Higgins and Stevens do,[15] rather than to protectionism which the unions supported along with manufacturers and governments of all stripes. It would be just as implausible to cast the union movement as the 'initiator of reform' battling the recalcitrant and traditional Hawke government during the 1980s.[16]

In any case, the union movement was relatively slow in turning its thinking away from protectionism. The transformation of public thinking that had occurred earlier in governments and bureaucracies was reflected, in due course, in the conversion of state organisations from protective to corrective purposes. Such changes are strikingly apparent in the freeing of the Tariff Board, under Alf Rattigan's independent leadership, from the pervasive protectionist ideology, interests and fiefdom of McEwen's Trade and Industry Department, and in its becoming an effective opponent of protection. This process of transformation was given institutional effect when the Whitlam Labor government restructured the Tariff Board into the Industries Assistance Commission in 1974, and subsequently carried further when the Hawke Labor government made it the Industry Commission in 1989. The Industry Commission has spearheaded the initiative for micro-economic reform of the public sector through critical reviews of government business enterprises, the provision of public infrastructure and services, and regulatory arrangements. Thus, the organisation that protected the private manufacturing sector for so long has now become the pace-setter in streamlining both the private and public sectors. Similarly, McEwen's old stronghold of the Department of Trade and Industry has been restructured in various ways: by creating a mega-department of Foreign Affairs and Trade that recognises that Australia's foreign interests are linked fundamentally with its trade; and by linking industry with technology and commerce in the Department of Industry, Technology and Commerce.

The corrective national industry policy of tariff reduction was adopted somewhat tentatively by the Hawke government when it came to office in 1983, but then with greater commitment after the collapse of the terms of trade and the scare in 1985–86 of Australia's becoming a 'banana republic'. After very extensive public discussion and despite some wavering by senior ministers such as John Dawkins in late 1990, the Hawke government finally committed itself to the virtual elimination of all tariffs by the turn of the century. This was unequivocally spelt out in the prime minister's statement on industry policy in March 1991.[17] Such commitment to tariff reduction, however, does not mean a reduced role for the state but rather a quite different one of encouragement, facilitation and promotion of industry – the provision of 'warm infrastructure', as Senator Button has put it[18] – as well as sectoral amelioration for troublesome industries through special plans. The patchwork of such policies that have been progressively put in place by the federal Labor government since 1983 is analysed in Chapter 4.

In its various initiatives for stabilisation of labour markets, amelioration of the adverse effects of tariff reduction on particular highly protected industries, and facilitation and promotion of more technologically advanced and export oriented industries, the Hawke government has been partly heir to Laborist traditions of union cooperation and statist action. But it has also used its Accord with the trade union movement[19] and the institutions of the state for corrective purposes of deregulation and industry restructuring that represent, in sum, a significant new orientation for an Australian government (and a Labor government at that). Similarly, the Labor govenment's sectoral plans have continued, but greatly changed the focus of, special industry arrangements that had been started by previous Liberal coalition governments.

In Chapter 4 we discuss a range of policies that the Hawke government has been putting in place, including the 'Partnerships for Development' scheme to secure a share of state-of-the-art manufacturing for Australian companies, trade facilitation, assistance for exporters, incentives for restructuring, and encouragement for reskilling in the workplace. The direction and motivation, if not the achievement, of this patchwork of policy initiatives show just how extensively the role of the state has changed in recent years away from protective policies towards corrective and facilitative ones and market solutions. And it is the state that is bringing about that transition through the deregulation of capital and exchange markets, phased tariff reduction combined with ameliorative sectoral plans for troubled industries and micro-economic reform of the public sector.

In Chapters 5, 6, and 7 we move from the macro-level of national policy to the meso-level of sectoral plans for specific industries. The three industry sectors examined in these chapters are the major ones of steel, motor vehicles, and textiles, clothing and footwear. Within the broad national policy environment of scaling down tariffs, or at least not increasing them, to alleviate temporary crises (such as threatened the Australian steel industry in the early 1980s), sectoral plans have been used to tailor special state intervention to phased restructuring of particular industries. These industry plans are instances of state intervention through quasi-corporatist schemes at the sectoral level. They are corporatist because they involve tripartite arrangements between government, business and unions, but only partly or 'quasi' corporatist because they have been devised and sustained by state initiative and the supporting state structures that have been put in place. That the government retains the whip-hand was shown most starkly when the Labor cabinet unilaterally changed the essential parameters of the textiles, clothing and footwear plan in March 1991 because, in cabinet's view, that sector was not shaping up quickly enough.

These Australian sectoral plans for troubled industries represent a fundamentally different approach to the liberal/pluralist response typical of countries such as the United States and Canada where interest group pressure typically leads to *ad hoc* tariff or other restrictive trade measures or, alternatively, to business bailouts. Even the controversial Kodak 'bailout' by the Hawke government before the 1989 national election was to save a major exporter of high value-added products that was threatened by corporate restructuring of its international parent.

COMPARATIVE PERSPECTIVES

Our purpose in this book, in addition to documenting and analysing the historical transformation of Australian manufacturing industry policy from protection to correction, is to locate Australia and

Australian developments in industry policy within a comparative, as well as a theoretical, perspective. Comparative analysis is included at appropriate places throughout the book; here it is sketched in broad outline using Peter Katzenstein's useful categorisation of the dominant political forms of contemporary capitalism as liberalism, statism and corporatism.[20] This threefold scheme captures essential attributes of the different ways in which nations with distinctive domestic structures, political cultures and histories interact with international market forces.

According to Katzenstein's typology, liberal countries such as the United States rely on market forces, and when those fail, adopt *ad hoc* protectionist measures to insulate threatened industries. This buys breathing space and tends to export the costs of change to other countries, at least in the short term. Statist countries such as Japan possess the means at national level to pre-empt change through redirecting industry to take advantage of longer term trends in world markets. Both these strategies for dealing with structural economic change are the preserve of large countries with extensive domestic economies. Liberalism has suited the United States because the enormous size and wealth of its domestic economy has both insulated it from, and allowed it to exercise influence over, the world market. Similarly the statist strategy is appropriate for Japan with its large and affluent domestic market and disciplined population because such a strategy requires a powerful state that can shape national economic development and pursue longer term structural change.

Katzenstein's main concern, however, was with explaining how small European states such as Austria and Switzerland cope in world markets. He did this brilliantly through developing his third category, democratic corporatism, to explain the economic affluence and political stability of small states. Being small polities with open economies, such countries can neither influence the world market nor insulate themselves from its effects. Instead, since the Second World War, they have learned to live with the consequences of change that stem from such dependency through a flexible system of domestic compensation. The smaller European countries benefit economically from being integrated into the dynamic world market, and they cope politically through a nationally integrated system of internal adjustment to change. Democratic corporatism enables 'low-voltage politics' and is characterised by three distinguishing traits:

an ideology of social partnership expressed at the national level; a relatively centralized and concentrated system of interest groups; and voluntary and informal coordination of conflicting objectives through continuous political bargaining between interest groups, state bureaucracies, and political parties.[21]

Australia does not fit this tripartite scheme, but has some attributes of all three types. It is small to medium in economic size and highly dependent on world markets for the sale of its primary agricultural and mineral products. In this respect, Australia is similar to the small European states in having a large export sector directly dependent on international markets. It is markedly different, however, in that its manufacturing sector, like their agricultural sectors, is highly protected and inefficient. Politically, Australia is quite different because its internal structures and processes are not corporatist, but have a combination of statist and pluralist characteristics. Australian politics is competitive between parties and divided among national and regional governments; interest groups, with the exception of trade unions, are fragmented and relatively decentralised and uncoordinated; and the political process is rather more formal, adversarial and incremental than corporatist bargaining, again with the partial exception of the bipartite Accord between the Hawke Labor government and the union movement since 1983. In this respect, Australia's domestic politics has similarities with the liberal pluralism of the United States. Australia differs fundamentally from the United States, however, in its relative economic size and dependency on the world market both for capital imports and commodity exports. It also differs in its extensive use of the state as 'a vast public utility' to cushion such dependency while at the same time facilitating development of its smaller domestic economy.

Thus, for Australia, the interrelationship between national structures and the world economy is quite different from any of Katzenstein's three types because of its dual economy. On one hand, its export sector is based on the exploitation of vast natural resources of minerals and energy and agricultural production, all of which are highly competitive in, and comprise a relatively large proportion of, world trade. On the other hand, its manufacturing sector has been import-substituting, inefficient and small scale. Hence, as a leading international primary producer, Australia competes favourably in world markets, but otherwise has shielded its secondary industry behind protective walls of tariffs and import restrictions.

In facilitating the former and protecting the latter, Australia has been profoundly statist but without being corporatist in any wider sense. In the past, continuing consensus on the great national policies allowed Australian politics to function tolerably well in managing conflict and adjusting to change in a pluralist way within the settled parameters of protective statism. Australia's overall policy of protectionism, which was dominant until the late 1980s, required national political consensus and a trade-off between the costs of domestic protection and the returns from world trade in primary commodities. That was achievable through pluralist and party politics as long as such commodity trade remained lucrative and the costs of domestic protection were not exorbitant. This was a lucky country's strategy of living off the benefits of trade in its natural endowments, and an egalitarian country's way of sharing the benefits among capital, labour and the weaker sectors of primary industry.

It should be noted that Katzenstein's 'statism' category needs to be distinguished in part from our 'statist' concept. He used the term to designate a particular type of state role in a typology of contemporary capitalist systems. We use statist in two ways. The first is in a more general sense where the primary focus is on political institutions and actors rather than social groups or economic forces. A similar statist orientation pervades Katzenstein's work including this typology, except that he reserves the term for one form of more directive industry policy that is typical of Japan. The second sense in which we use statist is similar to Katzenstein's in that it designates an active and formative role for the state rather than a passive and reactive one. There is a difference, however, in the scope of state activity that is referred to, with our usage covering the setting in place and dismantling of broad national policies such as tariff protection whereas Katzenstein's usage is restricted more narrowly to directive industry policy at the sectoral level.

In a recent book, Francis Castles criticised Australia's move away from protectionism without any compensating welfare policies having been put in place to cushion the impact of international market fluctuations.[22] Taking as his paradigm the smaller European states, Castles adapted Katzenstein's framework to come up with a rather different, and more pessimistic, analysis than the one developed here. Castles thus laments the dismantling of Australia's established 'politics of domestic defence' – by which he means the traditional policy of protectionism combined with the historic trade-off of enhanced national wages through the arbitration system – without the substitution of an adequate 'politics of domestic compensation' (his characterisation of Katzenstein's notion of democratic corporatism).

According to our analysis, however, such corporatism at the macro-level is not feasible because it has no basis in Australia's political history, its public culture or its established institutions and processes of government. These are all predominantly pluralist and statist rather than corporatist, as is argued at length throughout this book. But neither is that the full story, for the Hawke government has implemented a series of industry plans which have helped to alleviate the wrenching process of structural adjustment in the hardest hit industries and which have compensated, to some extent, for the painful impact of such changes through the policies of quasi-corporatism at the sectoral level. But Castles was right in highlighting the inadequacy of the Labor government's compensatory policies to cushion change and compensate losers. The failure to take greater responsibility for the dislocation being caused by the government in pursuing tariff reductions is taken up in the concluding chapter.

The other key point to be made in evaluating the critics' case is the fact that Australia had little choice but to abandon protection because it was a policy that could no longer be afforded. The political economy of protective statism that established and consolidated Australia's manufacturing industries depended on the economic strength of the sheep's back and the coal truck, but as they have declined in relative terms, so protective statism has become untenable. What then should be done? Because of its geographical isolation, Australia does not have the luxury of entering a major trading bloc as Canada did through its bilateral Free Trade Agreement with the United States in 1989, or as most of the European countries are now doing through the European Community. 'Closer Economic Relations' with New Zealand is not quite the same sort of thing because it adds only about four million people to Australia's own population of seventeen million. Nevertheless, achieving a more complete union would help focus the practical attention of Australians on supranational issues of trading and political ties that are of increasing importance for smaller countries. But, closer ties with New Zealand aside, Australia's only realistic option is to move beyond protectionism and to encourage other trading nations and blocs to do likewise through GATT and other international and regional forums.[23]

BEYOND PROTECTION

No matter how Australia might fare in exposing its manufacturing sector to international markets which are currently dominated by unsympathetic trading blocs, one thing is now certain: it will do so without a policy of national protection. The final nail in the protectionist coffin was Prime Minister Hawke's March 1991 industry statement reaffirming the Labor government's commitment to tariff reduction, adopting the goal of moving by steps to 5 per cent nominal rates by the turn of the century and accelerating the special rates of reduction for the intractable textiles, clothing and footwear industries. There was virtually nothing in the March 1991 industry policy statement to console the so-called 'new Keynesians' and 'new protectionists' who favour greater state intervention and support.

Having settled the phasing out of protection, the federal Labor government in the early 1990s shifted its attention to associated areas of national inefficiency. Two key sets of initiatives were undertaken: first, micro-economic reform of public sector services, provision of infrastructure and regulatory regimes; and, second, a major review aimed at reforming federal arrangements and intergovernmental relations through a series of Special Premiers Conferences and associated reviews by teams of Commonwealth and state officials. Progress on these fronts has been slow with 'New Federalism' stalled by Paul Keating's spirited rejection of any proposal for returning powers of taxation to the states and his subsequent wresting of the prime ministership from Hawke in December 1991. For their part, manufacturers and business groups have turned the demands for greater efficiency back on government; they blame the government for their competitive disadvantage because of inefficiencies in public services.

A third area of national contention is the whole system of centralised national wage-fixing that was patched up by the Hawke government as recently as 1988, but which remains highly precarious in a deregulated economy. Until 1991, the Industrial Relations Commission (IRC) worked in tandem with the Accord process, endorsing the revised Accord agreements (Accords Mark I–V) between the government and the ACTU. This process held down real wages in exchange for some additional non-wage trade-offs. This harmonious working relationship was shattered by the 1991 national wage decision when the IRC reasserted a more independent role for itself by refusing to endorse the Accord Mark VI agreement. This government–union deal included a component of modified enterprise bargaining designed to loosen the Accord strait-jacket that had delivered real wage cuts, and was intended to allow stronger unions to win better increases. With the Labor government and the unions at odds with the IRC, and the Liberal coalition parties pledged to scuttle the whole centralised system. Should they win office, this last pillar of Australia's protective state seems ripe for demolition.

At this point, it seems unlikely that the Labor government will have either the inclination or time to deal with these three large and messy items of unfinished business: micro-economic reform of the public sector, overhauling federalism and intergovernmental relations, and saving the Accord without jettisoning entirely the central wage-fixing system. This disinclination persists because the country remains mired in 'the recession we had to have' - the phrase which Keating as Treasurer used to describe the current recession before its severity was fully recognised and to justify the government's restrictive monetary policies that exacerbated the downturn. With unemployment persisting above 10 per cent, the Australian dollar weak and the terms of trade so vulnerable and volatile, it seems unlikely that the Labor government, despite the leadership change from Hawke to Keating that freshened its image and renewed its vigour, will have time to grapple with the tough but pressing question of the role of the government beyond the protective state.

Both sides of Australian politics have recently published their respective blueprints for the medium term, but neither has anything much to say about the role of the state beyond protection. Not surprisingly, with an election due by April 1993 and the national economy in the doldrums, both parties are focusing on current economic strategies. The Liberal coalition's 'Fightback' package released in November 1991 proposes substituting a broad-based goods and services tax for some existing taxes and slashing government expenditure.[24] The hope here is that a 'more level playing field' with a broader-based but flatter tax regime and further squeezing of the public sector will promote greater private initiative and enterprise. The Labor government's alternative package released by the new prime minister, Paul Keating, in February 1992, reaffirms the deregulatory reforms of the 1980s but endorses modest stimulation of private investment by means of an investment allowance and boosting public spending on major infrastructure.[25] Thus, while there is now a clear difference between the major parties on tax and expenditure policies, both remain committed to phasing out tariffs and neither has given much attention to life after protection.

Our purpose in the book is to tell the story and explain the theoretical implications of Australia's move beyond protective statism; it does not attempt to devise an appropriate role for the state in the precarious terrain beyond protection as Australia approaches its centenary of nationhood. It should become apparent through the centenary decade that Australia needs a new synthesis of political economy far more than it needs a new Constitution. The main challenge of the 1990s will be to work out this new synthesis within the established constitutional system which is unlikely to change much. This book, we hope, prepares the ground for such a national enterprise.

NOTES

1. This is the title of a well-known book, sponsored by the American Social Science Research Council, by Peter B. Evans, Dietrich Rueschemeyer & Theda Skocpol, eds, *Bringing the State Back In*, Cambridge University Press, Cambridge, 1985.
2. Elizabeth J. Harman & Brian W. Head, eds, *State, Capital and Resources in the North and West of Australia*, University of Western Australia Press, Perth, 1981; and Brian Galligan, *Utah and Queensland Coal: A Study in the Micro Political Economy of Modern Capitalism and the State*, University of Queensland Press, St Lucia, Qld, 1989.
3. Brian W. Head, ed., *State and Economy in Australia*, Oxford University Press, Melbourne, 1983.
4. Martin Painter, *Steering the Modern State: Changes in Central Coordination in Three Australian State Governments*, Sydney University Press, Sydney, 1987.
5. W. K. Hancock, *Australia*, Ernest Benn, London, 1930, pp. 73, 86.
6. In *R. v Barger* (1908), 6 CLR 41.
7. John Rickard's revisionist account of the failure of New Protection focuses too narrowly on the elements of Deakin's initiative that failed: see Chapter 2 of *Class and Politics: New South Wales, Victoria and the Early Commonwealth, 1890–1910*, Australian National University Press, Canberra, 1976.
8. Edward Shann, *An Economic History of Australia*, Cambridge University Press, Cambridge, 1948 (first edition 1930), p. 430.

9. ibid., pp. 427, 446.
10. L. F. Giblin, 'Some costs of marketing control', *Economic Review*, vol. 4, 1928, p. 154.
11. Hancock, *Australia*, p. 89.
12. Patrick Dunleavy, 'Paradoxes of an ungrounded statism', in *The Comparative History of Public Policy*, ed. Francis Castles, Polity Press, Cambridge, 1989.
13. P. Ewer, W. Higgins & A. Stevens, *Unions and the Future of Australian Manufacturing*, Allen & Unwin, Sydney, 1987, p. 5.
14. ibid. (quoted in), p. 2.
15. ibid., p. 6.
16. ibid., pp. 136, 151.
17. Department of the Prime Minister and Cabinet, *Building a Competitive Australia*, Australian Government Publishing Service, Canberra, 12 March 1991.
18. Interview with Senator Button, 19 June 1991.
19. The Accord (or, to give its full title, 'Statement of Accord by the Australian Labor Party and the Australian Council of Trade Unions Regarding Economic Policy') was originally an agreement between the Labor Party and the ACTU in 1983. It has provided the federal Labor government with a flexible incomes policy, allowing it to restrain wages through tax cuts and related social security trade-offs while maintaining relative industrial harmony. The Accord has been periodically renegotiated – six times under Prime Minister Hawke and again in early 1992 following Prime Minister Keating's 'One Nation' economic statement. For a full account, see Gwynneth Singleton, *The Accord and the Australian Labor Movement*, Melbourne University Press, Melbourne, 1990.
20. Peter J. Katzenstein, *Small States in World Markets*, Cornell University Press, Ithaca, 1985, p. 23.
21. ibid., p. 32.
22. Francis G. Castles, *Australian Public Policy and Economic Vulnerability*, Allen & Unwin, Sydney, 1988.
23. There is a substantial recent literature by international political economists on the significant developments that have been taking place: see especially Richard Higgott, 'The politics of Australia's international economic relations: adjustment and two-level games', *Australian Journal of Political Science*, vol. 26, 1991, pp. 2–28.
24. *Fightback: the Way to Rebuild and Reward Australia*, Liberal Party of Australia, Canberra, 1991.
25. *One Nation*, Statement by the prime minister, the Hon. P. J. Keating, Australian Government Publishing Service, 1992.

CHAPTER 2

Reinstating the State

For more than a decade there has been a resurgence of interest in the state among political theorists and practical researchers.[1] In part, this has been due to belated recognition of the enormous growth in the size and role of the modern welfare state, its diffuse range of economic and business functions in managing the overall economy, promoting and sustaining private business enterprises and development projects, and directly providing numerous services through its own corporations. But it is also due in part to the revival of statist theory and perspectives which has come from critical reappraisal of the pluralist orthodoxy that dominated post-war political science, and dissatisfaction with alternative Marxist and corporatist models that have been used to explain political and economic relations within advanced capitalism.

Some 'old-guard' political scientists like David Easton criticised this renewed interest in the state as a retrograde step: 'The state, a concept that many of us thought had been polished off a quarter of a century ago, has now risen from the grave to haunt us once again'. Advocate of a sanitised 'systems' approach to political analysis, Easton acknowledged with regret that 'the state has slipped back into the vocabulary of conventional social science' and 'has now laid siege to the political system'.[2] Bringing the state back into primary focus, however, enables political analysts to come to grips with one of the essential parts of post-war advanced capitalist democracies and to go beyond the constraining assumptions and dogmas of both liberalism and Marxism that have coloured political analysis in both traditions.[3] Moreover, a statist focus ensures that political actors and institutions rather than sociological groups or economic forces are the main objects of attention.

In the post-war years of the 1950s and 1960s political science ignored the massive role of the modern state because it took for granted an earlier liberal political economy that assumed a minimum role for the state, or, alternatively, a pluralist world of competing interest groups in which the state was largely responsive to dominant coalitions that had their way. Moreover, because of the artificial distinction between the political and the economic that had grown up and been intellectually formalised in the separate disciplines of political science and economics within the liberal tradition, political science focused narrowly on the institutions and processes of government and on parties, voting and pressure groups. Marxists, unlike liberals, acknowledged the state which they assumed was an instrument of class rule; but like liberals they too neglected to study its large and complex role within advanced capitalism. This began to be corrected in the 1970s with leading pluralist scholars such as Lindblom directing attention to the central relationship within capitalism between business and government, and claiming that 'much of politics is economic, and most of economics is also political'.[4] Marxists too began to acknowledge that politics in general and the state in particular had an autonomy of their own that was, to a large extent, independent of economic forces.[5]

In the preceding decades, however, the term 'state' had virtually disappeared from the conceptual universe of American political science, which is most of political science. This was due to the overthrow of the older formal-legal tradition, which had concentrated on institutional structures of the state, by the behavioural revolution. During these decades, as Stephen Krasner points out, political scientists wrote about 'government, political development, interest groups, voting, legislative behaviour, leadership, and bureaucratic politics, almost everything but "the state"'.[6] This has now changed with an increasing number of writers focusing on the state, emphasising its autonomy and structural shaping of politics, and its interdependent relations with business and interest groups.[7] Thus, the behavioural movement had 'buried the memory of the institutionalists, only to have a "statist" counter-revolution take place', as Gabriel Almond has put it.[8] The state had not withered away in the interim couple of decades: it had simply been ignored.

Such scholarly neglect of the state was also prevalent in Australian political science during the earlier post-war decades despite the state's continuing extensive role and a reasonably well-developed statist political economy before the Second World War. In 1953, S. J. Butlin pointed out for the related discipline of history that:

> Australian economic history is the major part of all Australian history; from the beginning economic factors have dominated development in a way that should gladden the heart of any Marxist. What is true of any particular strand of economic growth – land settlement, labour relations and labour organization, immigration, secondary industry – is also true of each major stage in the development of the community as a whole: each is characterised by economic changes which conditioned political, social and cultural changes.[9]

Our argument is that political economy is the major part of Australian politics and the role of the state in industry policy and its relations with business are major parts of political economy.

The distinction between politics narrowly conceived and political economy was better appreciated by an earlier generation of less specialised scholars. W. K. Hancock, for example, divided his classic treatise on Australia between political economy and politics. Political economy was concerned with the role of the state as 'a vast public utility' in providing the great national policies of land settlement, immigration, protection, utilities and transport infrastructure that developed and shaped the nation. Hancock devoted most attention to such structural policies, and gave politics, which was concerned with parties and elections, only a minor role.[10] Brian Fitzpatrick concluded his review of Australian politics to 1945 with the telling observation that, in all its phases, Commonwealth political history was only 'superficially a story of contending parties and their rival policies', and that there was 'actually very little . . . abrupt or remarkable departure from previous major policy'. Despite the earlier presence of a strong Free Trade Party that formed government with protectionist Liberals on a number of occasions, 'there was no abrupt reversal of established protectionist tariff policy at any time'.[11] Thus, in bringing the state back into the forefront of political analysis, we are reviving an earlier venerable tradition of Australian political economy that is reinforced by current trends in the discipline.

Our renewed focus on the state in analysing national political economy complements and extends two other strands in Australian political studies that have sustained a major emphasis on the state. The first is international relations which has been prominent in post-war Australia and has treated the nation state as the primary actor in international affairs.[12] Australian academic specialists in international relations 'almost without exception', according to Martin Indyk, 'have remained firmly within the bounds of Realist-Rationalist discourse':

> they have chosen either to examine the foreign policy *process* of individual states or the wider *systemic* relations between states – particularly the great powers. In other words, whether they chose to analyse system or process, their unit of analysis was the state.[13]

In recent years, the dominant realist paradigm, which focused exclusively on the nation state's political manoeuvring in international affairs, has been supplemented by political economy perspectives emphasising the importance of world economic forces. Like Australia's foreign policy that used to be conducted largely in an economic vacuum, the study of Australia's international relations, mirroring its formal conduct through the Department of Foreign Affairs, paid little attention to economic issues.[14] Both of these things changed in the 1980s with the amalgamation of the Departments of Foreign Affairs and Trade and with scholars giving greater attention to the international economic environment and its impact on Australia's domestic political economy.[15] With the increasing deregulation of Australia's national economy during the 1980s, the dynamic impact of international economic forces on domestic policy has quickened. Yet, so far at least, this has not been recognised sufficiently in the study of Australia's domestic politics and policy.[16]

The second strand of Australian political studies that has focused on the state, although for the most part much less overtly than international relations, has been public administration and, in recent times, public policy. Several generations of scholars in public administration have consistently documented and analysed the structures and operation of various component institutions of the Commonwealth government and state governments. Much of this work dealt with the nuts and bolts of the administrative state and with the intricacies of its internal processes. Like international relations, public administration asserted its autonomy as a distinct sub-discipline, but unlike international relations it tended to focus on component parts rather than the whole. However, in the pioneering work of Bland[17] and in recent studies of administration and policy, there is a much more overt focus on the state both at the national and regional state level.[18]

In this chapter we examine the theoretical perspectives that have been used by various scholars at different times in trying to make sense of Australian politics and public policy. We discuss in turn the following paradigms: Australia's pre-war political economy that had an exaggerated concern with the state; post-war pluralism, predominant in the 1950s and 1960s and still continuing in the 1980s, which rejected the earlier political economy with its primary focus on the state in favour of interest groups and pressure politics; new left Marxism of the 1970s and early 1980s which mounted a spirited reaction to pluralism but focused mainly on class analysis; and corporatism which gained some currency in the 1980s as a way of articulating the Labor Party's Accord with the trade union movement and the Hawke government's tripartite approach to aspects of economic and industry policy. Our purpose is to bring to the fore theoretical paradigms that have often been implicit or have escaped critical debate within Australian political writing, and to indicate how these have coloured empirical analysis and critical diagnosis. Given this approach, our treatment of authors is illustrative rather than comprehensive. In the final section of the chapter, we explore further the statist approach that informs our own approach throughout the book.

Our purpose then in this chapter is to provide the theoretical framework for understanding Australia's national industry policy of protective statism (explained from a historical perspective in Chapter 3), and the extent of the transformation towards a corrective state (examined in Chapter 4 and subsequent chapters).

PRE-WAR POLITICAL ECONOMY

The most influential Australian writers who used the concept of the state extensively were W. K. Hancock and F. W. Eggleston who, writing in the early 1930s, gave definitive expression to a long-established tradition that emphasised state action and 'colonial socialism' in early Australia. Hancock's central thesis regarding the state was that:

> Australian democracy has come to look upon the State as a vast public utility, whose duty is to provide the greatest happiness to the greatest number . . . . To the Australian, the State means collective power at the service of individualistic 'rights'.[19]

It is important to note that Hancock's discussion of the state comes within Part II of his book and is titled 'Political Economy'. This is the central section of the work and deals with the great national policies of protection, arbitration, immigration and land settlement, with state action at the regional state level by departments and public bodies, and with the complications of a federal system of government and administration. Part III, a shorter section of the book, is headed 'Politics' and deals with political parties and foreign policy. Unfortunately, Hancock is often remembered by political scientists because of Henry Mayer's critique of the 'initiative-resistance' thesis. Mayer was in the forefront of the new Australian political science and used pluralist rhetoric against a much exaggerated caricature of Hancock's treatment of political parties.[20] Hancock's more important point about political parties, which seemed to have been lost on his pluralist critics, was that party politics were less important than, and in fact subservient to, the established structures of political economy. It is unfortunate that Hancock used the 'resistance' tag for his chapter on the non-Labor parties because his major argument was that the two political parties were much alike and, in any case, had little immediate impact on the larger national and regional state policies for which there was overall political consensus.

The point needs to be emphasised because Hancock is often associated with a tradition that is supposed to have attributed the interventionist Australian state to the Labor party. For example, Sol Encel, one of Hancock's more sympathetic post-war critics, sums up the early treatment of the state as follows: 'The character of this [interventionist] state was determined during the formative period of Australian politics between 1890 and 1914 as the result of the emergence of the Australian Labor Party, which throughout its history has been the lodestar or positive pole of Australian politics'.[21] This is quite untrue of Hancock. In Hancock's view, 'state socialism' (a handy way of referring to state action, mainly at the regional state level and particularly in Victoria) and the major national policies such as protection and arbitration were not the product of any political party but were rooted in deeper, more substantial political economy and political culture factors. More specifically with respect to the Labor Party, Hancock pointed out that between 1891 and 1908 Labor overthrew the government of the radical Liberal prime minister and apologist, Alfred Deakin, but not the Deakinite policy which it was 'content to make . . . more emphatic'. Moreover, Hancock underlines the fact that, between 1916 and 1929, 'the Labor party was in disarray because of the conscription split' and had little impact on Australian national politics.[22] In short, Hancock's view was that the Labor Party was an heir to, and had only minimal impact upon, 'state socialism' and the major settled national policies.

In his chapter on 'State Socialism', Hancock acknowledged his debt to Eggleston 'who ha[d] for several years been collecting, with great industry and skill, a vast mass of facts' and who had published various articles 'as preliminary sketches for his exhaustive work, soon to be published, on *State Socialism in Victoria*'.[23] Eggleston's book had a much narrower focus than that of Hancock, namely the state of Victoria, which he claimed had 'possibly the largest and most comprehensive use of State power outside Russia'.[24] His work was ideologically motivated by a strong commitment to extreme *laissez-faire* economics which was something of an idealised alternative to which Eggleston turned after his own disillusioning experience as a Victorian politician and minister.[25] Eggleston traced the history of Victoria's extensive use of public enterprise as a means to stimulate development, provide social and economic infrastructure, foster local manufacturing, resettle returned soldiers and alleviate depressions. He produced detailed case studies of the giant public enterprises such as the Metropolitan Board of Works, Country Roads Board, Electricity Commission and the State Railways that continued to dominate Victoria's public sector until recent times. Eggleston defined 'state socialism' simply as 'the operation of common services by the State'.[26] At times he acknowledged that state action was undertaken for practical rather than ideological reasons, the result of 'the mass instinct to use the handiest instrument to relieve the situation'.[27] At other times, however, Eggleston's judgement was affected by his ideological purpose: for example, when he claimed that, in practice, Marxist society was only a more extreme example of the Victorian experiment.[28]

Eggleston's view of the Labor Party was equally ambivalent: on the one hand, he claimed that in the 1890s 'a Labor Party professing the Marxism creed entered politics, with nationalisation as its main plank', yet, on the other hand, he described the Labor Party more aptly as 'not socialistic but an opportunist representative of a unionist machine without any thought of ultimate economic effect'.[29] The traditional pragmatic state socialism of the non-Labor parties had been less extreme than that of Labor, but they too had become tainted when the renegade Labor prime minister,

Billy Hughes, assumed leadership of the Nationalists after his expulsion from the Labor Party in 1916 because of his pro-conscription stance. Eggleston's damning of public enterprise relied on the dubious methodological strategy of comparing actual inefficiencies of Victorian state enterprises with the idealised efficiency, dynamism and individual freedom of an imagined *laissez-faire* system.

In their heavy emphasis on the state, Hancock and Eggleston were picking up and articulating an established view that went back to nineteenth-century colonial experience. Noel Butlin, who has examined the character and extent of nineteenth-century 'colonial socialism', points out that early commentators tended to be 'unduly conscious' of government intervention.[30] This exaggerated concern with state action was also characteristic of Hancock and Eggleston, but there were good reasons for such emphasis. In the first place, public enterprise in Australia was extensive compared with that of other countries. Before the First World War, public expenditure as a percentage of gross domestic product for Australia was twice the level of Britain or the United States (23 per cent compared with about 11 and 9 per cent respectively), while the proportion of the workforce in public employment was also twice that of Britain and the United States (12 per cent compared with 5 and 6 per cent).[31] Public employment by Victorian state bodies peaked in 1927, a few years before Hancock and Eggleston were writing, at 14 per cent of the workforce and has been declining ever since.[32] It was hardly surprising that state action, which was high for Australia in both absolute and relative terms around 1930, should be given heavy emphasis by Hancock and Eggleston. They were following the tradition set by certain European visitors such as Albert Métin who several decades before characterised Australia as a country of pragmatic state socialism.[33]

A second probable reason for the early emphasis on state action was the rise of the Labor Party which gave colonial 'state socialism' heightened significance. Early Labor backers romanticised state action as an established means of achieving their socialist goals. In his public debates with Reid in 1906, Holman, who was to lead the Labor Party to electoral victory in New South Wales in 1910, eulogised the state in these terms:

> We regard the State not as some malign power hostile and foreign to ourselves, outside our control and no part of our organized existence

> but we recognize in the State, we recognize in the Government merely a committee to which is delegated the powers of the community . . . only by the powers of the State can the workers hope to work out their emancipation from the bonds which private property is able to impose on them today.[34]

In writing *The Case for Labor* in 1910, Billy Hughes, who was a rising star in the federal Labor Party which won national office in that year, claimed that 'Socialism would come to Australia just as manhood came to a boy'. The process would be gradual but inevitable: 'Complete collectivism', when it came, 'would appear the most ordinary natural, and inevitable thing'. Hughes was confident because he believed that socialism was already present in an incomplete form and would evolve further because of the favourable social environment.[35]

There were obvious advantages and disadvantages in this early emphasis on the state. By focusing on the state, writers such as Hancock were able to explore the great settled national policies and established regional state enterprises that constituted a major part of Australian politics. These were not contentious but rather matters of national consensus that had become largely depoliticised in the narrower party-political arena. Their broader focus on the state enabled such writers to capture the larger political economy aspects of national policies and state enterprises that were no less important in determining the pattern of Australian politics for being established and settled.

If there was much of worth in this early emphasis on the state, there was also much confusion, particularly with respect to the term 'socialism' and its adoption by the Labor Party. It was rather unfortunate that such state action was called 'socialism' at all, and this confusion was compounded when Labor adopted a socialisation objective. The French scholar Albert Métin had pointed out that public debate in early Australia was characterised by a 'poverty of ideas' and that the theoretical arguments were ignored or avoided.[36] Métin had given a perceptive account of the Labor Party:

> Labor parties in Australasia resemble the English movement in their trade-union based structure, their exclusively practical nature, their pursuit of minor and immediately realizable reforms and the scarcity and vagueness of any declarations of socialist and other general principles to be found in their official publications. On the other hand they resemble French socialist groups in their organisation of their own

> political party, something which exists in England only as a much-canvassed plan for the future. In appearance they constitute what we know as a *class party* leading the struggle against the bourgeoisie: in practice they accept private ownership and the wages system, seeking simply to ensure good working conditions in the world as it is. That should suffice as a brief sketch of the general character of Australian Labor.[37]

Métin also summed up nicely the misleading appearance of the 'state socialism' of many government instrumentalities: 'from a distance it is socialism; from close at hand it is simply a colonial expedient'[38] - hence *Le Socialisme Sans Doctrine.*

The diagnostic problem was often exacerbated for subsequent commentators because of their ideological commitment to more extreme positions than were reflected in the actual spectrum of Australian politics. Eggleston, for example, was intent upon damning state action and socialism in favour of a system of individual free enterprise. On the other side, many Labor historians romanticised Labor's achievements and painted Australia as an egalitarian, radical nation. Hancock was often brilliantly perceptive, as for example, when he pointed out that 'the old Australian experimentalism which some people called socialism was not really socialism at all, but rather the practical utilitarianism preached by John Stuart Mill in his later days, running towards State action under pressure of circumstances'.[39] But insights such as these tended to be forgotten in the subsequent obsession with Hancock's exaggerated treatment of parties.

The major omission in both Hancock's and Eggleston's work was a surprising one: namely private enterprise. As a result there was little detailed consideration of the crucial relations between government and private business, and no attention given to the purpose behind much state action in the Australian economy. In Hancock's political economy, the actors are the state and individuals: the state being a vast public utility for providing the greatest happiness to the greatest number, collective power at the service of individual rights.[40] Except as a beneficiary of protection, private enterprise is missing. As noted above, Eggleston contrasts the actual inefficiencies of state enterprises with an idealised efficient and dynamic system of *laissez-faire*. But Eggleston did not bother to look at the actual state of private enterprise in Australia, nor its relations with the state. Had he done so, he would have found that much state enterprise was undertaken specifically to boost private investment, and hence was not socialism at all but rather developmental and facilitative state action.

POST-WAR PLURALISM

If the state had been exaggerated by early Australian political writers, it was to be virtually ignored by political scientists when that discipline was established and expanded in Australian universities in the 1950s and 1960s. Political science in Australia essentially continued the pragmatic British traditions of description and analysis typical of the established disciplines of history and law in which many of Australia's first political scientists were schooled. However, it also adopted the specialised focus on political institutions and processes from American political science.[41] The earlier concerns of Hancock and Eggleston with political economy and particularly with the state were abandoned. The standard Australian political science text or reader even today is indicative of this tradition, being mainly concerned with politics narrowly defined as institutions, parties, voting and pressure groups, but lacking a political economy dimension and typically omitting any mention of the state.

This is surprising because, during the 1940s, state action in Australia was raised to a new plateau under the strong, centralising Labor governments of Curtin and Chifley. During the first half of that decade, Australia was put on a total war-footing and was ruled virtually by ministerial decree; and in the post-war period the familiar plethora of Keynesian economic management techniques and policies of a modern welfare-state system were put in place. In the informed debate of the time, as evidenced for example in the pages of the *Australian Quarterly*, there was a preoccupation with this increased level of state action and its implications for democracy. Despite the enhanced role of the state, there was a concern to distinguish sharply Australian liberal democracy from the hated European brands of totalitarian statism: fascism, nazism and communism. Some writers noted with concern that the 'trend towards State control and ordering of social and economic life' within liberal democracies was taking them in the direction of totalitarian countries, and so were intent on emphasising the differences.[42] Increasingly, writers used a pluralist theory of democracy to highlight the competitive and libertarian aspects of liberal democracy.

For example, one writer in 1943 saw the state as one organisation among others within a competitive, pluralist system:

> the theory of political pluralism . . . regards the State (here taken as equivalent to the government) as one organisation among others, and social order as the balance resulting from the pressure upon each other, and upon the government, of the diverse and conflicting interests and movements which go to make up the life of a community.[43]

This was a curious transitional use of the term state within a pluralist framework. As pluralism became more dominant, the term state was dropped, probably because it did not fit with pluralist theory and also had unsavoury totalitarian overtones.

The greatly increased role of the state in the Chifley period of post-war reconstruction was continued in the Menzies era. The welfare state and Keynesian management techniques were consolidated rather than challenged and so became settled parts of Australian political economy for the next three decades. The 1950s and 1960s were years of sustained economic growth and stable, if unadventurous, government by the Menzies Liberal–Country Party coalition. After the earlier traumas of the two World Wars and the Great Depression, Australians settled down to the undistracted pursuit of material acquisition and comforts. The successful Liberal slogan for the 1958 general election, 'Australia Unlimited', nicely summed up aspirations of the time.[44] There was no need to reformulate and implement basic national policies – neither the older policies of tariff protection for the manufacturing industry, assisted immigration and arbitration which had been basic features of Australia's political economy in Hancock's day, nor the newer post-war politics of Keynesian management of the economy and the welfare state which had been put in place by the Chifley Labor government. There were no world wars or major depressions requiring or inviting basic changes to the level or type of state intervention at the national or regional state levels. Because all this was settled and therefore off the political agenda, political writers could focus more narrowly on political parties, voting, institutions and pressure groups.

Of course there was very extensive state action during this period. Public employment was now higher than ever before, absorbing 20 per cent of the workforce, and public expenditure accounted for between 35 and 40 per cent of gross domestic product.[45] In addition, there was extensive state intervention and regulation of business which Butlin, Barnard and Pincus sum up in their chapter title for the period 1945 to 1975 as 'All the Restrictive Practices Known to Man'. The Menzies Liberals integrated state interventionism, particularly for national development purposes, with private business enterprise both in their party ideology and their practical administration. As Marian Simms has pointed out:

> It was a traditional Liberal idea (shared by the business community) that governments could provide infrastructure, but this established idea was given a novel twist from the mid-1940s onwards. The recognition of a partnership between the state and private capital was expressed in terms of the Liberal Party as a progressive force. According to Liberal writers such as R. Casey, R. G. Menzies and A. G. Price, Liberalism did not entail the principled curtailment of state expansion but its 'creative' encouragement.[46]

In fact, during the 1950s and 1960s, there was a quickening of established national policies – tariff protection, massive immigration and the continuation of national wage-setting by arbitration to consolidate and expand Australia's post-war manufacturing industry. The 'McEwenism' of the ruling Liberal–Country Party coalition government was a remodelled version of traditional Australian statism.

For Australian political science at the time, however, this increased level of state action did not attract much attention. Perhaps this was partly because Australia was no longer exceptional either by comparison with other countries or by reference to the reigning orthodoxies which were now those of a moderate welfare–Keynesian kind. Earlier, when Hancock and Eggleston were writing, Australia's high level of state action was more at variance with accepted liberal–free enterprise theories and perhaps therefore more noteworthy. Probably the main reason why the state was largely ignored, however, was because of the pluralist, interest-group orientation of political science and the restrictive boundaries that were drawn around the discipline. Political science was interested in political institutions and processes narrowly conceived. According to its dominant paradigm the political world was constituted of diverse elites and powerful groups all freely pursuing their interests in a political market-place in competition with one another. Government consisted of a subgroup of political elites and institutions that responded to the dominant pressures of the system with policies and legislation. In any case, political scientists were thin on the ground and not much given to theoretical reflection: most of them simply got on with the business of describing and analysing the institutions of Australian government.

Pluralism was so strongly rooted that even writers such as Sol Encel and Alan Davies, who retained the earlier concern for the state, attempted to rework the insights of Hancock and Eggleston to fit the pluralist model. Encel sifted critically through the pre-war literature and came up instead with a pluralist version of the state as 'a machine, or perhaps a collection of pieces of machinery, available for manipulation by sufficiently powerful interested groups or syndicates'. For Encel in 1960, as for pluralists generally, the character of the state and the scope of things political had been considerably downgraded. In his view, the state was 'a body where the organs of government and their concomitant institutions, like the party system, exist[ed] not to frame national policy but to execute the expressed demands . . . [of] organised bodies'.[47] The earlier romanticised views of Labor historians and others who lionised political parties were a favourite target for pluralists. In Encel's view, major political conflict was provided not by parties or classes but by extra-party groups. Parties were 'convenient devices for forming a government' rather than 'agencies for formulating basic policies'.[48] Unfortunately Encel and mainstream political science did not seem to appreciate the implication of this, that by focusing on political parties and groups they would ignore basic policies that were settled and not on the political agenda narrowly defined.

In his study of Victorian politics, Alan Davies continued Eggleston's focus on the public sector, emphasising 'the overwhelmingly administrative character of State government'.[49] In Davies' account, the real business of managing public affairs was performed not by politicians but by 'rational' administrators in the state's bureaucracy and giant public corporations. Public policy was not produced by political parties but by the administrative system in response to pressure group activities.[50] So again we have a version of the pluralist, interest-group model applied to the state, but in this instance combined with assumptions about a Weberian rational bureaucracy plus interest groups from pluralist theory.

In their concern with the state, albeit within a pluralist framework of analysis, Encel and Davies were atypical. For the most part, pluralism was taken for granted and earlier concerns with the state were either ignored or dismissed as old-fashioned. For example P. H. Partridge, one of Australia's most senior political scientists, dismissed Ralph Miliband's book, *The State in Capitalist Society*, which was a powerful stimulus to new left thinking in English-speaking countries,[51] as follows:

> Mr Miliband writes about the state and its functions, and this is a rather unfashionable thing to do: as long ago as 1953 David Easton demonstrated to his own satisfaction that the state is a concept useless for the purposes of political science. Mr Miliband writes about capitalism, also an eccentric thing for an academic political scientist; we can speak of pressure groups, interest groups, political cultures, even perhaps industrial society, but capitalism is a little old fashioned . . . So far as Anglo-American political science is concerned (of course things are different in countries like Italy or France which have not arrived at the ultimate stages of political modernisation) Miliband is like a survivor from an earlier vanished world; he writes about politics rather in the way in which Laski, Tawney and Cole - formidable men in a world which hadn't heard of the political system, systems analysis and structural-functionalism - used to do.[52]

Such confidence in pluralism and systems analysis, and such slighting dismissal of the alternative radical paradigm, belong to a vanishing era of doctrinal certitude among political scientists.

Contrast this with the more recent admissions of Charles Lindblom (one of the American pioneers of pluralism) that the key insights into the relationship between business and government, which he articulated in *Politics and Markets*,[53] are incompatible with the pluralist paradigm. In response to a critical article arguing that he and Robert Dahl, a fellow leading Yale political scientist who was also backing away from the pluralist paradigm that he had helped to pioneer, were trying to save an inadequate pluralist theory by amending it in the direction of class analysis,[54] Lindblom admitted:

> It is true that many of the amendments can be described as trying to save pluralist theory rather than as abandoning it, and indeed they are in the direction that would be urged by class analysts. But some are better characterised as outright departures from pluralist theory . . . I consider some of my amendments - specifically the arguments on the privileged position of business and on circularity through indoctrination - to be antagonistic to pluralism rather than resuscitating it.[55]

Lindblom went on to say that social and political pluralism was itself an ideal that he preferred rather than a reality that was practised: 'I see only a limited amount of it in contemporary polyarchies'. In many issues, Lindblom admitted, 'including many of the most fundamental issues concerning political and economic structure, there exists no pluralism of opinions or of political initiatives'. As a result, he concluded that 'politics is pluralist only on secondary issues, not on primary issues'. And even among the secondary issues that do reach the political agenda, many were 'settled largely by interchange greatly restricted to businessmen and government officials'.[56] Consequently Lindblom, one of the giants in developing pluralism, admitted to being only 40 per cent pluralist.

In Australia there has not been a similar rethinking of ingrained pluralist assumptions, perhaps because there is no concern for articulating theory or critically assessing paradigms that are implicit in more practical work. This can be illustrated by reference to Leon Glezer's study of tariffs during the 1960s golden period of protectionism and the early 1970s when, despite increased questioning and sporadic attempts by government at corrective action, tariff politics seemed to be dominated by entrenched interest groups. Glezer's pluralist assumptions reinforced his diagnosis of the dominance of interest groups in determining industry policy. While stressing that tariff charges were always more than the outcome of the demands of interest groups and emphasising, in particular, the independent influence of the Tariff Board and the IAC, Glezer's account of industry policy put interest groups rather than government in the driving seat. Private interests, Glezer argued, defined the specific purposes of tariff policy and through a cumulative effort influenced the broad direction of tariff policy:

> As the immediate beneficiaries and bearers of the costs of tariff-making, the interest groups were the direct implementors of the aims inherent in industry policy. The aims of politicians and bureaucrats were dependent on how they were viewed by the interests.[57]

Glezer's interpretation is essentially one of manufacturers turning government initiatives to their advantage. For example, the creation of industry councils by the Whitlam government in response to the Jackson Committee's recommendations boiled down to a 'major opportunity to increase manufacturers' influence on industry policy-making'.[58] More generally, manufacturing interests had usurped public opinion and captured the regulatory institutions of state. Glezer concluded that, for much of the 1960s and 1970s, the practical meaning of public opinion in the tariff area was essentially groups' preferences: 'what had been a mass issue early in the century had been rechannelled, with the help of the partial consensus among the political parties and the Tariff Board mechanism, into almost a monopoly of interest groups and the elite'.[59] Even the IAC, which Glezer acknowledged as playing an independent advisory role during the 1970s, was accommodated within this pluralist perspective as a pressure group within government that served as 'an insulating mechanism to cope with conflicting pressures'.[60]

There is a certain plausibility in Glezer's use of interest-group theory because, during the period in question (1960 to 1980), manufacturers' interests tended to predominate with the established policy of national protection remaining in place despite increasing dissatisfaction in many quarters of government. But a better explanation is given by John Warhurst who also used an interest-group framework in his study of tariff policy-making in the 1970s, focusing on the IAC. While cautioning against over-estimating the extent to which a government can influence structural change, Warhurst nevertheless concluded that governments and agencies within governments 'possessed a great deal of autonomy and independence'.[61]

Perhaps due to residual interest-group assumptions and the period he studied, however, Warhurst too under-estimated the capacity of governments for autonomous action. He predicted, on the basis of backsliding by the Whitlam and Fraser governments in the 1970s, that:

> The experience of the ALP was such that it is unlikely to again leave itself open in the foreseeable future to charges of not being willing to protect Australian industry. Nor is the Liberal Party likely to change its present cautious stance.[62]

With the benefit of a longer time-span which can encompass the pre-war erection and the more recent dismantling of national protection, our study is able to give a more coherent account of the decades of status quo and backsliding by governments. We do this in terms of compliant or facilitative state action where state and business preferences are not divergent; in other words, the policies pursued by the state coincided with the preferences and interests of business. A historical account of the extension of Australia's protective state into the 1960s and 1970s is given in the next chapter, while the theoretical explanation of such a compliant mode of state action is developed in the final section of this chapter. The next two sections take up the new left reaction to pluralism and its resurfacing in the 1980s debate over corporatism under the Hawke Labor government.

NEW LEFT MARXISM

The resurgence of Marxism among radical students and academic activists that swept universities in Western countries in the 1960s also had some impact in Australia. Much of the early energy of the new left writers went into practical polemics and activism, first in warnings of an impending doom when all around was affluence and apathy, and then in providing a rationale and motive for dissent as the various counter-culture and anti-Vietnam war movements got under way. The issues were raised and territory was staked out, but more serious scholarship came later. The primary concern of the bulk of this scholarship was with corporate power, class relations and political socialisation.[63] The better work, such as that of Connell and Irving,[64] was grounded in a study of Australian phenomena, work which has been mainly concerned with class but which has also been extended to analysis of the state.

Connell and Irving used the concept of the state quite extensively in their historical analysis of class formation in Australian history. That should hardly be surprising given the prominent role that the state has played in Australian society and political economy since the first convict settlements. Connell and Irving noted that 'the autonomy of the state emerged in the 1850s and grew rapidly in the 1870s in the form of a massive program of public capital formation'; that, at various stages in Australian history, the state has enjoyed 'economic autonomy' in order to preserve its legitimacy and 'integrative function'; and that, through concessions, the state has both integrated the working class into the capitalist system and underpinned the growth of the corporate form of business organisation.[65] Although the concept of the state was used fairly extensively in these ways, it was not systematically explored, nor were the complex and subtle relationships between class and the state in Australian mass democracy fully articulated. To do so would have required two things that were lacking: first, an analysis of how the Labor Party fits into the overall class picture as the organised political arm of the working class; and second, a more sophisticated account of the state.

Connell's earlier book, *Ruling Class, Ruling Culture,* also focused on the ruling class, but had some specific discussion of the state as well.[66] In examining the character of the ruling class Connell asked two key questions regarding the state: what is the relationship between the ruling class and the state? and what is the role of bureaucratic state elites? In answering the first, Connell gave a definition of the capitalist state:

> The state is one section of the total organisation of power that defines a capitalist society: a crucially important section, in terms of the maintenance of the structural pattern: but not the section from which the principal dynamic of the system arises.[67]

The principal dynamic of the system came from capitalism. In answering the second question regarding the role of state elites, however, Connell emphasised their power and autonomy: 'In an executive sense, the top civil servants in Canberra along with a few of the more influential ministers, are certainly the most powerful men in the country'. Top bureaucrats were acknowledged to be more powerful than corporate directors of the largest companies such as BHP or CRA. According to Connell, 'the top civil servants can be seen as bureaucratic entrepreneurs parallel to the business and political [Liberal] entrepreneurs', but unlike them they are separate from the ruling class. Connell himself remarked on the irony of his position which treated the most powerful executive figures as independent of the ruling class.[68]

In reaching such a conclusion Connell jettisoned much of the simplistic new left dogma, derived from C. Wright Mills' power-elite theory[69] and Miliband's instrumentalist view of the state,[70] that made senior bureaucrats an arm of the ruling class through shared attitudes and common social background. Connell also partly rejected the related view that the ruling class is held together through common socialisation and education, and that it exercises power through the networks of corporate directors and powerful families. He criticised Playford[71] and Encel,[72] who placed great store on such matters, for confusing real domination, control and power with the potential for exercising domination, control and power: 'The studies of market concentration . . . yield, at best, inferences about a potential for control of an industry (or an economy)'. Connell introduced the key concept of 'mobilisation' as being necessary to activate such potential for organisation.

Connell only partly rejected an instrumentalist model of the state (where the state is manipulated by the ruling class to protect its own privileged position). He oscillated between a modified instrumentalist view of the state and a minimal structuralist view (where the state is autonomous and capitalism reproduces itself independently of the personal motives and networks of corporate and state elites). This was evident in the concept of mobilisation: on the one hand, there are in place networks of elites that can be mobilised; on the other hand, Connell claimed that the behaviour of such key elite groups as businessmen would not be very different if there were no such networks.[73] Connell fell back on a minimal structuralist view of what a ruling class entails when he excluded the powerful bureaucrats from it. Ruling class meant 'collective domination, the maintenance of an institutional structure within which the class appropriates benefits - the choking off of alternatives - the only sense in which a class can intelligibly be said to rule'.[74] But on the instrumentalist side, he made Liberal–National Party politicians a 'political specialisation' within the ruling class. This immediately raises some fundamental questions that Connell, surprisingly, failed to address: what about the Labor Party? Would it really make much difference if Labor had governed federally for most of the time? Probably not, because the reproduction of capitalist relations, the maintenance of settled national policies, and the continuation of the privileged position of business does not require the dominance of the capitalists' political party in politics. As Poulantzas has argued, the capitalist system is less vulnerable in a democracy if business interests are altogether separate from politics.[75]

Other authors such as Playford, Wheelwright and Theophanous, who focused more directly on the state in the 1970s and early 1980s, transposed theories and models from critical theorists and third world experience. Most of the new left work that focused more directly on the state was flawed either because of problems with the original theory or with fitting it to Australian phenomena. Playford's early work which directly transposed Miliband's theory is an example of the former tendency; Wheelwright's and Theophanous' examples of the latter. A couple of examples should suffice to illustrate some of the pitfalls in applying to Australia's political economy theories and explanations that have been worked out in alien contexts.

Most of Wheelwright's empirical work was concentrated on the large corporate sector, particularly transnational companies, but his overall interpretive model was 'the Client State'. This incorporated a version of dependency theory that had been developed by Marxists to explain third world national economies. Wheelwright argued that, as a result of developments in modern capitalism (mainly transnational corporations and the new international division of labour),

Australia had become 'a client state of international capitalism'.[76] As a client state, its main function was 'to shape the future development of the economy in such a way that the profile of foreign corporations have first priority, and the needs of the Australian people the last priority'.[77] Crough and Wheelwright emphasised the weakness of our fragmented political system for dealing with the integrated power of transnational corporations. Yet, in their counsel on what ought to be done, these authors abandoned their conclusions of the client state model and reverted to optimistic voluntarism: 'In a democracy these centres of power (transnationals) must be brought under public ownership and control'.[78] A state with such an option is hardly a client state: either the client state model is an exaggeration or there is no such scope for the state dealing so severely with transnationals.

Theophanous argued that Australia was experiencing a legitimacy crisis of the state. In fact this was only one, or one aspect, of a multitude of interrelated social, economic and political crises.[79] Theophanous took over and combined the central theoretical arguments of both O'Connor[80] and Habermas[81] which had some currency at the time. According to O'Connor, governments in advanced capitalist economies could no longer afford their two necessary functions of promoting capital accumulation through fiscal support for the ailing business sector which benefits the ruling class, and buying legitimation from the popular electorate through increased welfare payments. According to Habermas, liberal-capitalist systems used to be characterised by 'a relative uncoupling of the economic system from the political'. As a result, whole areas of socio-economic life involving property, production and exchange transactions were depoliticised. In advanced capitalist economies there had been 'a recoupling of the economic system to the political'. The consequence was that economic crises had become re-politicised as legitimacy crises.

Regardless of the plausibility of O'Connor's and Habermas' theoretical analyses or their applicability to Europe and America (in retrospect they seem superficial and contrived), there were obvious problems in applying such crisis theory to Australia. In Australia the state had always been deeply involved with accumulation, either directly through public enterprises or indirectly by actively fostering private enterprise. There had not been a recent recoupling of the political and economic in Australia because there was never an uncoupling. The whole logic of legitimation had worked rather differently for Australia with the accumulation and legitimation functions of the state going hand in hand: the state had always been deeply involved in accumulation precisely in order to legitimate itself.

The 'new left' treatments of the state that were fashionable in the 1970s and early 1980s were by-products of theorising about class or derived from experience elsewhere in the world and gave only selective attention to Australian politics and history. As scholars of the left became more immersed in the latter through the 1980s, they tended to jettison Marxist interpretive baggage.[82]

Perhaps the most notable of such authors is Kosmas Tsokhas who, in a series of political economy studies on a range of topics, has moved beyond Marxism and dependency accounts of Australian development. Tsokhas' first book, *A Class Apart?*, was a detailed study of the relations between peak business groups and government, but with a Marxist superstructure tacked on. This provided the book's approach and its purpose which was to explore the complex relationship between the state and social classes. This was to be done, in Tsokhas' words, 'by examining how the capitalist class mobilised itself', in particular by studying the mechanisms used by business 'to transform economic control into political power'.[83] The problem in that book, which Tsokhas never surmounted, was establishing the transformational links.[84] It does not follow that just because business often gets the policy outcomes its leaders want it controls the political system. Such a crude voluntarist and instrumentalist model neglects alternative explanations: for example, a structuralist one in which both business and compliant governments are articulating and responding to the requirements of the political and economic system, or a simpler one in which the government's view of policy needs coincides with the business leaders' articulated interests. Either or both are plausible for a democratic capitalist system and sufficient to explain the phenomenon.

Whether for these or other reasons, Tsokhas abandoned any Marxist framework in his two subsequent books and rebutted the applicability of the dependency thesis (a central tenet of new left theorising) to key aspects of Australian political economy. At the micro-level, he showed conclusively that Australia's leading mining companies had moved beyond dependence on their transnational parent companies.[85] At the macro-level, he argued that, far from Australia being exploited by imperial Britain in its earlier trade in wool, the country had manipulated imperial preferences and massive wartime deals to its own advantage.[86]

One notable scholar who retains a fairly orthodox, although subtle and carefully articulated, Marxist line in the contemporary study of Australian business-government relations is Doug McEachern. He distinguishes between the *economic/structural* and the *political* dimensions of business power and business politics. The political dimension is contingent on particular events and incidental to the deeper structural power of business. The latter is explained in classic Marxist terms as 'a force which empowers business as a class and is concerned with and derives from the basic social relations which constitute private business as an effective economic and social force'.[87] According to this view, it does not matter that business is politically weak and fragmented, nor should it be surprising that the Hawke Labor government and the trade unions have worked to improve the profitability and restructuring of private business.

There is a good deal of plausibility in this structuralist account of business power - certainly much more than in the instrumentalist alternative that Tsokhas abandoned. Business power, as McEachern concluded, is 'not marked by a succession of policy victories but by the security of the basic social order assigning to business important benefits and advantages'.[88] But that tells us both everything and nothing, and is of the same order as Lindblom's theory of the privileged position of business in a capitalist system. The state within a basically capitalist political economy is clearly part of the system which it has to maintain. Steering, tinkering, reforming and system maintenance are all part of the state's role and the focus of political analysis. Whatever the systemic factors of private ownership and privileged position of business tell us about the basic character of the system, they tell us little about the dynamics of its operation. Nor is an economic determinist explanation, such as that of C. Bulbeck - that 'as the structure of the economy changed, the structure of assistance-advising institutions and their ideology also changed' - of much plausibility or value.[89]

CORPORATISM

The concept of corporatism was revived as an alternative paradigm for explaining the role of the state in modern capitalist economies during the 1970s. It was applied typically to European countries with social democratic governments or traditions where peak associations of business and unions were closely involved with government in addressing major issues of industry policy, international competitiveness, industrial relations and social welfare.[90] Corporatism received little attention in Australia, however, until the election of the Hawke Labor government in April 1983.[91] This was due partly to the barriers of established patterns of thinking that neglected political economy and the role of the state. But, in addition, neither the politics nor the economics of the decade to 1983 seemed conducive to corporatist explanatory models, being dominated by the Fraser Liberal–National Party coalition that was widely seen as the harbinger of the 'new right'.[92]

In fact, Fraser's government was fairly traditional, of the sort that has dominated Australian politics particularly since the 1950s: mildly conservative in its commitment to traditional Australian values, professed champion of liberal individualism and the economic virtues of the market, but generally satisfied with the status quo and otherwise given to muddling through and responding to issues on an *ad hoc* basis. If the Fraser government seemed to be much more reactionary to its reformist critics, it was because their hopes had been dashed in 1975 by the dramatic dismissal of the Whitlam Labor government which, like Halley's comet, had been brighter in anticipation than performance.

After the brief interregnum of the Whitlam government that coincided with the ending of the long post-war boom, it seemed by the end of the 1970s that Australian politics and economics had returned to normal. Australia's easy affluence appeared to be assured once again by an energy boom that was a crisis for most industrial countries in the rest of the world. The problems of stagflation that had swamped the Whitlam government in 1974 and plagued its successor, the Fraser government, throughout its first term of office were replaced by the challenges of managing affluence in yet another minerals and energy boom. The Fraser government exaggerated the energy boom for the 1980 election and claimed credit for the resurgence of investment in large resource projects that was taking place. At the same time, it ensured, through the Foreign Investment Review Board, that Australian investment had a reasonable share of the new bonanza through enforcing foreign investment controls.[93]

There were certain worries about the skewing of capital and labour markets that threatened to starve the manufacturing sector of scarce resources, and some concern with the distorting effect that a resources-driven exchange rate might have in further inflating the price structure for imports and protected manufactures. The Fraser government, or at least some of its leading 'dries', were more or less committed to reducing tariffs but, because of internal divisions and a lack of political will, very little was done. Consequently, the structural inefficiencies of Australian manufacturing, which had been accumulating through decades of protection to service a growing but relatively small domestic market, remained. The political imperative for such action was blunted because basic manufacturing industries, such as steel and heavy equipment, were also booming due to the construction demand from the resources sector and a flow-on to the rest of the economy that produced a certain affluence and optimism. Time had been bought, but the opportunity was wasted. Australia's established political economy of domestic protection could be sustained, it seemed, because once again it was underpinned by strong export markets for primary commodities.

Such hopes for the continuing prosperity of the Australian economy were dashed in 1982, however, with the collapse of commodity prices that coincided with severe drought in the rural sector and the onset of a more general recession. The Labor government that swept into office at the snap election in early 1983, mistakenly called by Fraser to capitalise on leadership instability within the Labor Party and to pre-empt further expected deterioration of the economy, brought with it a new style of politics. The Hawke Labor government was characterised by a commitment to consensus rather than traditional partisanship, a style epitomised by its new leader Bob Hawke, who had previously been president of the Australian Council of Trade Unions. The new Labor government adopted a managerial and technocratic, rather than a blustering and ideological approach in order to distance itself from its erratic Whitlam predecessor.[94] Most important of all, it had in place the Accord with the trade union movement which provided a basis for industrial stability and a wages policy that previous governments had lacked. When the first major act of the new government was to call a National Economic Summit Conference in order to formulate a national economic strategy and establish tripartite institutions, it seemed to some that corporatism had arrived in Australia.

The macro-corporatist debate

The ensuing discussion among political scientists as to whether, and if so to what extent, Australia was turning corporatist proceeded in an intermittent manner over the next few years. For the most part, established scholars of business–government relations and industrial relations, the two fields most relevant to the debate about corporatism in Australia, already had entrenched positions that were theoretically incompatible with corporatism. The dominant paradigm in both areas was still a version of pluralist interest-group theory. This had been justified in contradistinction to the traditional orthodoxy of Australian political studies, responsible party government, and the tendency to idealise the Labor Party and the trade union movement. Interest-group pluralism was taken for granted by most, and was defended against the new corporatism by leading scholars such as Ross Martin in industrial relations and Peter Loveday in business-government relations.

Martin had written extensively on Australian trade unionism, and had subtitled his definitive study of the British Trades Union Congress as 'The Growth of a Pressure Group'. In that book Martin used pressure group terminology to describe the TUC, which he saw as occupying 'a singular position in the hierarchy of contemporary British pressure groups', and set his explanatory framework in terms of pressure group determinants and questions.[95] His justification and defence of a pressure group approach was made in a subsequent article criticising the 'new corporatism' in which he argued that the whole notion was either conceptually confused or, as in 'liberal corporatist' terminology, merely a variant of pluralism under a fancy name. Martin declared that 'the new corporatists are primarily concerned with the relations between government and organised groups' and hence concluded 'that liberal corporatist forms are essentially outgrowths of tougher and more basic pluralist forms'.[96] One benefit of new corporatism, according to Martin's self-serving argument, was that it 'revived interest in pressure group studies':

> Group power is precisely what pluralism and corporatism, in the end, are both about. The transition from the former to the latter hinges at least on the power of a group becoming such that government leaders choose, or are obliged, to engage it in the kind of arrangements characterized as liberal corporatist. The crucial aspect of such incorporation is that government leaders negotiate, rather than control, the

ensuing outcomes. The relationship involved is thus a bargaining relationship, varying only in degree from pluralist forms of group-government dealing.[97]

In his major study of the interaction between government and industry in Australia, published the year before the Hawke government won office, Loveday barely mentioned corporatism. The theoretical thrust of his book was to debunk the orderly Westminster model of responsible government that lay at the heart of much Australian political science in favour of a pluralist model of fragmented state administration, diverse interest groups and interactive policy processes. Loveday's book belatedly brought the pluralist revolution to the study of Australian industry policy. This was nicely summarised in his concluding comments:

> When governments negotiate with firms . . . they do something quite different from issuing commands. In the course of these activities much is done without the minister's concurrence, and some things are deliberately put beyond his - or parliament's - direct knowledge and control; responsibilities for outcomes are shared and attenuated; the legally based elements of the policy process are mixed in with and modified by non-legal components to such an extent that Westminster ceases to be an appropriate model.
>
> But this is not to say that power . . . has been concentrated in the hands of those at the top of the hierarchies and organizations of industry, labour, and administration. These hierarchies are too fragmented and their interests are too diverse and in conflict for power to be concentrated at this level beyond the reach of parliament. And the field of industry policy is so broad that no government could have an overall policy for it . . . Government policies are bound to be ad hoc, reactive to some degree, dependent on the activities and fortunes of non-governmental organisations.[98]

We can see here an oblique rejection of corporatism in that the preconditions for a strong form of macro-corporatism - concentration of power in the hands of state, industry and labour hierarchies - are denied. In a subsequent article published the year after the Hawke government's election, Loveday tackled squarely the question of 'Corporatist Trends in Australia?'[99] The concept of corporatism that Loveday used, however, was based on the rather extreme definition of Winkler that 'corporatism is an economic system in which the state directs and controls predominantly privately owned business according to four principles: unity, order, nationalism and success'.[100] Not surprisingly, such directed and ordered corporatism was absent in Australia. Loveday's vision of post-war Australia, as set out in some length in his earlier book, was essentially a pluralist one: government's relations with industry were 'too complex a combination of elements of partnership, mutual influence, competition, some monopoly and some duopoly, some controls and unregulated enterprise to be summed up in one word except "mixed" '.[101]

Loveday admitted that in the Australian context it was not difficult for corporatists to find evidence of the incorporation of interest groups by government into a more tidy system of representation. In particular, there was evidence of groups moving from conflictual to cooperative relations with government; of groups being given official recognition through participation in boards close to government; of groups carrying out government tasks and keeping their members in order; and of unwelcome groups being denied government recognition. But all of that could be accommodated under pluralism and an interest-group paradigm, as Martin had claimed. Similarly, Loveday concurred with Martin in rejecting corporatism on the grounds that it required a strong and directive state that was obviously lacking in Australia. He used a strong test of what corporatism required: the state becoming 'dominant over other groups in economic policy making in Australia', and 'the government, as the instrument or embodiment of the state, [being] a well-oiled and smoothly operating machine of great power'. The state in Australia was simply not like that, Loveday claimed, but hedged in and constrained from without by constitutional arrangements such as federalism and fragmented internally by quarrelling departments.[102]

Such spirited rebuttals of corporatism by established pluralist scholars did not foreclose the Australian debate after the accession of the Hawke government. The National Economic Summit, called in April 1983 to legitimise the Accord and address the economic crisis in a consensual way, and the Economic Planning Advisory Council (EPAC), established as a continuing forum for participation by a range of groups in longer term economic assessment, provided concrete institutions of a broadly corporatist form. Stewart and Ballard were quick off the mark with a strong corporatist interpretation of EPAC that proved to be much too hasty, because the senior Departments of Treasury and Finance quickly marginalised its role.[103] Subsequent debate was directed at characterising the tripartite initiatives of the Hawke government, and towards critically interpreting the more substantial Accord between the Labor Party and the trade union movement that, in various forms, has remained the core of the federal Labor government's incomes policy and its industrial relations strategy.

The major contribution to that debate has been made by Gwynneth Singleton who argued that both the Accord and EPAC are to be understood in traditional party and political terms of laborism and responsible party government. In an article in 1985, Singleton argued that the tripartism of EPAC was superficial and largely symbolic because EPAC lacked any decisive role in government policy-making. By careful analysis of how EPAC was constituted and operated, Singleton showed that it was but a pale imitation of corporatism: the body was purely advisory and rather peripheral to government policy-making; the non-union participants retained their distinct and often conflicting group interests; they were not incorporated into any meaningful national consensus; and there was no agreement on key matters such as taxation reform and industry restructuring. EPAC was not so much a manifestation of corporatism that would require 'bargained, negotiated agreement, a collaboration among the groups and between government and the groups, of self-subordination of special interests', as an exercise in Hawke-style political consensus concerned with symbolic participation and the mobilisation of consent for government policy.[104] Such consensus seeking and group intermediation was 'nothing new' and could be substantially explained in terms of responsible party government, Singleton argued. There 'was no legitimate reason to suggest that any real form of corporatist intermediation has supplanted the party in the policy formulation and decision-making process'. Rather, Singleton concluded by quoting an earlier article by Parkin on the character of Australian political science: 'the focus remains on "... the institutions and processes of parliament, cabinet, and the public service, on the periodic and highly-structured legitimation of the system through elites" '.[105]

Singleton's 'nothing new' interpretation of the Hawke government also characterised her book-length study of the Accord as a laborist alliance or partnership in government between the Labor Party and the trade union movement:

> The Accord is the product of the interdependence of the political and industrial wings of the Australian labour movement. It is the facilitator for the achievement of their disparate but related political, economic and social objectives.

> There is nothing new in this relationship. It has its basis in the long-standing tradition of laborism that has been an integral feature of the Australian trade union movement's association with the Australian Labor Party, that is, the idea that the capitalist state can be managed to the advantage of the working people by a combination of a strong trade union movement with a parliamentary labour party.[106]

Singleton explained the Accord in terms of the Labor Party's political base within Australian trade unions, party ideology of humanitarian concern for workers, close personal relationships among like-minded parliamentary and ACTU leaders and, above all, mutual self-interest of the Labor Party to win government and the unions to share in the spoils through having congenial economic and industrial policies implemented. In sum, 'The Accord is Australian labourism dressed in contemporary clothing'.[107]

The case against a corporatist interpretation of Australia was reinforced by both Trevor Matthews and Doug McEachern from quite different perspectives. From his detailed study of business organisation from an interest group perspective, Matthews argued that Australian business was relatively weak and fragmented. He also emphasised that the institutional representation of business and even unions was not the sort of intermediation that corporatism would entail.[108] Adapting the characterisation of Japan as 'corporatism without labour', Matthews has recently suggested that even the depiction of the Hawke regime as 'corporatism without business' is somewhat problematical because the Accord is highly contingent on Labor Party politics.[109]

From a leftist perspective, McEachern agrees that Australian business is *politically* weak and fragmented and hence corporatism cannot apply. But, that does not matter because business remains strong *economically* and does not need to mobilise politically. Business benefited from the Hawke government's Accord which delivered wage restraint and industrial harmony. In this period, business may have been 'a loser in politics' but it was 'a winner in the economy'.[110] As well, this neat account of how business gets what it wants without having to control politics overcomes the impass on which Tsokhas' earlier attempt at establishing businessmen's transformation of economic power into political power foundered.

Not all the earlier commentators on the Hawke government were as negative in their dismissal of corporatism as an explanatory concept. Stewart argued that what was involved in the Accord and the tripartite arrangements was 'partial corporatism' which benefited business disproportionately and excluded the most vulnerable sections of society – women, welfare recipients and the unemployed. From a quasi-Marxist perspective, Stewart claimed 'that business is organised as a class in partial corporatism even though it may be fragmented as a peak organisation and thus may appear to be the weaker partner'. In this analysis, he persisted with a behind-the-scenes explanation: 'Corporatist politics are simulated. The real decisions are hidden from view. The substantive decisions take place behind closed doors where only the tripartite partners are accorded privileged access.'[111] Partial corporatism was thus a 'political strategy' or subterfuge perpetrated by the dominant tripartite partners that excluded the less powerful and less privileged.

In the more sophisticated and subtle analysis of the Hawke government, Gerritsen blended the three elements of Labor traditionalism, business pluralism and 'partial' or 'consensual' corporatism that had been highlighted by other commentators. Agreeing with the Labor traditionalists' interpretation, he acknowledged that the Accord was 'a refinement and institutionalisation of a strong, traditional interpenetration between the ALP and the trade union movement', with the difference being greater acceptance by a Labor government of the ACTU.[112] There was no formal and compulsory tripartite collaboration but only 'two sets of bilateral relations – one more or less formal and bargained, with the ACTU, and one informal, pluralist and uncertain, with the pressure groups of capital'. That meant an asymmetric set of relations that tended towards pluralism with business and 'bargained bilateral corporatism' with the unions.[113] But in any case, the tripartite collaboration was only 'consensual' and hence was fragile to exogenous shocks or general economic recovery.

The federal Labor government and the Accord have proved more robust and enduring than Gerritsen and others anticipated, although interest in corporatist interpretations of them has waned. In a paper presented at the Australian National University in 1990, Wyn Grant, one of the British leaders of the corporate charge, characterised the 1980s as 'the decade of corporatism that never was'. That is probably also an apt summation for Australia during the 1980s because, as the Hawke government consolidated its grip on government, corporatism seemed to have little relevance. As a result, the

Australian corporatist literature has been rather incidental and haphazard, resulting from occasional forays by scholars who are established in, or concerned mainly with, particular fields such as industrial relations, Labor politics, business organisation or class analysis. Alternatively, or in addition, many of its Australian critics have used corporatism as a foil for restating their own pluralist, Marxist or traditionalist assumptions. Partly as a result of this self-vindication of established mind-sets and partly due to the largely domestic focus of Australian political analysis, little attention was given to the broader political purpose of corporatism which is to facilitate national economic management in the context of international volatility.

That purpose of corporatism has been best articulated by Katzenstein's classic study of smaller European states, referred to in Chapter 1.[114] These states have small, open and affluent economies, benefiting from export trade in international markets. Corporatism provides the political means for pursuing such an economic strategy by facilitating internal adjustments to the fluctuations caused by international markets. The smaller European states have been able to benefit economically from being open to greater international competition because they have also compensated politically for the shocks and adjustments through domestic corporatism.

From his background in comparative European politics, Castles adapted Katzenstein's perspective to expose what is, in his view, the error of the Labor government in pursuing policies of greater international competition without adequate domestic arrangements to cushion and accommodate its consequences. Australia's traditional policy of tying protectionism to enhanced national wages, the 'politics of domestic defence', is being eroded by the Labor government's policies of deregulation and greater exposure of the national economy to international market forces, without the provision of an adequate alternative 'politics of domestic compensation'.[115] The problem with Castles' analysis is that it leaves unexplained how the federal Labor government was able to pursue such deregulation without domestic compensation and yet did not jeopardise its continuing trade union and electoral support. Moreover, there seems little point in hankering after a form of European national corporatism that has no grounding in Australia's political culture or history.

Sectoral corporatism

The absence of corporatism at the national level need not preclude a kind of corporatism at the sectoral level. While Australian political scientists were reacting to the generic concept of corporatism and demonstrating that it had little salience for Australia under the Hawke government, the focus of much overseas interest was shifting from macro- to 'meso'-corporatism, a more fruitful field for corporatist analysis in the more pluralist democracies that are comparable to Australia. It is worth examining the theory of sectoral corporatism because it, rather than macro-corporatism, has more relevance to industry policy under a Labor government and has been virtually neglected by Australian scholars.[116]

In the early 1980s, Wassenberg proposed a three-level analysis of politico-economic systems: the 'macro', national or peak association level; the 'micro' or individual firm level; and the 'meso' or intermediate level of complete industries and industry-wide associations. He suggested that if we relaxed the exclusively macro-societal focus of our approach and allowed for the possible coexistence of different regime types: 'the contrasting ideal-types may be accommodated – in a more or less pragmatic fashion – to the analysis of inter-level relations, without driving out or supplanting each other in time or without merging into some sort of coherent Gestalt'.[117] The same point was made by Cawson in introducing a collection of 'Studies in Meso-Corporatism': 'When we fix our sights below the peaks of class organisation, and study organisation and interest intermediation within specific sectors and policy fields, a much more complex picture appears.'[118] Empirical studies of the Anglo-American democracies (Britain, the United States, and Canada) that are usually considered to be non-corporatist, as well as European countries, show that corporatist practices are prevalent at the sectoral level. This concept of sectoral corporatism has obvious relevance for characterising the Labor government's industry plans which were sectoral and tripartite. These plans will be discussed in detail in Chapters 5, 6 and 7.

Since corporatism remains a contested concept with no general agreement on its precise meaning by its users,[119] it is important to specify what is meant by the term. Essentially, sectoral corporatism might be considered to have four defining components. The first is its sectoral character: it is concerned with relations between the state and functional groups within an industry sector and has nothing to say about the national society or macro-economic relations. The second has to do with the state which needs to be sufficiently autonomous so as not to be captive of sectoral interests nor to limit its actions merely to responding to interest group pressures; nor for that matter can the state be sufficiently dominant and authoritative to direct action without the cooperative agreement of affected groups. The third component is sufficient concentration in the organisation of both business and labour to enable their participation in tripartite negotiations at the sectoral level that produce binding commitment on longer term policy and shared responsibility for its implementation. The fourth entails the state's recognition of the functional interest groups and their incorporation into the process of policy-making and implementation.

Sectoral corporatism is to be distinguished from a free market, preferred by economists, because of the state's role in recognising and co-opting the functional interest groups to participate in a sectoral plan and, through state intervention in the economy, to ensure its implementation. Likewise sectoral corporatism also differs from pluralist models, which are favoured by political scientists and which presuppose some approximation to a market place of interest pressures, because of the autonomous role of the state and the concentration of representation of sector-wide interests of business and labour. Obviously, sectoral corporatism also differs from Marxist models, which are grounded in an underlying societal division of antagonistic class relations, because of the collaborative association of business and labour and a quasi-autonomous state.

Much of the literature on meso-corporatism has been unduly concerned with the organisation of industry-specific business associations and 'private interest government'.[120] There has been insufficient attention to the politics and the role of the state; as Allen has pointed out: 'what the meso-corporatist literature is still lacking is an explicit treatment of the politics of industrial adjustment'.[121] In the federation of Germany with which Allen was concerned, subnational governments have played a key role in industrial adjustment. More significant in Australia during the 1980s was the federal Labor government's use of tripartite plans for sectoral adjustment in troubled industries.

Sectoral corporatism is possible where macro-corporatism with its encompassing national requirements for interest association and policy coordination is precluded. We suggest that a version of this has been the case for the motor vehicle and the textiles, clothing and footwear industry plans that are analysed in detail in Chapters 6 and 7. Fragmentation of business, the weak link in any scenario for a corporatist Australia, may be overcome, to a large extent, at the sectoral level, particularly for highly protected industries such as the textiles, clothing and footwear industry, and the motor vehicle industry which have been under threat and have long traditions of defensive action. In fact, it is precisely in restructuring this sort of industry that one would expect sectoral corporatism to apply.[122] The structured tripartism of sectoral corporatism also applies partially to the steel plan, although with a virtual monopoly of the BHP company on the business side it was clearly a special case. Moreover, as we shall see in Chapter 5, the fragmentation was actually on the union side with ruptures between the national leaders who negotiated the plan and the local branch leaders who controlled the shop-floors.

If the Labor government's industry plans can be characterised as quasi-corporatist, they are corporatist with a strong statist element. The state, through a strong minister and his officials, has been the predominant architect, catalyst and actor in devising the plans and securing tripartite argreement. The state has also put in place the support machinery for coordination and monitoring. The senior Labor minister who has held the industry portfolio since the Hawke government came to office in 1983, John Button, used the organisations and powers of the state to establish tripartite arrangements, coordinate the negotiation of acceptable industry plans, and implement these by offering a range of incentives to business and labour. For its part, labour has had close bilateral relations with the Labor government through its traditional union affiliation with the Labor Party and formally through the Accord at the national level, while at the sectoral level it has had an immediate stake in protecting, and some hope of enhancing, its shrinking domain.

Recognition of the corporatist dimension of its sectoral plans enables us to sketch a more plausible account of this Labor government's overall approach to national economic management than has been given so far. On the one hand, traditionalist Labor proponents have lamented the betrayal of laborist values in pushing for greater reliance on market competition rather than government regulation and intervention.[123] On the other hand, comparativists such as Castles, whose reference is the smaller European states, have lamented the demise of Australia's established 'politics of domestic defence' (protectionism combined with enhanced national wage conditions) without the substitution of an adequate 'politics of domestic compensation'.[124] Our suggestion is that the Hawke-Keating government has indeed changed the direction of macro-policy in favour of deregulation and less protection but has compensated the industries most affected through the policies of sectoral corporatism in its industry plans. This is the sort of trade-off that one would expect from a Labor government committed to deregulation but with a strong trade union base and within a country that has an established tradition of statist intervention, although not previously in such tripartite plans at the sectoral level. Moreover, such an explanation resolves the political gap in Castles' account as to why the Labor government has been able to demolish protection without alienating either the unions or business.

REINSTATING THE STATE

From our critical review of Australian (and other) pluralist, Marxist and corporatist writers, it is clear that whether or not the idea of the state is used depends on the conceptual assumptions of the author and the intellectual fashion of the time. For political science, as for most disciplines, what is studied and what is found depend very much on the presuppositions that have been made, either explicitly or implicitly, about the nature and scope of the discipline and of the subject studied. The writing on Australian politics, as is the case with most of the social sciences, is as much a reflection of the conceptual framework of the writer as of the phenomena being observed. Our critical examination of various schools of Australian political writing in different historical periods that focused on the concept of the state (whether the concept had been used or not and the variable meanings that it had been given when used) shows how the intellectual framework and assumptions determine the approach and findings of political research.

It is suggested here that the scope of political science has been too narrow and its predominant pluralist orientation unsuited to coming to grips with the aspects of Australian politics that concern the state's leading role in national policy in general and industry policy in particular. Many of the most significant events of politics occur off the political agenda of partisan contention – which has tended to be the focus of pluralist political science. Such events can occur as a result of the impact of international market forces on Australia's relatively small and dependent economy; because of the continuing effect of settled national policies and established state departments and public corporations that are only occasionally and indirectly politicised; or because of corporate decisions and special arrangements between corporations and governments, state departments and public bodies. Such was the case for Australia's national policy of protection that was not politically contentious for much of the country's history.

Moreover, changes in structural policies, like Australia's present move beyond protectionism, are, in important ways, driven by and reflected in the changing attitudes and purposes of state officials and state organisations. An obvious example, discussed in some detail in Chapter 3, is the influence of Alf Rattigan and the Tariff Board in turning around protectionist thinking and practice in the late 1960s. But, as well, politicians and the political process that normally function within well-established institutional structures and routines, and with settled policies that are anchored in established state departments and bureaus, can, in special circumstances, restructure state institutions and practices in fundamental ways. To an extent, McEwen did that in creating the Department of Trade and Industry in 1956 and in manipulating the Tariff Board into a subservient role which served his grand protectionist purposes. More recently, after its third electoral victory in 1987, the Hawke Labor government carried out a major institutional restructuring to form mega-departments, revamped the Industries Assistance Commission and transferred it from the department with responsibility for industry, now the Department of Industry, Technology and Commerce, to a more independent base in Treasury.

The pivotal role of the state was articulated by earlier Australian writers such as Hancock, so that in advocating a statist approach within a broader political economy framework we are in part resurrecting that earlier Australian tradition. If it is true in America that only 40 per cent of significant political issues fall within pluralist politics, as Lindblom claimed, in Australia that figure would no doubt be lower. Therefore, to study the more than 60 per cent of politics that is not on the agenda of pluralist political science, we need a broader approach for the discipline that includes political economy and focuses on the role of the state.

What we have in mind is both an approach to studying politics and an interpretive framework in which to study them. Any serious study of politics necessarily entails both elements, although the interpretive perspective is often implicit and unarticulated, either because the author takes it for granted or it is assumed to be obvious or shared by the readers. The statism we are proposing is theoretically informed by critical reflection on what it entails compared with alternative conceptual paradigms; it is also practically grounded in the historical analysis of Australia's politics and development.

The new statism, or really the revival of an older statist approach that we are proposing, entails an orientation and an agenda for research that eschews both the simplifying assumptions or grand theorising of pluralism and Marxism. Both those paradigms are essentially society-based in assuming that the primary actors are interest groups or classes, and that the state either resonates or reflects their influence. Both pluralism and Marxism assume that the real explanation for politics and public policy is to be found beyond the political system in social forces and groups. A statist approach switches attention back to the state and the processes of government on the grounds that these have an autonomy and a determining force that is at least partly independent of social groups and forces, and indeed instrumental in shaping them. Just how independent and in what ways the state interacts with society depend on the complex balance of factors, both domestic and international, at particular periods of time. Again, McEwen provides an apposite illustration: through the 1950s and 1960s he dominated the Tariff Board, appointing Rattigan as Chairman in 1966 because he was perceived to be both 'saleable' and 'manageable',[125] but by the late 1960s McEwen had lost control of the Tariff Board and the tariff debate. The reasons for this about-face need to be sought in history and politics, not *a priori* theories of the state.

In similar vein, Skocpol has insisted on the 'inherent historicity of sociopolitical structures'.[126] She and the other authors of *Bringing The State Back In* give a nice summary of the research strategy and method of the new statism:

> Heuristically, at least, it is fruitful to assume both that states are potentially autonomous and, conversely, that socioeconomic relations influence and limit state structures and activities. The challenge for researchers is to identify, conceptualize precisely, and explain variations through time and space.[127]

This approach needs to be extended to state-political relations in addition to socio-economic ones, and also from the macro-level of aggregate state action to the meso-level of sectoral policy where particular state organisations interact with business, labour and consumer groups.

The new statism can be characterised by three features. The first is a holistic approach to the study of domestic politics that preserves the larger unity of government institutions and public policies in the entity of the state. This is something that scholars of international relations and comparative politics retained, but pluralists and others studying the hard core of domestic politics tended to lose sight of – hence the strong influence of internationalist and comparative scholars such as Krasner, Katzenstein and Skocpol in bringing the state back into modern political analysis. The second is an emphasis on political institutions and state officials because these are considered to be important in shaping public policy. This 'new institutionalism' in political science is grounded in a renewed appreciation of the organisational basis of politics and the independent role of state officials that had tended to be swamped by pluralism and Marxism.[128] The third characteristic is a strong preference for historical investigation of what has developed and why during periods of stability and change, rather than static analysis of conceptual categories or the exposition of implications from doctrinal positions.

While acknowledging the historical contingency of its particular structural arrangements and relations, we do need to define, albeit in a very general way, the enduring entity of the state that is the subject of our historical research. This can be done in terms of broad propositions which specify what the state is, what it does, and how that varies over time. First, the state is a distinct but complex organisation; second, it formulates and implements public policies which influence groups and individuals in society; and third, both its organisational shape and its influence are variable over time. If nothing more, this is a way of structuring research questions. First, how independent and organisationally coherent is the state? Second, how influential is it? And third, how does the state's independence and influence change over time? Alternatively, this threefold attention to state attributes and relations might be ordered in terms of autonomy, strength and dynamism.

Autonomy of the state

The autonomy of the democratic state can be articulated, drawing on Nordlinger's classic account, in terms of its ability to implement state preferences generated by state officials into authoritative actions in terms of binding policy. Nordlinger has a useful categorisation of three types of state autonomy: type I is where state–society preferences diverge but public officials have their way; type II is where state–society preferences at first diverge, but public officials reshape society preferences to bring them into line with public views; and type III is where state–society preferences are not divergent and the state acts upon its preferences.[129] Clearly, the first two are instances of state autonomy, but even the third might just as plausibly be also. However, it is not uncommon among both pluralists and Marxists alike to assume that because interest groups or business want some policy which the state provides that their very wanting and demanding it will cause it to be granted. It might simply be that the state independently appreciates what is good for business or employment, for example, so provides policies that benefit business and unions. The more general methodological point is that the autonomy, or any other aspect, of the state cannot be determined solely or primarily from the societal end, by looking at interest groups and peak associations and their relations with the state.

The autonomy of the state depends on two key variables: the organisational coherence and concentration within its own structures, and its independence from society generally or the particular social groups with which it deals. Policy relations are by definition reciprocal since they involve both the state and affected groups. Hence, the organisational coherence and strength of the social groups are also important in determining what the state can do and the shape of its policies. Katzenstein has pulled these relational aspects together in the concept of a 'policy network', arguing that the amount of concentration in the state and in society and the degree of independence between the two are crucial in determining the character of policy networks. Katzenstein argues that a centralised state bureaucracy that is independent from private business enables successful sectoral policy to be put in place, as in the case of Japan, whereas in the United States a decentralised state that is interpenetrated by fragmented business and labour groups precludes strong sectoral policy and produces its celebrated pluralism.[130]

Strength of the state

Atkinson and Coleman, who are concerned with the strength or weakness of the state in industry policy, have adopted the framework of Katzenstein's 'policy network' but questioned his attempt to explain industry policy from an analysis of the overall state system. Industry policy, they claim, is typically made by parts of the state, in agencies or bureaus, and for particular sectors of industry. So they adapt Katzenstein's macro-analysis to the meso-level, substituting state agency or bureau for the state, and business interest groups for society. The state is strong in industry policy, they argue, if decision-making is centralised in state officials and agencies, business is well organised, and the two are independent of one another. In other words, to be strong the state has to be concentrated within its internal organisation and have an organisationally coherent respondent to deal with at arm's length.

The problem with the Atkinson and Coleman approach, and its application to Australia, is the pluralist bias that puts too much weight on the structure of pressure groups and not enough on the state. In their analysis, the state is overly determined by the 'pressure pluralist network'. To quote them:

> The nature of industry policy employed in a sector is closely linked to the character of the policy network. In the United States, Britain, Canada, *Australia* and New Zealand, the most common arrangement involves a reactive approach to industrial policy and a pressure pluralist network. Even at the sectoral level, where business organization is often mobilized and state structures more variable, the state is predisposed to leave business alone. *Policies are responses to political pressures from business.* They tend to be *ad hoc*, uncoordinated with previous decisions, and oriented almost entirely to the short term. Other than discussions about specific, short-term problems, the state administration requires little from business and business makes few demands of the state.[131]

Just how wrong this is with respect to Australia is brought out in subsequent chapters which demonstrate the primary role of the state in the establishment, consolidation and dismantling of the national policy of protection. It is sufficient at this point to expose the conceptual error of overgeneralising the features of policy networks from corporatist and statist countries such as the smaller European states and Japan. A strong state does not necessarily require a corresponding concentrated organisation of business groups in order to implement industry policy. In fact, state action may well be a substitute for strong business, as was the case with 'state socialism' in early Australia. Alternatively, the state may effect a concentration of business at the sectoral level sufficient to implement corporatist plans as the Hawke government has done. Furthermore, strong state policy may obviate the need for business mobilisation, just as business may not need to organise if what it would require is provided by the state anyway.

Dynamism of the state

The third key attribute of both state structures and relations is their dynamic variability over time. This is a leading theme of our book which focuses on the transformation of Australian industry policy from protectionism to corrective state policies and sectoral plans.

The dynamic aspect of business–government relations with which we are concerned has become a central theme in some recent research; for example, the work on the fluctuating fortunes of American business by David Vogel using a pluralist perspective,[132] and on the Australian Tariff Board's besting of McEwenism by Stephen Bell from a Marxist perspective.[133] Vogel breaks the arid debate over Lindblom's claims that business enjoys a privileged position, between those claiming that it does and opponents claiming that it does not, by pointing out that both claims are incomplete because the political power of business has actually varied. Such variations are explained in terms of three main variables: the first is public perception of the economy's long-term strength, with business paradoxically weaker when the economy is stronger; the second is the degree of cooperation within the business sector; and third is the dynamics of the political system and the ability of business to influence politics.[134] As a pluralist, Vogel eschews any notion of the state and seeks explanation from the business side. Bell, on the other hand, looks to both the state and business, concluding that we 'need to take seriously the state's capacities for independent initiatives', a finding that is of significance for him because he persists with a larger Marxist framework that assumes the structural dominance of business.

Our focus in the following chapters is primarily on the state because we see it as the primary focus and instrument of policy change. We locate the main source of dynamism not in the fluctuating strength or weakness of business or the organisational coherence of business interest groups but primarily within the political process and the state in its relations with business and interest groups.

NOTES

1. Influential earlier works included a 'Special Number on the State', *Daedalus*, 1979; Eric A. Nordlinger, *On the Autonomy of the Democratic State*, Harvard University Press, Cambridge, Mass., 1981; G. Poggi, *The Development of the Modern State*, Stanford University Press, Stanford, 1978. For subsequent discussions, see a 'Special Issue on the State in Comparative and International Perspective', *Comparative Political Studies*, Vol. 21, No. 1, April 1988; and Bert A. Rockman, 'Minding the State - or a state of mind? Issues in the comparative conceptualization of the State', *Comparative Political Studies*, Vol. 23, No. 1, April 1990, pp. 25–55.
2. David Easton, 'The political system besieged by the State', *Political Theory*, Vol. 9, 1981, pp. 303, 322.
3. See Peter B. Evans, Dietrich Rueschemeyer & Theda Skocpol, *Bringing the State Back In*, Cambridge University Press, Cambridge, 1985. For an Australian perspective see Brian Head, 'Recent theories of the State', *Politics*, Vol. 19, 1984, pp. 39–45; and Brian Head, ed., *The Politics of Development in the Australian States*, Allen & Unwin, Sydney, 1984.
4. Charles Lindblom, *Politics and Markets*, Basic Books, New York, 1977.
5. F. Block, 'The ruling class does not rule', *Socialist Revolution*, Vol. 33, 1977, pp. 6–28; B. Frankel, 'On the state of the State: Marxist theories of the State after Leninism', *Theory and Society*, Vol. 7, 1979, pp. 205–27; B. Jessop, *The Capitalist State*, Martin Robinson, Oxford, 1982; Claus Offe, 'The theory of the capitalist State and the problem of policy formation', in *Stress and Construction in Modern Capitalism*, eds L. Lindberg et al., Heath, Lexington, 1975; N. Poulantanzas, 'The problem of the capitalist State', in *Ideology and Social Science*, ed. R. Blackburn, Fontana, London, 1972; N. Poulantanzas, *The Problem of the Formation of the Capitalist State*, New Left Books, London, 1978.
6. S. Krasner, 'Approaches to the State: alternative conception and historical dynamics review article', *Comparative Politics*, Vol. 16, 1984, pp. 223–46.
7. S. Krasner, *Defending the National Interest*, Princeton University Press, Princeton, 1978; P. Katzenstein, ed., *Between Power and Plenty*, University of Wisconsin Press, Madison, 1978; T. Skocpol, *States and Social Revolutions*, Cambridge University Press, New York, 1979; A. Stepan, *The State and Society in Peru*, Princeton University Press, Princeton, 1978; R. Hass, 'The primacy of the State . . . or revisiting

the revisionists', *Daedalus,* Vol. 108, 1979, pp. 125–35; M. Klapp, 'The State - landlord or entrepreneur', *International Organisation,* Vol. 36, 1982, pp. 575–607.

8. G. Almond, 'Corporation, pluralism and professional memory', *World Politics,* Vol. 35, 1982, p. 252. Almond is partly critical of the new statism, but also points out that it has strong roots in mainstream political science which has been more diverse than is often credited. For a more critical rejection of the concept of the state, see H. Eckstein, 'On the science of The State', *Daedalus,* Vol. 108, 1979, p. 120.
9. S. J. Butlin, *Foundations of the Australian Monetary System 1788–1851,* Sydney University Press, Sydney, 1953, p. 1.
10. W. K. Hancock, *Australia,* Ernest Benn, London, 1930.
11. Brian Fitzpatrick, *The Australian People 1788–1945,* Melbourne University Press, Melbourne, 1946, p. 239.
12. See for example Hedley Bull, 'International relations as an academic pursuit', *Australian Outlook,* Vol. 26, 1972, pp. 251–65; and J. D. B. Miller, *The World of States,* Croom Helm, London, 1981.
13. Martin Indyk, 'The Australian study of international relations', in *Surveys of Australian Political Science,* ed. Don Aitkin, George Allen & Unwin, Sydney, 1985, p. 267.
14. ibid., p. 298.
15. For example, Harry Gelber, 'Australia in a changing world economy', *Australian Economic Papers,* Vol. 5, 1986, pp. 1–20; S. F. Harris, 'The linking of politics and economics in foreign policy', *Australian Outlook,* Vol. 40, 1986, pp. 5–10; and R. A. Higgott, 'Of territorial borders and intellectual barriers: the State in international politics', in *New Directions in International Relations: Australian Perspectives,* ed. R. A. Higgott, Canberra Studies in World Affairs, No. 23, Australian National University, Canberra, 1988.
16. Richard Higgott, 'The politics of Australia's international economic relations: adjustment and two-level games', *Australian Journal of Political Science,* Vol. 26, 1991, p. 3.
17. F. A. Bland, *Shadows and Realities of Government,* Workers' Educational Association of NSW, Sydney, 1923; and *Planning the Modern State,* Angus & Robertson, Sydney, 1934.
18. Martin Painter, *Steering the Modern State,* Sydney University Press, Sydney, 1987
19. Hancock, pp. 72–3.
20. Henry Mayer, 'Some conceptions of the Australian party system', *Historical Studies,* Vol. 7, 1956, pp. 253–70.
21. S. Encel, 'The concept of the state in Australian politics', *Australian Journal of Politics and History,* Vol. 6, 1960, p. 62.
22. Hancock, p. 227 ff.
23. ibid., p. 130.
24. F. W. Eggleston, *State Socialism In Victoria,* King, London, 1932, p. 1.

25. See Warren O. Osmond, *Frederic Eggleston: An Intellectual in Australian Politics*, Allen & Unwin, Sydney, 1985, pp. 161–5.
26. ibid., p. 7.
27. ibid., p. 30.
28. ibid., pp. 283–4.
29. ibid., pp. 234–5.
30. N. Butlin, 'Colonial socialism in Australia 1860–1900', in *The State and Economic Growth*, ed. H. G. J. Aitken, Social Science Research Council, New York, 1959.
31. N. G. Butlin, A. Barnard, & J. J. Pincus, *Government and Capitalism: Public and Private Choice In Twentieth Century Australia*, Allen & Unwin, Sydney, 1982, pp. 5–6.
32. Public Bodies Review Committee, *Fifth Report, The Economic Impact of Public Bodies in Victoria*, Government Printer, Melbourne, 1981.
33. Albert Métin, *Socialism Without Doctrine*, ed. D. Aitkin, translated by Russel Ward, Alternative Publishing Co-operative Ltd, Chippendale, 1977.
34. Quoted S. Encel, 'The concept of the state in Australian politics', p. 71.
35. W. Hughes, *The Case For Labor*, Worker Trustees, Sydney, 1910, pp. 85, 91.
36. Métin, *Socialism Without Doctrine*, pp. 255–6.
37. ibid., p. 51.
38. ibid., p. 165.
39. Hancock, *Australia*, p. 82.
40. ibid., p. 73.
41. For a survey of Australian political science, see Don Aitkin, 'Political science in Australia: development and situation', in *Surveys of Australian Political Science*, ed. Don Aitkin, Allen & Unwin, Sydney, 1985.
42. E. Tapp, 'Planning and democracy', *Australian Quarterly*, September 1945, p. 76.
43. A. Stout, 'Self interest versus The Common Good', *Australian Quarterly*, December 1943, p. 29.
44. M. Simms, *A Liberal Nation*, Hale & Iremonger, Sydney, 1982, p. 58.
45. Butlin, Barnard, & Pincus, *Government and Capitalism: Public and Private Choice In Twentieth Century Australia*, pp. 5–6
46. Simms, *A Liberal Nation*, p. 162.
47. Encel, 'The concept of the state in Australian politics', pp. 72, 73.
48. ibid., p. 74.
49. A. F. Davies, 'The political system of Victoria', in *The Government of the Australian States*, ed. S. R. Davis, Longmans, London, 1960, p. 185.
50. ibid., p. 233.
51. R. Miliband, *The State in Capitalist Society*, Weidenfeld & Nicolson, London, 1969.

52. P. H. Partridge, 'The capitalist State', *Politics*, Vol. 5, 1970, p. 235.
53. Charles Lindblom, *Politics and Markets*, Basic Books, New York, 1977.
54. J. Manly, 'Neo-pluralism: a class analysis of Pluralism I and Pluralism II', *American Political Science Review*, Vol. 77, 1983, pp. 368–83.
55. Charles Lindblom, 'Comment on Manly', *American Political Science Review*, Vol. 77, 1983, p. 384.
56. ibid., p. 385.
57. Leon Glezer, *Tariff Politics: Australian Policy-making 1960–1980*, Melbourne University Press, Melbourne, 1982, p. 218.
58. ibid., p. 248.
59. ibid., p. 278.
60. ibid., p. 285.
61. John Warhurst, *Jobs or Dogma? The Industries Assistance Commission and Australian Politics*, University of Queensland Press, St Lucia, Qld, 1982, pp. 231, 234.
62. ibid., p. 235.
63. As was the case in the above discussion of early and mainstream views of the state, no attempt will be made here to give a comprehensive account of the variety of work. For example, no attempt will be made to assess the prolific output of the political economy group at Sydney University: see E. L. Wheelwright & Frank J. B. Stilwell, eds, *Readings in Political Economy*, Vols 1 & 2, Australia and New Zealand Book Company, Sydney, 1976; and E. L. Wheelwright and Ken Buckley, eds, *Essays in the Political Economy of Australian Capitalism*, Vols 1-5, Australia and New Zealand Book Company, Sydney, 1975–1983.
64. R. W. Connell & T. H. Irving, *Class Structure in Australian Society*, Longman Cheshire, Melbourne, 1980.
65. ibid., pp. 111–13.
66. R. W. Connell, *Ruling Class, Ruling Culture*, Cambridge University Press, Cambridge, 1977.
67. ibid., p. 55.
68. ibid., pp. 56–8.
69. C. Wright Mills, *The Power Elite*, Oxford University Press, New York, 1956.
70. Miliband, *The State in Capitalist Society*.
71. J. Playford, 'Who rules Australia?', in *Australian Capitalism*, eds J. P. Kirsner &. D. Kirsner, Penguin, Melbourne, 1972.
72. S. Encel, *Equality and Authority*, Cheshire, Melbourne, 1970.
73. Connell, *Ruling Class, Ruling Culture*, p. 45.
74. ibid., p. 58.
75. N. Poulantanzas, 'The problem of the capitalist State', in *Ideology and Social Science*, ed. R. Blackburn, Fontana, London, 1972; N. Poulantanzas, *The Problem of the Formation of the Capitalist State*, New Left Books, London, 1978.

76. E. L. Wheelwright, *Transnational Corporations and the New International Division of Labour: Some Implications for Australia*, Occasional Paper No. 4, Sydney University Press, Sydney, 1980.
77. G. Crough & E. L. Wheelwright, *Australia a Client State: A Study of the Effects of Transnational Corporations*, Working Paper No. 9, Sydney Transnational Research Project, Sydney University, Sydney, 1981.
78. ibid., p. 19.
79. Andrew Theophanous, *Australian Democracy In Crisis*, Oxford University Press, Melbourne, 1980.
80. J. O'Connor, *The Fiscal Crisis of the State*, St Martins Press, New York, 1973.
81. Jurgen Habermas, *Legitimation Crisis*, Cheshire, Boston, 1973.
82. An exception is Rick Kuhn who maintains a bold Marxist perspective: see 'The Accord and business: the distinctiveness of the Hawke government's approach to capital accumulation', in *Business and Government Under Labor*, eds B. Galligan & G. Singleton, Longman Cheshire, Melbourne, 1991, pp. 47–74; and R. Kuhn & T. O'Lincoln, 'Profitability and economic crisis', *Journal of Australian Political Economy*, No. 25, 1989, pp. 44–69.
83. Kosmas Tsokhas, *A Class Apart? Businessmen and Australian Politics 1960–1980*, Oxford University Press, Melbourne, 1985, pp. xi, xiv–xv.
84. See B. Galligan, 'A class apart?', *Arena*, No. 70, 1985, pp. 199–202.
85. Kosmas Tsokhas, *Beyond Dependence: Companies, Labour Processes and Australian Mining*, Oxford University Press, Melbourne, 1986.
86. Kosmas Tsokhas, *Markets, Money and Empire: The Political Economy of the Australian Wool Industry*, Melbourne University Press, Melbourne, 1990.
87. Doug McEachern, *Business: The Power and Politics of the Hawke Era*, Prentice Hall, Sydney, 1991, p. 141.
88. ibid., p. 154.
89. C. Bulbeck, 'State and capital in tariff policy', in *State and Economy in Australia*, ed. B. W. Head, Oxford University Press, Melbourne, 1983, p. 234.
90. P. C. Schmitter & G. Lehmbruch, eds, *Trends Towards Corporatist Intermediation*, Sage, Beverly Hills, 1979.
91. See John Ballard, The corpus of neo-corporatism: insights into the State in Australia or corpus delicti?, mimeo, Australian National University, 1980. This was one of a number of seminar papers in a series Ballard organised in 1980.
92. Marian Sawer, *Australia and the New Right*, Allen & Unwin, Sydney, 1982; A. Patience & B. W. Head, *From Whitlam to Fraser: Reform and Reaction in Australian Politics*, Oxford University Press, Melbourne, 1979.
93. Brian Galligan, 'The regulation of direct foreign investment in the Australian mining sector', *Politics*, Vol. 22, No. 1, May 1987, pp. 35–46.

94. B. W. Head & A. Patience, eds., *From Fraser to Hawke: Australian Public Policy in the 1980s,* Longman Cheshire, Melbourne, 1989; and C. Jennett & R. G. Stewart, eds, *Hawke and Australian Public Policy,* Macmillan, Melbourne, 1990.
95. R. M. Martin, *TUC: The Growth of a Pressure Group 1868–1976,* Oxford University Press, Oxford, 1980, pp. vii, 1–2.
96. R. M. Martin, 'Pluralism and the new corporatism', *Political Studies,* Vol. 31, 1983, pp. 87, 89.
97. ibid., pp. 101–2.
98. Peter Loveday, *Promoting Industry,* University of Queensland Press, St Lucia, 1982, pp. 208–9.
99. Peter Loveday, 'Corporatist trends in Australia?', *Politics,* Vol. 19, May 1984, pp. 46–51.
100. ibid, p. 46, quoting J. T. Winkler, 'The corporatist economy: theory and adminstration', in *Industrial Society: Class, Cleavage and Control,* ed. R. Scase, Allen & Unwin, London, 1977, pp. 43–58.
101. Loveday, 'Corporatist trends in Australia', p. 47.
102. ibid., p. 50.
103. R. G. Stewart & J. Ballard, The Summit as simulated politics - staging corporatist legitimation in Australia, mimeo, Australian Political Studies Association Conference, Sydney, 1983; but see Randal Stewart, 'The politics of the accord. Does corporatism explain it?', *Politics,* Vol. 20, May, 1985, pp. 26–35.
104. Gwynneth Singleton, 'The Economic Planning Advisory Council: the reality of consensus', *Politics,* Vol. 20, May 1985, p. 23.
105. ibid., p. 24, quoting Andrew Parkin, 'Pluralism and Australian political science', *Politics,* Vol. 15, No. 1, May 1980, p. 51.
106. Gwynneth Singleton, *The Accord and the Labour Movement,* Melbourne University Press, Melbourne, 1989.
107. ibid., p. 198. See also Gwynneth Singleton, 'Corporatism or labourism?: The Australian labour movement in Accord', *Journal of Commonwealth & Comparative Politics,* Vol. 28, No. 2, July 1990, p. 192.
108. T. V. Matthews, 'Business associations and the State, 1850–1979', in *State and Economy in Australia,* ed. B. Head, Oxford University Press, Melbourne, 1983, p. 144.
109. T. Matthews, 'Interest groups politics: corporatism without business?', in *Australia Compared,* ed. F. G. Castles, Allen & Unwin, Sydney, 1991; T. J. Pempel & K. Tsunekawa, 'Corporatism without Labor? The Japanese anomaly', in *Trends Toward Corporatist Intermediation,* eds Phillipe C. Schmitter & Gerhard Lehmbruch, Sage Publications, Beverly Hills, 1979.
110. Doug McEachern, 'Corporatism and business responses to the Hawke Government', *Politics,* Vol. 21, May 1986, p. 26.
111. Randal Stewart, 'The politics of the Accord. Does corporatism explain it?', *Politics,* Vol. 20, May 1985, p. 33.

112. Rolf Gerritsen, 'The necessity of "corporatism": the case of the Hawke Labor government', *Politics*, Vol. 21, May 1986, p. 51.
113. ibid., pp. 49, 50.
114. Peter J. Katzenstein, *Small States in World Markets: Industry Policy in Europe*, Cornell University Press, Ithaca, 1985.
115. Francis Castles, *Australian Public Policy and Economic Vulnerability*, Allen & Unwin, Sydney, 1988.
116. The following analysis was first developed and applied in A. Capling & B. Galligan, 'Sectoral corporatism with a difference: the textiles, clothing and footwear plan', *Australian Journal of Public Administration*, Vol. 50, No. 1, 1991, pp. 47–60.
117. A. F. P. Wassenberg, 'Neo-corporatism and the quest for control: the cuckoo game', in *Patterns of Corporatist Policy-Making*, eds G. Lehmbruch & P. C. Schmitter, Sage, London, 1982, p. 88.
118. Alan Cawson, *Organized Interests and the State: Studies in Meso-Corporatism*, Sage, London, 1985, p. 221.
119. See Alan Cawson, *Corporatism and Political Theory*, Basil Blackwell, Oxford, 1986.
120. W. Streeck & P. C. Schmitter, *Private Interest Government: Beyond Market and State*, Sage, London, 1985; and W. Grant, ed., *Business Interests, Organisational Developments and Private Interest Government*, Walter de Gruyter, Berlin, 1987.
121. Christopher S. Allen, 'Corporatism and regional economic policies in the Federal Republic of Germany: The "meso" politics of industrial adjustment', *Publius*, Vol. 19, Fall 1989, p. 150.
122. M. M. Atkinson & W. D. Coleman, 'Strong States and weak States: sectoral policy networks in advanced capitalist economies', *British Journal of Political Science*, Vol. 19, 1989, p. 64.
123. G. Maddox, *The Hawke Government and Labor Tradition*, Penguin, Melbourne, 1989; and D. Jaensch, *The Hawke-Keating Hijack*, Allen & Unwin, Sydney, 1989.
124. Castles, *Australian Public Policy and Economic Vulnerability*.
125. These are Rattigan's own words: Alf Rattigan, *Industry Assistance: the Inside Story*, Melbourne University Press, Melbourne, 1986.
126. Theda Skocpol, 'Bringing the State back in: strategies of analysis in current research', in *Bringing the State Back In*, eds P. Evans, D. Rueschemeyer & T. Skocpol, Cambridge University Press, Cambridge, 1985.
127. Preface to *Bringing the State Back In*, pp. viii–ix.
128. J. G. March & J. P. Olsen, 'The new institutionalism: organizational factors in political life', *American Political Science Review*, Vol. 77, 1983, pp. 281–97; and *Rediscovering Institutions: The Organizational Basis of Politics*, Free Press, New York, 1989.
129. Eric A. Nordlinger, *On the Autonomy of the Democratic State*, Harvard University Press, Harvard, p. 29.

130. Peter J. Katzenstein, 'Conclusion: domestic structures and strategies of foreign economic policy', in *Between Power and Plenty*, ed. Peter J. Katzenstein, University of Wisconsin Press, Madison, 1978.
131. Atkinson & Coleman, 'Strong States and weak States: sectoral policy networks in advanced capitalist economies', p. 60, emphasis added.
132. David Vogel, *Fluctuating Fortunes*, Basic Books, New York, 1989.
133. Stephen Bell, 'State strength and capitalist weakness: manufacturing capital and the Tariff Board's attack on McEwenism, 1967-74', *Politics*, Vol. 24, No. 2, November 1989, pp. 23-38.
134. Vogel, *Fluctuating Fortunes*, pp. 6-8, 290-1.

CHAPTER 3

The Protective State

Once set in place shortly after federation, the tariff level in Australia moved inexorably upwards: the average tariff level for manufactures virtually doubled in the decade to 1920, and doubled again by 1932. By 1927 Australia had jumped to the top of the protective league, being only second to the inward-looking United States; and by 1970 it shared with New Zealand the dubious distinction of having the highest manufacturing tariffs among industrial nations.[1] The 'protective ratchet', as Anderson and Garnaut describe the mechanism of Australian tariff policy,[2] was ever upwards, usually incrementally through the application of routine procedures and the extension of established policy settings, but occasionally by dramatic leaps in response to grave national crises such as the Great Depression.

This chapter explains how tariff protection was established and consolidated as the cornerstone of Australia's national industry policy, and how it meshed with other key policy areas including industrial relations, White Australia, national development and immigration. Hence the emphasis is on the earlier decades before the Second World War when protection was being put in place, justified and publicly reviewed, and extended to aspects of primary industry as well as manufacturing industry. We show how this national policy was further embellished by Sir John McEwen in the post-war decades of the Menzies Liberal coalition government.

Our justification for concentrating on the earlier period is in part because the post-war period has been so extensively researched by others. Until recently, the study of business–government relations and the politics of economic policy-making was quite neglected by Australian scholars - with the notable exception of tariff politics. Major studies by Leon Glezer and John Warhurst covered the 1960s and 1970s in great depth and with particular focus on business interest groups.[3] In addition, Alf Rattigan has given us 'the inside story' of industry assistance from his vantage point of Chairman of the Tariff Board-cum-IAC during the watershed period 1963 to 1976.[4] Kym Anderson and Ross Garnaut, quoted at the beginning of the chapter, also give an extensive critical account of protectionism from an economist's perspective. Also covering the modern period are two theses: Stephen Bell's study of manufacturing and the state which ranges more widely over non-tariff industry policy,[5] and Jenny Stewart's study of manufacturing industry policy, 1965 to 1985, from a policy-making perspective.[6]

Our pre-war focus in this chapter, however, gives an enhanced historical perspective that has theoretical implications for understanding state action in Australia. The longer sweep of Australian political history needs to be kept in mind when interpreting the state's capacity and its substantive policy role in any period – whether it be for McEwenism in the 1960s, the persistence of protectionism despite increasing state ambivalence in the 1970s, or the switch to corrective policies in the 1980s. Otherwise, one can be beguiled by the apparent role of the state in a particular period, or equate the actual policy direction with policy capacity. For example, the plausibility of Glezer's pluralist interest-group approach was enhanced because he focused on the high period of protectionism when the state's role appeared secondary to that of interest groups in determining tariff policy. But such an interpretation neglected the fact that the larger national policy of protection was firmly anchored in place by the state.

Similarly, a more extensive historical perspective provides a corrective to pessimistic conclusions about state capacity. According to Bell, the federal state's capacity has declined throughout the post-war period, as has its ability to pursue a consistent and coherent approach to industry restructuring since the 1970s.[7] Such conclusions derive from focusing on the transitional decades, from high protectionism under McEwen to part way through its dismantling by the Hawke government, and from contrasting the coherence of the former with the apparent incoherence of the latter. But, we argue, Bell has confounded the switch in direction and character of state policy with a loss of capacity. Stewart's conclusions that undue fragmentation has led to incapacity for coherent industry policy are also conditioned by her 1965–85 time-frame which ends just as Labor's transformative corrective policies were coming into play.[8]

Our account of the federal state's switch to corrective mode in winding down tariffs and providing special plans for the most highly protected and troublesome sectors is one of state strength rather than weakness. This is documented at length in Chapters 4 to 7. This chapter outlines the policy scale and historical extent of the protective state that had to be dismantled.

FEDERATION AND THE COLONIAL HERITAGE

Import duties provided the principal source of revenue for the Australian colonies prior to federation in 1901. The history of tariffs in the Australian colonial period can be neatly divided into two eras: before 1850, when tariffs rates were established under direction from the imperial power, Great Britain; and after 1850, when the granting of responsible government allowed each colony to determine its own tariff rate. The legislation, however, prohibited preferential rates on inter-colonial trade and this effectively militated against the establishment of a customs union of the colonies.[9]

In 1866, Victoria became the first Australian colony to adopt an overtly protectionist tariff. The move to protectionism had occurred in the context of a rapid population increase during the 1850s gold rush. When the rush ended in the early 1860s, Victoria was left with large numbers of unemployed. The political and economic imperative to prevent depopulation by creating new jobs fuelled the protectionist views of Melbourne's influential newspaper editor, David Syme, who espoused his opinions in the pages of the *Age*. Syme wielded his political influence like a club and convinced the Victorian government to implement a tariff policy which would encourage manufacturing, create and sustain jobs and maintain high wage levels. Tariff protection once offered proved almost impossible to remove and, as a result, Victoria remained avowedly protectionist.[10]

By contrast, Victoria's colonial neighbour, New South Wales, was staunchly committed to free trade. The most vocal proponents of free trade were the pastoralists who favoured a commercial policy which kept down the cost of living and the cost of production. They were supported by the manufacturing community which enjoyed a natural advantage in coal and other raw materials. The views of the free-traders also coincided with the fiscal position of the New South Wales government which relied on the sale of crown lands, rather than import duties, to generate its revenue.[11]

The rest of the colonies fell between the two extremes. After Victoria, South Australia was the most protectionist colony. The other colonies supported free trade in principle but protected aspects of their domestic economies. Western Australia protected its local manufacturers and food producers. The Queensland government effectively protected the local sugar industry through production bounties and duties against refined sugar. Tasmania advocated inter-colonial free trade and used tariffs largely as a retaliatory measure. With the exception of Western Australia, all the colonies favoured a customs union. They differed, however, on the subject of external tariffs. Victoria and South Australia desired a protected continent-wide market for their manufactured goods while the other states resented the prospect of becoming saddled with a high external tariff which would increase local prices.[12]

In the preparation of the Australian Constitution, the tariff was a major stumbling block, described by Victorian premier, James Service, as 'the lion in the path' of federation.[13] Under the provisions of the new Constitution, the Commonwealth government was given exclusive responsibility for customs and excise. However, the opponents of federation had two reasons for not wanting to yield colonial control of tariff policy to the federal government. The first was a problem of fiscal federalism: depriving the states of the right to collect customs duties would sharply reduce the government revenue of all except New South Wales. The financial issue was resolved, at least for a while, by section 87 of the Constitution known as the 'Braddon clause' which required the Commonwealth to pay to the states 75 per cent of customs and excise receipts as well as any surplus revenue, after Commonwealth expenditures, for ten years.[14] In theory, this meant that in setting the tariff rate the federal government would take into account the fiscal needs of each state. In practice, it did not work because the Commonwealth pleaded poverty while the states demanded more money.

Others opposed federation on the grounds that a uniform national tariff spread unevenly the burden and benefits of protectionism. In particular, farmers in Western Australia feared that tariffs designed to protect secondary producers in south-eastern Australia would increase the price of farm equipment and imported meat and foodstuffs in the outlying states. Moreover, section 92 of the federal Constitution required the states to trade freely with one another. This left Western Australian manufacturers with no means of protecting their relatively young industries against competition from established firms in South Australia, Victoria and New South Wales. The tariff issue threatened to keep Western Australia out of federation until a concession was made to allow that state to retain a tariff on interstate produce for five years.[15] Opposition to a uniform national tariff had been quelled for the time being but regional grievances against the protective tariff became a recurrent issue in national politics, leading to an abortive secessionist movement in Western Australia in the 1930s.

Despite continuing support for free trade in some quarters after federation, the constitutional settlement had made a tariff absolutely necessary for fiscal reasons. The states had always looked to customs duties for the bulk of their revenue as colonies and so required grants from the Commonwealth to compensate for surrendering the right to levy customs. The states would not substitute by levying direct taxes of their own, nor would public opinion permit the Commonwealth to exercise its power of direct taxation while it had 'the Customs House under its thumb'. As Deakin explained, 'Free Trade in its familiar sense [was], indeed, impossible in Australia' and there could be 'no escape from a heavy tariff'.[16] The tariff had to support both the existing establishments of the states and the new departments of the Commonwealth. This was done through the 'Braddon clause', but only for a period of ten years after federation, so that Australian fiscal federal arrangements remain unsatisfactory and contested today.

Of course, the obvious protectionist consequences of a high tariff were controversial because they benefited Victoria with its highly protected manufacturing industries rather than New South Wales which lived by trade. If high duties were introduced, people in New South Wales would have to purchase from Victoria or pay more for imported goods. Again Deakin put the issue succinctly to his London audience on the eve of the first great debate over a national tariff: 'Shall Melbourne secure mastery of the Australian market at once, or shall her industries decline and Sydney dominate as the chief emporium of distribution?'[17] The question was answered in favour of Victoria, Deakin's home state, by the fiscal requirements of the new federation which also ensured that protection was high. Prime Minister Barton's watchword was 'revenue without destruction', by which he meant revenue was the primary goal of the tariff but preservation of established industry was an important secondary purpose. The tariff that was adopted by Barton's protectionist government and the first Australian Parliament served both these purposes.

NEW PROTECTION

There were three political groupings in the early years of federation: Protectionists, Free-traders and the Labor Party, whose members were divided on the issue of protectionism. Neither the Protectionists nor the Free-traders had numbers sufficient to form a government in their own right and, as a result, tenuous alliances were formed and broken, often over a single issue.[18] Despite the shifting coalitions, the Protectionists, led by radical Liberals such as Deakin, and the Labor Party both sought to extend the scope of the Commonwealth's involvement in socio-economic policies.

This proved to be difficult because, under the Constitution, the Commonwealth's jurisdiction was limited to enumerated powers that were of national significance such as external affairs, interstate trade, defence, navigation, customs, immigration and communications. The states retained important residual powers which were not spelt out but included education, agriculture and much of industry. This division of powers left issues such as wages, labour disputes and industrial conditions under state jurisdiction unless they became the subject of 'industrial disputes extending beyond the limits of any one State' and thereby came within the Commonwealth's conciliation and arbitration power (section 51(xxxv)). Moreover, the Commonwealth was given a specific power over corporations but this was couched in terms that left extensive scope for the states to regulate the incorporation and intra-state activities of corporations (section 51(xx)).

Early Commonwealth governments sought innovative ways to extend national influence and control, but their legislative schemes had to pass the critical scrutiny of the High Court. The early Court was dominated by a triumvirate of the most eminent founding fathers, Griffith, Barton and O'Connor, who applied a restricting method of interpretation whereby the scope of Commonwealth powers was curtailed by 'implied' limitations which respected the immunity of state instrumentalities and 'reserved' state powers.[19] The tariff, which had a measurable impact on domestic prices and wages, seemed to be an ideal instrument by which the federal government could achieve sweeping social and economic objectives. Achieving a national customs union through slaying the lion in its path had been a major purpose of federation. That achievement had been recognised institutionally in granting the Commonwealth *exclusive* power over customs, and, as a consequence, fiscal supremacy over the states. Extending the instrument of tariff policy beyond protection and revenue raising to the regulation of industrial conditions for the benefit of the labour force was an ambitious initiative for cementing a political coalition of Protectionist Liberals with the Labor Party, and more generally of forging a protected national union of capital and labour.

The Protectionists and the Labor Party had different historical antecedents and political constituencies, but converging ideologies that sanctioned statist action for social reformist purposes. The Labor Party was the political arm of the trade union movement but had inherited the ideology and practices of the colonial radical liberalism that was also dominant among the Protectionists.[20] Both groups proposed that businesses which benefited from tariff protection should pass on to their employees some of the fruits of protection in the form of 'fair and reasonable' wages and working conditions. The convergence of Protectionist and Labor views on the tariff, together with raw political ambition, led Labor to support Protectionist governments headed by Alfred Deakin in 1902–04 and 1905–08.

In legislation passed between 1905 and 1908, the Deakin government implemented the 'New Protection', which coupled protection with enhanced wages and conditions of workers. One Act allowed companies to affix a 'Commonwealth Trade Mark' to goods which had been produced under 'fair and reasonable' conditions. Two other bills established bounties payable to sugar and iron producers on the condition that their (white) workers received a fair wage. Linking a tariff policy to fair wages proved to be a more vexing issue because a customs duty gives blanket protection across a specific industry. To overcome this, in 1906, the government devised the Excise Tariff Act which levied an excise tax, equivalent to the protective tariff, on agricultural machinery made in Australia. The excise tax would be waived for manufacturers who proved that they paid fair wages. The Act was subsequently overturned by the High Court on the ground that it regulated business activity that was reserved within state jurisdiction. For the purpose of wages policy, however, that did not matter because the Commonwealth Arbitration Court was only too willing to pass on a proportion of the benefits from tariff protection through the system of wage fixing. Thus, the notion that the New Protection was the foundation for a workers' paradise in Australia - a notion which Deakin said was fixed in the public's mind - was in effect implemented through the arbitration system.[21]

The influence of free-traders declined rapidly in the early Commonwealth Parliament. Free-traders had a minority voice in the Parliamentary Commission that reviewed the tariff in 1907 to 1908, but the government of the day went beyond the recommendations even of the protectionists on this Commission. Customs Minister Sir William Lyne raised tariffs considerably above the original 1902 levels to an average rate of 20 per cent (including the free list). The passing of this second tariff in 1908 was, according to another early commentator, 'a single victory for the protectionists, and henceforward protection was the policy of Australia'.[22]

The First World War contributed further to the rhetoric of protectionism: national pride combined with a sense of isolation and vulnerability to revive Syme's old argument for tariff protection to promote national self-sufficiency through industrial development. In accordance with these sentiments, tariffs were raised in 1921 and new penalties against dumping were introduced.[23] At the same time, a new party representing primary producers had entered federal politics and threatened to re-open the debate on tariff protection. This paralleled the formation of the Canadian Progressive Party in 1920, which represented the anti-tariff views of commodity producers on the prairies. However, unlike the Progressive Party in Canada, the Australian Country Party was not irrevocably opposed to protectionism. Only a minority of the Country Party members desired completely free trade; most supported tariff protection to manufacturers contingent on assistance to primary producers in the form of bounties, reduced duties on staple necessities, and free entry for implements and tools of trade from Empire countries.[24]

PROTECTION AND THE PUBLIC INTEREST

Once the tariff had been put in place, it became primarily a protective rather than a fiscal instrument. While 'New Protection' might have been formally defeated, it was replaced by 'Effective Protection' which emphasised the interrelated goals of national development through industry promotion, 'fair wages' for workers and 'fair prices' for consumers. The protective tariff was cemented by the community of interest between manufacturing capital and industrial labour, with the arbitration system effectively passing on a share of the benefits to workers. This was 'new protection' by another name and became the cornerstone of Australia's manufacturing industry policy.

But it was even more than that, being integrally linked with powerful sentiments of White Australia and national independence. Moreover, through differential rates of 'imperial preference', the tariff could also be made to serve the maintenance of strong imperial trade links with Britain which early Australians also cherished and the Great War reinforced. Tariff policy was a multifarious instrument, as F. A. Bland pointed out in 1923:

> It has been used as a weapon to further the interests of manufacturers, to improve the standard of living of employees, to maintain the policy of White Australia, and to foster closer trade relations with the United Kingdom and the various dominions.[25]

For all these reasons Hancock described protection in Australia as being a faith and a dogma as much as a policy. The result was that the critics of protection who lost the debate at federation were marginalised during the second decade of the twentieth century, dwindling to 'a despised and detested sect suspected of nursing an anti-national heresy'.[26]

If Australia's turning protectionist resolved the colonial division over free trade versus protection, it nevertheless raised a new set of political and administrative issues for national policy. In such a sheltered environment, how was the rank growth of protectionism to be curtailed, given the powerful forces feeding it? And who would protect the public interest of consumers? The Australian solution was the state, or a special institution of the state. Just as the state had put in place the protective regime, it would also seek to monitor and check its progress through an independent institution. Initially, this was the Interstate Commission until it was rendered impotent by a jealous High Court; it was then replaced by the Tariff Board through its various protective and corrective phases from 1921 until the 1970s, then superseded by the Industries Assistance Commission and, finally, by its mutant the Industry Commission in the 1980s. Australia's propensity for using independent state institutions to develop and monitor government policy is as old as protectionism itself.

The need for such a monitoring body was obvious even if its success in such a difficult task was not assured. Both these points were strongly made by Edward Shann, one of Australia's early economists, in explaining 'How Tariff Protection Grows':

> The voice of the special pleader is never stilled. New Protection, developing through wages fixation, tariff schedules, Navigation Act restrictions and subsidies on export, has wrapped Australian industry in a net of legal rules. The Australian business man is tempted to become a suave concessionaire, exploiting his small corner while yet the system admits it, but explaining that he would gladly treat his clients better if the newest board would but give him a little larger scope and check the unpatriotic greed of others.[27]

The democratic state must endeavour to contain the coalition of special pleaders pushing for ever greater protection at the expense of the consumer, but Shann was deeply sceptical of its ability to do so successfully. Hence, his pessimistic conclusion:

> In the politics of a protectionist country there is no ease. Having given certain industries an advantage in the home market, your protectionist is torn with anxiety that they will take advantage of the consumer. Hence his addiction to boards. Subconsciously aware that he has run a risk of high prices and slack service, he calls on a board of experts to guard against it.[28]

The task, according to Shann, was too complex and, in any case, would be short-circuited by manufacturers going directly to the government. Hence, for him, the story of one board contained the lesson of them all.

The Interstate Commission

Shann's generalisations were based on his critical analysis of the Interstate Commission's findings on the consequences of 'scientific protection' during the second decade of federation. The Commission's terms of reference in tariff inquiries required it to give attention to 'lessening the costs of the ordinary necessities of life'. Yet, of the 666 applicants for tariff assistance reported in its first annual report, whose products ranged from motor cars to insecticides, corsets and canary seed, none had any such concern. The problem, the commissioners reflected, was one of collective action: 'The cost of living is everybody's business, but not the special affair of each citizen . . . Any increase in the cost of living resulting from Tariff taxation produces its effect only by a total of separate imposts on many separate items.'[29] Yet, on the other side, 'the applicants stood in separate and urgent need of protection'. As a result, it was hardly surprising that protection was a means of passing increased costs on from manufacturers to consumers.

The boast that protection could lower the costs of local producers by securing for them an expanded market which would allow them to spread overheads over larger production runs was a hollow one. Manufacturers simply passed on to consumers their cost increases and lacked the market discipline which might have compelled efficient practices. Despite its critical review of the consequence of the tariff, however, the Commission ended up endorsing most of the requests from manufacturers on a cost-plus basis. Hence, Shann concluded that a scientific tariff would turn out to be 'like the French criminal who, after being "psycho-analysed", found that his character consisted entirely of defects'.[30]

The demise of the Interstate Commission was not due to the economic contradictions that Shann had articulated, but rather to its legal shortcomings. The High Court ruled that commissioners appointed for a term of seven years could not exercise a judicial function which was an integral part of the the Interstate Commission's judicial-administrative role, because such a role must be reserved for tenured judges of courts.[31] As a result, the Interstate Commission was wound up when the terms of its first commissioners expired, to be revived by Whitlam in the 1970s but once again wound up by the Hawke government in the 1980s.

The demise of the Interstate Commission meant that the task of administering the tariff was thrown back on the Trade and Customs Department. The number of items on the tariff schedule had increased to between 600 and 700 by 1921, and rates were raised to accommodate the new and expanded manufacturing establishments which had burgeoned to supply a captive market during the First World War. With these increases in its extent and significance, tariff protection had become the central pillar of Australian industry policy. Its administration overloaded the Trade and Customs Department, despite its rapid expansion, and tended to swamp the minister. Hence, in conjunction with a further round of tariff hikes in 1921, the Tariff Board was established to administer and oversee the tariff.

The Tariff Board

The idea of an independent board of 'distinguished experts' had been around for some time, and had been endorsed by a number of Australian political leaders. In introducing legislation to establish the Tariff Board, Massey Greene claimed the government was following the United States model. The Tariff Board was to be set up under legislation as an independent advisory body to the minister for trade and customs, with a full-time chairman and two part-time members drawn from the business community. It was to be a semi-judicial body which substituted for the minister in the determination of cases involving the interpretation of the Customs Act. As well as undertaking reviews and making recommendations on specific items, the Board was also required to make an annual report, to be tabled in Parliament, on the overall operation of the tariff and the development of industries.

As one government spokesman put it, the Tariff Board would 'be required practically to determine questions of high administrative policy' in applying the tariff.[32] It was expected that such an independent board could be more objective and systematic in administering the tariff than government and the Parliament because it could be more single-minded in developing the necessary expertise and would be less swayed by political pressures. With most of the secondary industries of Australia 'crying out for increased duties', this was an attempt to approximate a 'scientific' tariff. It was considered a qualitative improvement on the 'happy-go-lucky' methods employed previously, as one senator put it, or, as another said, 'an earnest attempt on the part of the Government to make Protection thoroughly effective'.[33]

Besides its technical function of administering an effective or scientific tariff, the Board was also supposed to be a watchdog of the public interest and to ensure that protection did not get out of hand. Such a body was essential for 'a Protectionist country like Australia', one government proponent argued, to ensure 'a fair deal for the people of Australia, and that the power of government shall be exercised for the benefit of the whole of the people of Australia, and not of any particular individuals'. Another justified the state's monitoring role in this way:

> If this country is good enough to put its full weight behind a manufacturer to help him to develop his industry, . . . the people should have full power to control him, in the interests both of himself and of Australia, if he attempts to do anything mean or despicable.[34]

The Board's strength was boosted in 1924 by amending legislation which required public hearings for inquiries relating to any revisions of the tariff, proposals for bounties, or complaints against manufacturers for taking undue advantage of the tariff.[35] This requirement of public hearings ensured transparency: special interests had to make a public case for measures that advantaged them and enabled opponents to put contrary arguments.

No doubt, having an independent state body such as the Tariff Board to police tariffs in an open and objective manner was a decided improvement on leaving it all for the minister and the officials of the Customs Department. Nevertheless, there was a good deal of confused thinking in this whole exercise of institutional design. The first and most obvious was the technical one of an objective and 'scientific' tariff that would deliver protection without inefficiency. Another was in making the Tariff Board responsible for the dual tasks of implementing and monitoring protection. This, added to the fact that the Board was only partly independent of the minister, meant that it was prone to becoming a captive of its clients or, more generally, an extension of the minister and an instrument of protectionist policy. Both propensities were reflected in the initial appointments to the Board: R. M. Oakley, Deputy Comptroller-General of Customs as chairman, Herbert Brookes as representative of manufacturers and Walter Leitch as representative of importers. The Board was expanded to four in 1923 to allow appointment of a representative of primary producers.

The subsequent story of the Tariff Board was one of uneasy tension caused by the conflicting roles of serving protectionism and protected interests on the one hand and, on the other, of guarding the public interest under the guise of an independent monitoring body.

Administering the tariff

Once established, the Tariff Board set about its task of administering the Commonwealth's Customs Tariff, which it described as 'a stupendous piece of legislation',[36] with energy and enthusiasm. In theory, the Tariff Board was merely an advisory body, but in practice successive ministers simply accepted and implemented its recommendations.[37] The Tariff Board was involved in the minutiae of individual applications for concessions, in making recommendations to government for increases and decreases in customs duties that required legislative amendment, and in investigating dumping and applying the temporary protection provided under the Industries Preservation Act. At the same time, it was expected to keep abreast of all the complexities of industry protection and ensure that some overall balance was struck which would allow the broader economic and social purposes of the tariff to be achieved while still keeping protection in check. This was indeed a stupendous task since it entailed substituting an institution of state for the market.

At least in its earlier reports, the Tariff Board kept its role in tariff protection in broad perspective. Its role was to administer the various Tariff and Industries Preservation Acts and provide industry (primary as well as secondary) with a 'general supervisory body and court of appeal'. Ensuring that the Tariff was 'adequately protecting the primary and secondary industries throughout the Commonwealth' required, in the Board's terms, 'systematic and complete investigation' as well as the prudent application of principles of equity and efficiency:

> The maintenance of a desirable high standard of living, the continued payment of liberal wages assured to workers by Arbitration Courts and Wages Boards, the necessity for providing a fair and reasonable return for capital, and the maintenance of the mechanical efficiency of production, call for the most thoughtful consideration. On the other hand, increased duties would defeat the object of protection if they merely raised the cost of production, for such a result would not relieve the local industries from the danger of ruin through external competition.[38]

The job of the Tariff Board was made even more difficult by the precarious economic conditions of the 1920s, as the Board itself pointed out:

> It must be obvious to all that in these days of grave economic crises, when whole continents are struggling to adjust themselves to post-war conditions after a period of industrial exhaustion, any Tariff enacted with a view to protecting the industry of a country such as the Commonwealth must call for continuous vigilance and considerable amendment.

The Tariff Board set a cracking pace in carrying out its multifarious duties, visiting all the states and inspecting all of the more important industrial establishments in its first years of operation. During the years 1922 to 1926, the Board notched up an impressive record of work, as R. C. Mills has documented:

> The Board has received deputations, held public and private inquiries, and attended various conferences. The scope of its work is indicated by the fact that, in addition to its annual reports of 1923, 1924, 1925 and 1926, it has presented numerous reports and recommendations to the

> Minister. During the month of September 1924, for example, 188 reports and recommendations were made; during the year 1924–25, it held 305 public inquiries and examined 654 witnesses; and during the year 1925–26 no less than 975 reports and recommendations were made. Most of these recommendations do not go beyond the Minister, but, in 1925, 56 reports were presented to Parliament, although only a few of them were printed.[39]

In the face of strong overseas competition, secondary industry in Australia was hampered by a number of severe disabilities. One was the high cost of capital that resulted in heavy overhead expenses. This was due in turn to the fact that many of the secondary industries had been set up during the First World War when the costs of erecting factories and installing plant were extremely high. In addition, both capital and production inputs from local sources were already becoming relatively more expensive because of expanding levels of protection. Another major competitive disadvantage for Australian industry was high wages. At the time, this was affecting major projects such as the construction of the Sydney Harbour Bridge; the Tariff Board had become embroiled in this because local tenderers claimed they were disadvantaged by high wage levels. According to evidence from the New South Wales government engineer, 80 per cent of the cost of engineering production was due to wages with Australian workers being paid twice as much as their British counterparts in the industry: from 96 to 130 shillings per week in Australia compared with only 48 to 55 shillings in Britain.

The Tariff Board was busy in the 1920s across a wide range of individual industries, including clothing and footwear, cars and steel, which were all cases for special protective plans in the 1980s. The Board noted that Australian requirements for boots and shoes could undoubtedly be met from local production, although some people persisted in wearing only the imported article. Against such imports, Australia exported virtually nothing in the mid-1920s despite having enjoyed a substantial export trade to New Zealand and South Africa during the war. Those export markets had dried up with the return of normal conditions to the United Kingdom which usually supplied manufactured goods for its imperial dominions, and with New Zealand having imposed higher protection against the Australian product. The clothing industry was by now well-established but enjoyed a 55 per cent general tariff and a 40 per cent British preference. In this regard the Board was considering a range of proposals for dealing with the increasing 'menace' from cheaper imports. Growth in the woollen industry was slower because of its high capital overhead and wage costs, and additional protection was necessary for some lines in order to enable the Australian manufacturers to secure a 'fair share of the trade'.[40]

Building motor car bodies had been established during the war to conserve shipping space and had become one of Australia's most important industries by the 1920s, 'giving work to many hundreds of employees and using thousands of pounds worth of Australian materials'. Of course, that had been achieved with the aid of 'substantial protective duty' from the 1921 Tariff Act. The Board was concerned that Australia's imports of rubber tyres were so high, noting that 'Australian demand would be enormously increased if it were not for the practice of importing tyres with motor vehicles'. Therefore, it brought together motor car importers and Australian tyre manufacturers with a view to the latter supplying tyres to the former. Regarding steel, which the Board saw as a 'basic secondary industry', import competition was threatening to become acute, 'notwithstanding the liberal measure of protection' provided in the 1921 Tariff Act.

In its work the Tariff Board did not simply administer the tariff, but was an enthusiastic promoter of Australian industry. At times, R. C. Mills notes, 'in its zeal for the encouragement of Australian industries', the Tariff Board went outside its ordinary functions to give advice to firms and played a brokerage role in bringing domestic manufacturers and suppliers together. On several occasions when demand was slack, the Board chairman solicited orders for Australian engineering shops in various states, thus preventing orders from being placed abroad.[41] In other instances, the Board put local suppliers in touch with clients and mediated in working out deals, as in the case of tyre makers and motor vehicle importers mentioned above. Nor were primary producers left out. On one occasion, the Board arranged meetings between brewers in the various states and Tasmanian hop producers to work out an agreement for the enhanced purchase of local hops and reduction of imports.[42] On other occasions, Board members lobbied British officials and industrialists to obtain preferences for Australian primary products in British markets.[43]

Overall, the Tariff Board was optimistic, advising in 1924 that despite 'the many adverse circumstances with which manufacturers have had to contend', the development of Australian secondary industry had been 'fairly satisfactory'.[44] One notable bright spot, with which every Australian child would become familiar in primary school, was the agricultural implement industry. Besides employing many people, the Tariff Board boasted that 'the outstanding advantage of the local industry' was its ability 'to develop farm machinery to suit Australian conditions'. Stump-jump ploughs and cultivators, combine-harvesters and combination grain and fertiliser drills and tyne cultivators were all Australian inventions. These, it was claimed, had saved Australian farmers millions of pounds and greatly extended the cultivation of wheat.

Through administration of the system of classification and by-law exemption, the Tariff Board could play a highly discretionary and flexible role in helping the establishment of new industries. The Tariff Act allowed the minister considerable power to alter, from time to time, the classification of goods, known as 'concession items', for purposes of duty. These included mainly machines, machine tools and appliances, tools of trade for artisans and mechanics, and materials and articles for use in manufacturing goods. Goods classified under these heads were admitted free of duty or at low rates. In practice the Tariff Board administered the exemption system, using the general principle of admitting classified goods free of duty if they were not manufactured commercially in Australia. Once they were manufactured, as increasingly they were with local industry taking advantage of the tariff umbrella, the Tariff Board conducted an inquiry and 'wherever possible' recommended cancellation of the by-law exemption.[45]

Nor were the primary industries left out. During 1924, the Tariff Board was involved in protective measures for tobacco, hops, grapes, broom millet, box timber and maize. Some of these referrals involved intricate negotiations and arrangements: for example, facilitating the absorption of domestic oversupply for special grape varieties and enhancing exports by recommending bounties for fortified wines; ensuring brewers bought increasing quantities of Tasmanian hops instead of importing the product, and giving forward guarantees of orders to stabilise production; and sponsoring conferences between tobacco growers and manufacturers to achieve the expansion of tobacco growing in Australia and reduction of imports of tobacco leaf. As well as assisting primary producers in these ways, the Tariff Board received a welter of requests from others demanding much higher protection or absolute prohibition of imports. The most notable ones concerned maize, millet, lucerne seed, hops, citrus fruits, dried fruits and butter. The Board was 'wholly sympathetic with these primary producers, who are forced to meet competition from countries where the standard of living is much lower', and made appropriate recommendations for revision of the tariff by Parliament.

Abuses all round

By 1927, the Tariff Board had become alarmed at the pervasive abuse of the protective system by manufacturers, primary producers and trade unionists alike, and used its 1927 Annual Report to highlight that fact. Being in 'most intimate touch with all phases of industry within the Commonwealth', the Board reported 'that there was a prevailing tendency which [was] calculated to abuse the protective system and by forcing the pace under disadvantageous conditions to actually endanger the efficacy of the system'. There was 'nothing but disaster ahead', the Board warned, unless the serious menace of rising production costs was squarely addressed by all parties.[46] The problem was that all the major interests had now learned to manipulate the tariff and were endeavouring to exploit it for their own benefit.

One key problem area was the link between protection and arbitration. The Board was being asked to consider large increases in duties for a range of important industries that included timber, engineering, iron and steel, brushware, copper, butter and cheese, glassware, clothing and textiles, 'with the object of enabling such industries to *exist*'. Simultaneously, however, applications were being lodged with the Arbitration Courts, both federal and state, to grant increased wages, improved conditions and shorter hours to workers in these industries. In effect, industrial unions were securing generous awards which threatened the existence of many Australian industries, while the Tariff Board was propping them up by granting increased protection. The Board warned that the system was becoming one of 'passing back and forth between the Federal Arbitration Court and the Tariff Board for increases in wages and duties, which can only result in an ever increasing wage rate, and an ever increasing Tariff'. Such a system must ultimately defeat itself and result in 'industrial paralysis'.[47]

There was particular concern that public sector and service unions were making inordinate claims and threatening the viability of industry. The Federated Clerk's Union was pushing for a basic wage rise in Victoria from £4 12s 6d to £6, and a working week of 35 hours with treble rates for Sundays and holidays. The concern was that such rates would flow on to rural workers and undermine the competitive advantage of Australia's primary industries. As the Board pointed out: 'the main primary products of Australia that are exported are sold in competition with the products of different oversea countries in many of which, by reason of lower standards of living, costs of production are much lower than those already obtaining in Australia'. In addition, as the early record shows, the Tariff Board was concerned with what has become known as 'micro-economic reform' today:

> The development of industry and facilities for transportation go hand-in-hand and it only required the seamen, who enjoy the benefits of possibly the most favourable Navigation Act in the world, to threaten to strike because they did not approve of a course of fish for breakfast or because they objected to jam being served in 5lb. tins instead of 1lb. tins, to make the whole position ludicrous, if it were not in reality too tragic.[48]

Manufacturers were abusing the system of protection in a number of ways. Some attempted to shelter plant and machinery that was out-of-date, and products which were inferior or more expensive, behind increased protection. While technological advances were revolutionising manufacturing processes and the quality of products around the world, Australian manufacturers were seeking to protect from competition their old-fashioned processes and lower quality products. The result, as the Tariff Board made clear, was that Australian people were being denied the benefits of modern technology and engineering. Another form of abuse, according to the Board, was the earning of excess profits by protected manufacturers. Parliament had imposed protective duties 'in the interests of the community as a whole and distinctly not for the purpose of enriching certain manufacturers', so that the first duty of a protected manufacturer was 'to see that the community gets an adequate return for the protection it has accorded him, and that local prices sheltered by the duty are kept down to the lowest possible limit consistent with a reasonable and legitimate return on capital'. Clearly, that depended on the ability of the Tariff Board to fine tune protection, a task thought at the time to be possible and one that would be assisted by the method of public inquiry that was required before increases in protection were recommended.

Least abusive of the system were primary producers who had to compete in world markets and take world parity prices for their products. Moreover, the primary producer had been saved by two additional factors: first, the application of machinery to production which had increased efficiency; and second, the natural pastoral advantages that Australia enjoyed. But these advantages were being eroded by rising costs due to protection, including the flow-on of wage increases from protected industries. Hence, primary producers were demanding immunity from external competition and not always guarding against inferior products and inefficient methods. Primary producers had demanded embargoes on all imports of sugar, hops, millet, maize, potatoes, bananas, peanuts, tomatoes, eggs, butter, cheese, wine, tobacco and dried fruits. The Tariff Board had some sympathy for the primary producers because they were caught between rising domestic costs of production and declining export prices.[49]

TAKING STOCK: THE BRIGDEN REPORT

The government too was being forced to take notice of the abuses of protection and the political pressures that its administration was causing; Australia's vulnerable economy was becoming increasingly threatened by international economic forces. Primary producers were caught in the pincers of declining world commodity prices and rising costs due to tariff increases for local industries. Fuelling further this inflationary spiral, workers were demanding higher wages in order to offset increases in the cost of living, while manufacturers were seeking higher protection in order to meet import competition, rising costs and stagnating demand. Charged with overseeing the administration of the tariff, the Tariff Board had highlighted widespread abuse of the system in its 1927 Report cited above. It had become too much the leading player in administering protection, however, to make an objective review of its overall effectiveness. As Mills pointed out in his 1927 review of the Tariff Board, 'It has always looked upon its function as being to carry out, not to question, the settled policy of protection'.[50] In fact, as we have seen from examples of its work and rhetoric, the Tariff Board was passionately devoted to protectionism. Hence, in 1927, Prime

Minister S. M. Bruce appointed a committee of five economists, headed by Professor J. B. Brigden and including L. F. Giblin and Douglas Copland, to inquire into the effects of the tariff.[51]

Brigden was a prudent choice for a government that was committed to protection yet concerned about certain aspects of its application. In his academic writing, Brigden had recognised the dangers of protection getting out of hand, noting that Australia was 'in the full flood of economic nationalism, captivated by the attractions of new industries and different employment'. The consequences, however, were a propensity to pay 'impulsively for our fancies' and 'no doubt . . . too much for some of our industries'. He admitted that this was at the expense of the consumer:

> The protection of manufactuers [sic] and of labour marches in one indissoluble unity, and in this manner, at least, the two lions of employer and employed lie down at the same feast with the same 'lamb,' consuming the consumer.[52]

Brigden was also acutely aware of the cumulative effect of protection in the decades since federation: 'the tariff has grown like a snowball, regardless of ultimate consequences and even of immediate costs. The war finally cemented it as a policy, both as a means of ensuring national self-reliance and as a means to revenue.'[53]

Yet, despite such tendencies of protection, Brigden was firmly opposed to 'academic arguments of free trade advocacy'. These, he said, had been 'translated from a different soil, old, remote, and heavy with different associations' and 'carried neither appeal nor conviction'. Foreshadowing the findings of his official inquiry four years later, Brigden argued in 1925:

> The main body of Australian manufactures could not have been established without the tariff, at the existing standards of living, and that natural production would have continued in the primary form until the standard had fallen sufficiently to allow manufactures to compete with free imports.[54]

Using the criterion of 'general welfare', which he defined simply as the standard of living in a community, Brigden concluded that protection had been as beneficial to Australia as free trade had been to Great Britain. The problem with protection, according to Brigden, had to do with its application to particular industries. The challenge for economists was to sort out which industries were 'economically or politically viable' and the degree of protection that each might require. There were also limits to the extension of protection, particularly to export industries. Clearly, Brigden insisted, 'we cannot subsidise everything, or, if we do, no one gets any benefit and we merely "take in one another's washing" '.[55]

A few avid free-traders were still lurking in academia and one of them, F. C. Benham from Sydney University, challenged Brigden's whole argument. That Australia had prospered was due, according to Benham, to its natural endowments and improvements in farming technologies. In addition, the 'apparent prosperity' of the last couple of decades had been due at least partly to high public and private borrowing from abroad which would have to be repaid in the future. Benham argued, with comparative data on the growth of manufacturing in pre-federation New South Wales and Victoria, that Brigden had grossly overstated the extent to which protection was responsible for the establishment of Australian manufacturing industry. Free trade, he claimed, would give Australia high exports and high imports, keener competition and, as a result of these, higher standards of living. Protection had obviously benefited the protected industries and, coupled with wage regulation, had probably given skilled workers somewhat higher real wages. But, manufacturing overall and lower-paid workers, who had to pay increased costs as consumers, had not benefited. Brigden had made 'a valiant attempt . . . to discover a sound economic defence for Protection in Australia', but Benham suggested, he had been 'hunting a Snark' and might 'find a Boojum'.[56]

Further debate in the learned pages of *The Economic Record* for the period failed to break the deadlock over theoretical and applied benefits of free trade versus protection. To the central question of whether protection in Australia resulted in greater real income per capita than free trade, Brigden answered unequivocally 'Yes' and Benham just as categorically 'No'. Benham insisted upon the gradual phasing out of tariffs because 'our whole economic organisation has adapted itself to the fact of Protection', with the eventual goal being free trade.[57] Not to be beaten by better arguments, Brigden finally dismissed his opponent by charging that he was merely restating 'the faith that is in him with all the ardour of a zealot'.[58]

L. F. Giblin, who was also soon to be appointed to the Brigden inquiry, entered the debate by pointing out the considerable costs of trying to extend protection to agriculture. Australia had been making a series of remarkable attempts to counteract the determination of prices by international market forces through domestic marketing schemes designed to 'obtain for the exporting primary industries the benefit of a protective tariff'. There were definite limits to this which were 'set by what the sheep will carry', Giblin insisted. He illustrated this vividly with his famous vision of 'Australia as one enormous sheep bestriding a bottomless pit, with statesman, lawyer, miner, landlord, farmer and factory and all hanging on desperately to the locks of its abundant fleece'.[59]

In view of this earlier exchange, it is hard to accept the prefatory remarks of the Brigden Report that the authors had 'no reasoned opinion' of the workings of the tariff and had therefore been able to pursue their inquiry 'quite unhampered by any preconceived opinions of what results would come of it'.[60] As we have seen, Brigden at least had previously set out his protectionist view and defended it quite vigorously. Therefore it was hardly surprising that the committee which he chaired came up with precisely that view.

The task of the Brigden committee was to investigate two central issues: the effects of tariff policy upon national prosperity and the principles for applying tariff policy to Australia. It was charged with making a fundamental and thorough review of Australia's entrenched system of protection, as Prime Minister Bruce made clear in his foreword to the committee's report. Bruce noted that the Australian policy of protection was based on the 'belief' that such a policy accelerated development and increased national prosperity. It had been endorsed by the people on many occasions and become an integral part of the structure of the country's economic life. Because of 'its permanence and profound bearing upon every material activity of the Commonwealth', it was important to inquire whether this established national policy was achieving its objectives.[61]

The Brigden Report recycled many of the Tariff Board's criticisms of tariff abuse, but found in favour of the national policy of protection and against the free trade alternative that was being advocated by a few economists such as F. C. Benham in academia. This was stated in various ways in the report: that available evidence did 'not support the contention that Australia could have maintained its present population at a higher standard of living under free trade'; and that, owing to the marginal quality of uncultivated land and the adverse effect of increased exports on international market prices, 'the same average income *for the same population* could not have been obtained without protection'.[62] The finding that Australia could not have had the same standard of living for the same population without protection was of great significance for vindicating this settled policy and its supporting national consensus. It was also a curiosity for the rising discipline of economics, as Chicago economist Jacob Viner pointed out in review: 'Comprehensive inquiries into the operation of tariff protection made by competent economists', he pointed out, 'had invariably resulted in verdicts unfavourable to protection as a long-run policy'.[63] Was Australia therefore unique as an economic laboratory, or was the Brigden Report flawed in its analysis?

The Brigden findings, in terms of population size and average income levels, were that Australia could not have sustained its population at such levels of average income without protection. It freely acknowledged that a larger national income per head could have been achieved but with 'a considerably smaller population': in fact, average incomes could be maximised 'by reducing [Australia] to one large sheep-run with the necessary subsidiary and sheltered industries and a few rich mines'.[64] The Brigden Report estimated that industries which could not survive without protection accounted for production worth £75 million, requiring and maintaining a population of 750,000. Their alternative no-tariff scenario was for the equivalent expansion of primary industries for export. They calculated that, in such a case, costs of production would be 8 per cent lower so that £47 million of additional primary export production maintaining 470,000 people could produce the same real national income. Hence, according to such calculations, free trade for Australia might produce the same total national income but higher average incomes for a rural-based population smaller by 280,000. But achieving such a boost in export industries was unlikely because of marginal land having to be brought into production, especially for wheat production, and the adverse impact of increased Australian primary production on world prices, especially for wool.[65]

This analysis was fundamentally flawed on economic grounds. Since free trade could have produced the same national income, the excess population was, in aggregate terms, unproductive. It could be supported under the free trade alternative by redistributions from taxation, rather than by wages in inefficient protected industries. A further methodological flaw was the assumption that the entire loss of production from abolishing protection had to be substituted by primary exporting industries. More likely, a reduced cost structure would allow some expansion in domestic manufacturing, as well as exporting industry. In any case, the excess 280,000 people might have been employed under free trade in activities that increased national wealth, such as building additional roads or parks, or even 'trapping rabbits', as Viner suggested.

One could only make sense of the Brigden analysis by assuming some criteria other than economic efficiency which Australians took for granted. Viner saw economic efficiency as being a primary concern with the average real incomes *'of the working classes only'*. Australians must take this for granted he thought, if senior economists felt that it was unnecessary to spell it out for readers of the report. According to Viner's re-interpretation, the report's real findings were as follows:

> The basic conclusion of the report is that under free trade the present working-class population of Australia could not have been supported at its present standard of living; that protection has made possible its support in the existing numbers and at the prevailing standard by transferring income from landlords and capitalists to workers; that under free trade, with workers maintained at their present standard, the aggregate real income of Australia would have been as great as at present, but the population would have been at least 230,000 smaller; and that the net economic effect of protection, assuming always a given standard of living for the workers, has been to make possible the support of a greater number of workers by indirect appropriation of the amounts necessary for their support from the incomes of landlords and capitalists.[66]

If the Brigden Report's conclusions were read in this restrictive way, they were not substantiated unless it was assumed that the burden of tariffs was not also borne by workers. That could not be assumed because, as consumers, workers had to pay higher prices. It was more likely that the growing burden of protection had harboured inefficient practices and prevented technological improvements from bringing about real wage rises.

The Brigden Report was a rationalisation, rather than an economically rigorous vindication, of Australia's established national policy of tariff protection. The authors, however, were restrained and cautionary: they were concerned that protectionism generated its own momentum, that its burden fell most heavily on exporters, and that it raised the general price level by nearly 10 per cent above what prices would have been with a purely revenue-based tariff. The report concluded that the tariff had reached its upper limit and that no further protection should be considered 'without the most rigorous scrutiny of the cost involved'.[67] Within a few months, however, the Bruce government was defeated and the stockmarket crashed. With the onset of the Great Depression, the Brigden recommendations were left to gather dust while the new Scullin Labor government battled the Great Depression with yet higher tariffs.

THE GREAT DEPRESSION AND THE 'SCULLIN TARIFF'

The Great Depression had a disastrous effect on the Australian economy. Declining demand and falling world prices dramatically reduced the earnings of staple exports (wool, wheat, hides and meat). Moreover, the international market shrank with many of Australia's most important customers, namely Belgium, France, Germany, Egypt and India, cutting back their orders. While exports declined, there was a corresponding slump in the industrial economy as consumer spending was curtailed and businesses reduced their capital expenditures. In addition to the economic consequences of the Depression, there was a tremendous social cost as unemployment rose, incomes fell, and breadlines grew longer.[68]

In dealing with the economic crisis, the Australian government resorted to the defensive strategy of raising tariff levels. In Australia, the new Labor government, elected in October 1929, acted swiftly with Prime Minister J. H. Scullin raising the tariff not once but seven times during his first year in office.[69] Economic orthodoxy dictated that trade barriers should fall, not rise, to stimulate depressed economies. Political necessity, however, deemed otherwise and, by jacking up tariff levels, Scullin hoped to stem the tide of rising unemployment.[70]

The Scullin government had the singular misfortune of being sworn in the very week of the New York Stock Exchange's collapse on 'Black Thursday', October 1929. For several years in opposition, Scullin had been warning of the dangerous trends in the Australian economy during the 1920s in terms with which we are only too familiar: the government was spending beyond its means and accumulating a deficit; its foreign debt had increased steeply with accompanying increases in overseas interest payments; and Australia's terms of trade had deteriorated with alarming falls in export prices for agricultural commodities.[71] But the state of the nation with which Scullin was confronted after the successful 1929 election was far worse than he or most others had imagined. Even before being sworn in as prime minister, Scullin recalled that he had been confronted with the figures on Australia's financial position in London by the chairman of the Commonwealth Bank Board and was 'staggered. Those obligations had to be met at a time when prices had tumbled and the volume of exports had fallen.'[72]

In many respects, the subsequent tale of the Scullin government is one of unmitigated woe as it sought to cope with the Depression without having control of the Senate, the banking system or, increasingly, its own parliamentary caucus and especially the Lang faction which dominated the leading New South Wales branch of the party. Treasurer Theodore's more ambitious schemes for deficit financing of public works were blocked by the Senate, while the banks forced the government to adopt a conservative package of drastic cuts to public spending. Finally, under enormous stress, the Labor Party split, the Scullin government was defeated on the initiative of its rebel members, and Labor languished in opposition for a further decade, slowly mending its party machine and electoral fortunes. Reflecting on Scullin's misfortune in being swamped by the catastrophe that he had partly foreseen, his biographer remarks: 'It is often the fate of prophets to be ignored; but it does not always follow that the prophet is destroyed by the calamity he has foreseen.'[73]

The notable legacy of the Scullin government was the 'Scullin tariff', an unprecedented hoist in protective rates and quotas implemented as a crisis measure to cut imports and correct Australia's precarious trade balance. The powerful coalition of beneficiaries ensured that this too was subject to the 'protective ratchet' of Australian tariff policy and absorbed into the fabric of national protection. Forty years later, Alf Rattigan, leading a reformed Tariff Board, could still single out the distorting effects of the 'Scullin tariff' for special attention. In the first comprehensive review of the effects of accumulated protection on Australian manufacturing industry made in the late 1960s, the Tariff Board concluded that about 40 per cent of Australian manufacturing industry had effective protection at rates in excess of 50 per cent and in some instances this far exceeded what was necessary for profitable manufacture in Australia. The manufacture of machinery and metal-fabricated products represented about half of the 40 per cent and enjoyed

> excess protection (i.e. the tariff was probably two or three times higher than that necessary to enable the manufacturers to operate profitably). The cause of the excess protection was the 'Scullin tariff' enacted at the beginning of the depression.[74]

The Scullin tariff is significant in its own right as a high point of protective measures for dealing with national economic crises caused by adverse international market forces, and because it raised the walls of the protective state to new and enduring levels. But it has extra salience for this study because of the contrast with the opposite corrective response of the Hawke Labor government when faced with a similar, although admittedly far less traumatic, crisis in the 1980s. Scullin's 'boldest and bravest experiment' was but an extension, albeit a dramatic one, of established protectionism, whereas the Hawke government's response to head off 'banana republic' status which, according to Treasurer Keating's much publicised warning, threatened Australia in 1986, has been the abolition of protectionism and a greater exposure of Australia's manufacturing sector to international market forces.

Even by the standards of the time and among opponents who were thoroughly protectionist in sentiment, Scullin's tariff proposals announced to Parliament in April 1930 were extreme. Scullin called his government's action 'drastic' and 'unprecedented', whereas the opposition spokesman, Gullett, said they were 'staggering': 'They represent the boldest and bravest experiment in economics and finance ever seen in this country, or, perhaps, in any country.'[75]

This was an emergency measure for a crisis, explained Scullin, whose purpose was not protection, he claimed, but saving Australia's financial viability. To meet interest charges on Commonwealth and state debts, Australia had to export commodities worth at least £25 million more than imports. But over the previous seven years, export prices had deteriorated so that the value of imports into Australia had exceeded exports and had been financed by overseas debt. With accumulated interest and despite export of gold bullion, the accumulated shortfall was in excess of £100 million. Thus, Australia was heading for a crisis in the 1920s well before the Great Depression struck. This was acknowledged by the opposition in terms that are all too familiar given our modern predicament:

> For some years our export values have not been equal to our import values. There has been a progressive deficit. In addition, there has been a yearly deficit, amounting to a great sum, in regard to our overseas interest. On top of that there has been a grave slump in wool prices, the partial failure of our wheat crop, and the drying up, temporarily or permanently, of the overseas loan market.[76]

The government's response to the crisis was to cut imports drastically through four protective measures: absolute prohibition of a selected list of import items; partial prohibition with the power to ration further items equivalent to 50 per cent of the previous year's imports; the imposition of a 50 per cent surcharge on goods that did not lend themselves to rationing because of administrative difficulties; and a combination of the previous two measures, namely a 50 per cent surcharge plus 50 per cent rationing of the previous year's imports.[77]

Scullin claimed that these proposals were not in any way associated with the government's protective policy, although in selecting the items it did recognise that its policy would have a beneficial effect on those Australian industries that were manufacturing the commodities concerned.[78] This was somewhat naive or disingenuous, as was his expectation that slashing imports and jacking up protection would lead to increased production and reduced cost for Australian manufacturers. Scullin's argument was that competition with imports had led to inefficiencies in distribution and selling costs for Australian firms. Without such 'intense competition' necessitating an 'army of sellers' and with government pressure, Scullin suggested local manufacturers could both increase production and reduce costs. The findings of the Tariff Board four decades later showed this was not to be the case.

If the Scullin tariff was a bold experiment in using protection to arrest Australia's chronic trade imbalance and save the country from bankruptcy, it was a policy response in keeping with the dominant protectionist mood of the nation and designed by a high priest of protectionism. Scullin was an out-and-out protectionist but also an exponent of the scientific tariff. In opposition he had blasted the Tariff Board for suggesting that protection was too high in certain industries, allowing employees to capture the advantages through higher wages granted by the Arbitration Court.[79] Scullin prided himself on his expertise in the tariff field and, soon after taking office in 1929, spent three weeks consulting with the Customs Department on a revised 'scientific tariff'. All items were examined to see whether Australian industries could make them or do without, and tariffs adjusted accordingly. Scullin boasted that this was 'the most scientific tariff' Australia had ever had because its purpose was solely to protect Australian manufacturing and not to raise revenue.[80] After the massive increases of the 1930 emergency tariff which applied proportionately to British preference goods, Scullin urged British manufacturers to set up manufacturing behind the tariff wall.[81] With some adjustments for selective trade liberalisation negotiated in the Ottawa Agreements, Scullin's emergency tariff became part of the fabric of the protective state that was embellished by McEwen in the 1950s and only seriously questioned by Rattigan and the Tariff Board in the late 1960s.

THE OTTAWA AGREEMENTS AND A 'BARGAINED TARIFF' POLICY

The policy of high protection had obvious costs that were apparent even in Scullin's time. Populist protectionism pleased industrial workers and their employers but alarmed many others. Tariff Reform Leagues, supported by importers and some rural organisations, were formed in most states to lobby against increased protection. The Scullin tariffs also capped longstanding regional grievances and contributed to a powerful secessionist movement in Western Australia.[82] Finally, Scullin protectionism was curbed by two events: the fall of the Labor government in December 1931 and Australia's participation in the Ottawa Agreements of 1932.

While there is considerable doubt about the utility of tariff increases to soften the effects of a depression, they were useful as a political tool in international economic relations. Australia's minister resident in London, former Prime Minister S. M. Bruce, perceived that protectionism was a useful bargaining chip in negotiating trade agreements. This was especially true with regard to Great Britain which was already suffering from unemployment and a declining share of Empire trade. As a result of protectionism in countries such as Canada and Australia, the British government agreed to send a delegation to Ottawa in July 1932 to negotiate a series of bilateral preferential trade treaties with other members of the Empire. Essentially, the Ottawa Agreements secured the British market for wheat and other foodstuffs from Canada, Australia and other Empire nations while, in return, these countries offered tariff reductions for manufactured imports from Britain.[83] As a result, by the end of the 1930s, Australia had a three-column tariff structure: the lowest tariff was the British preferential rate, followed by the intermediate rate for most-favoured nations, and the highest rate, the general tariff.

This new national policy of bargaining tariff reductions for trading favours was not universally acclaimed. One critic of the day, none other than the redoubtable J. B. Brigden who had moved from an economics chair at the University of Tasmania to become Director of the Queensland Bureau of Industry, confessed to being 'an utter sceptic' as to the benefits of the Ottawa policy. Brigden objected to Australia joining the prevalent fashion in the regulation of international trade 'with its usual sublime confidence in the efficiency of government regulation'.[84] In his view, Australia's 1930 emergency tariff was so restrictive in its penalties, prohibitions and embargoes that some relaxation was necessary even in the interests of the protected industries themselves. The policy of extending favours only to select countries hurt domestic consumers and offended non-favoured nations such as Japan. Having been the largest buyer of Australian wool during the Depression, Japan had now withdrawn totally from the wool market because of high Australian tariffs imposed upon Japanese clothing imports. This led Brigden to warn that Australia was courting disaster with excessive protection which was burdening wool with internal costs while undermining its external markets through restrictive trade agreements.

Brigden's fellow economists from the 1920s inquiry, Professor Douglas Copland and L. F. Giblin, remained committed to protectionism even at the increased levels of the 1930s and wrote pamphlets in its defence. The Depression experience confirmed the findings of the Brigden inquiry, Copland argued, with tariff policy making 'a substantial contribution to our economic welfare'.[85] Increased protection had been something of a gamble in 1931–32, Giblin admitted in a public lecture in 1936, but it had 'turned out a winner', so there could be 'little disagreement about the necessity of the protective policy today'.[86]

Thus, by the late 1930s, Australia's national policy of protection had been expanded and consolidated by more than three decades of practice. Except for some selective reductions for Britain and other imperial dominions in the 1932 Ottawa Agreements, the tariff ratchet had produced higher levels of protection. War and depression alike furthered the process, while the Arbitration Court worked in tandem with the Tariff Board to spread the benefits to labour. Primary producers in weaker agricultural sectors were also brought under the protective state umbrella.

As the inefficiencies and abuses worked themselves through and fed off one another, it seemed that the whole system might be at risk. The Tariff Board was certainly not up to administering the system while simultaneously keeping it in check. At most, the Tariff Board ensured a somewhat more orderly and even-handed application of the tariff than political 'ad hockery' might have produced. Nor, with a few exceptions, did the small economics academy of the day provide an alternative view. Its leading members, through the Brigden inquiry in the 1920s and in public addresses and pamphlets in the 1930s, endorsed the national policy of protection.

There were persistent doubts, however, about pushing the system too far. These doubts, and indeed the overall picture of Australia's early political economy, were reiterated by Brigden in his article of 1936 referred to above. This is worth quoting at length because it sums up nicely the settled policy that was firmly in place before the Second World War and which McEwen would embellish in the 1950s and 1960s:

> We have presumed a great deal on our wool, and the men who produce it have been almost as helpless as the sheep they tend. Their efficiency and their organisation might no doubt be improved, but where is there in Australia a finer type of men, [sic] or a finer product, or as good a voluntary organisation for its marketing? I wonder do we take this all too much for granted.
>
> The great wool industry of Australia is scattered over a territory half as large as all Europe, and it is one of the wonders of the world. This occupied inland territory is often included as part of our 'empty spaces' but it is not empty . . .
>
> It produces practically the only Australian commodity, except the wasting asset of gold, that stands by itself in the world's markets. It produces what is indeed for us 'the golden fleece'. Except for the episode of 'the gold rush', wool has been historically and economically the foundation of our nationhood.
>
> The superstructure that has been built on this foundation is something to be proud of, but do not let us forget the foundations . . .
>
> We have used natural resources which employ comparatively little labour, in relation to the value of the product, to maintain other labour at high standards of living, and if sometimes this has been rough on individuals it has for the most part been legitimate national policy.
>
> How much more can the foundation stand? There may be no commodity in the world more securely established. The competition of

> substitutes may do no more than absorb the growing world demand for wool and all of its competing substances. Our producing territory is so large that its production per acre or per square mile can afford to be relatively small. No other inhabiting population of the same size enjoys a more lavish heritage. The asset is rich. How much are we asking from it?[87]

McEWENISM: PROTECTION ALL ROUND

During the 1980s, as Australian public opinion swung against tariff protection, it became fashionable to lampoon McEwenism as a shallow economic doctrine and to paint Sir John McEwen as the progenitor of all the country's economic woes. Although understandable because of the personal stamp that McEwen had put on national protection policy, this was unfair. Unfortunately, because there is still no biography of this leading politician, he was condemned largely by default. As well, many protagonists, lacking a historical perspective, blamed McEwen for half a century of national protection. While we await a biography to set the public record straight, there does need to be at least some account of McEwenism in a chapter on Australia's protective state.

McEwenism was essentially Australian protectionism writ large. The settled national policy was extended and embellished to meet post-war economic and political needs, but in variations of very traditional ways. National security was to be enhanced and national development promoted through accelerated immigration, with jobs being generated by expanding manufacturing industry behind tariff walls. Increased protection would place greater cost burdens on the weaker primary industries, but an enlarged population of consumers would also provide a bigger domestic market into which primary produce could be sold under state marketing schemes. McEwen came closer than any of his predecessors to squaring the circle of 'protection all round'.

The policy itself epitomised the man who was its mastermind and enforcer. John McEwen was a 'soldier settler' who had made good by sheer hard work and shrewd expansion despite the collapse of rural prices and the shortcomings of the ambitious state scheme that had put him and other raw soldiers onto inadequate settler blocks in the early 1920s. As he recounts:

> Difficult times soon fell upon us. When I first bought a herd of dairy cows the price of butter-fat was as high as 2/9d a pound. As soon as

> I was married the price of butter-fat fell to 1/3d a pound. Later it came down to 6d or 7d a pound. By this time I knew what being really hard up meant. But we struggled through it.[88]

McEwen succeeded where others failed, switching from dairying to sheep, and buying up or leasing adjacent farms when 'soldier settlers were walking off their properties all over the place' during the Great Depression.

McEwen's response was to enter politics because he saw both the problem and the solution as being state ones. 'My early farm experience formed the basis of a lot of my later views as leader of the Country Party', he reflected after his retirement. And just as an ill-conceived state scheme and some haphazard marketing arrangements had caused the soldier settlers' woes, so state intervention and stabilisation schemes were to be their salvation.

> Almost from the beginning, I became involved with the problems of soldier settlement in my own district. It was an irrigation area that, recurringly, did not have enough irrigation water. The settlers did not have enough land or enough capital. All of these things were within the authority of the government: to give us more land, to give us more capital, to give us more water and so on.[89]

McEwen's maiden speech in the national Parliament in 1937 was an eloquent plea for a national wheat stabilisation scheme to save an export industry that had been hard hit by the Depression. His proposal was to set a 'reasonable price' for the domestic market, and pool its proceeds with those of overseas trade where prices fluctuated. The rationale for government assistance to wheat farmers was simply an extension of the logic of protection:

> It is quite logical for persons engaged in our export industries to say that . . . the same measure of protection as is enjoyed by other industries should also be enjoyed by them . . . We have a properly constituted tribunal which wage-earners can approach in order that they may receive reasonable wages for their labour. The arbitration system is one of which I approve. The manufacturers engaged in secondary production can also approach the Tariff Board for higher protective duties, but unfortunately those engaged in essential primary industries have no tribunal to which they can appeal in order to secure a reasonable return for their labour. Protection to the wheat-growers in this respect is long overdue.[90]

As minister for commerce and agriculture in the Menzies coalition government in the early 1950s, McEwen began developing a series of stabilisation plans for primary industries. The mechanism was essentially the two-price system he had advocated as a novice member of Parliament. This entailed setting a higher price for the domestic market 'because we could exercise more influence on prices in Australia than on overseas prices', and pooling the proceeds of export and domestic sales in a common fund from which to pay producers.

McEwen's political purpose, however, encompassed far more than stabilising agricultural prices for his rural constituency. He championed large-scale immigration to bolster Australia's continental security and fostered the expansion of manufacturing industry to provide sufficient additional jobs. That in turn necessitated the high tariff protection for which McEwen is now vilified. As McEwen recounted:

> I argued that it would be unacceptable, in world affairs, if we sought to own and occupy a whole continent with so few people. But it was equally clear that it would be quite wrong to attract migrants to the country unless jobs were available on arrival. This linked up with ideas I was to develop concerning tariff protection. By far the greatest base for employment is in the industries enjoying tariff protection and in the tertiary activities that serve these protected industries, their direct employees and their families. Therefore, I have consistently argued that the manufacturing industries should have adequate tariffs to protect their capacity to sustain employment which is basic to any policy of substantial immigration.[91]

As minister for the interior, McEwen re-opened assisted immigration from Britain in 1938 and initiated a deal with Holland to encourage Dutch migrants to come to Australia. He saw himself as a precursor to Arthur Calwell and the Chifley Labor government's policy of massive post-war immigration.[92]

McEwen's determination to boost population for national security reasons was hardened by the threat to Australia in the Second World War. Back in office by 1950, McEwen preached this message tirelessly even to the Country Party faithful: 'Our very security requires that we have population carrying industries and the secondary industries are the principal vehicles of this.'[93] The central place of protectionism and manufacturing within McEwen's grand view of Australia's destiny was summed up in the final reflections of his oral memoir towards the end of his life:

> My own view has always been that it would be ridiculous to think that Australia was safe in the long term unless we built up our population and built up our industries. So I have always wanted to make Australia

> a powerful industrialised country as well as a major agricultural and mining country.
>
> This basic attitude meant that I was bound to favour broadly protectionist policies aimed at developing our manufacturing sector.

While agriculture, mining and manufacturing were the three 'basic wealth-producing industries' for McEwen, technological advances in agriculture and mining were resulting in contractions of the workforce. McEwen looked to manufacturing to carry the additional population load as it was 'the only wealth-producing sector with the potential to increase jobs in sufficient numbers'.[94] And that meant a policy of high tariff protection.

McEwen's dominance of manufacturing industry policy resulted from his appointment as the minister of trade after a reorganisation of ministries in January 1956. Trade (later renamed Trade and Industry) was a new portfolio established in the first instance to overcome problems with managing the system of import licensing which had been adopted in the early 1950s to maintain Australia's precarious balance-of-payments position. The requisite control over imports had been administered poorly by the old Department of Trade and Customs, so the new Department of Trade was set up with McEwen as minister and Crawford as permanent head to oversee the administration of import licensing, with the Department of Customs and Excise applying the policies. 'Of course', as McEwen relates, the new Department of Trade 'had a much wider set of functions than this', including trade policy and policy responsibilities for the Department of Primary Industry. 'So Trade became the central policy department of a triumvirate that covered nearly all aspects of Australia's trade and her primary export industries.' Trade's functions were further widened with the setting up of an office of Secondary Industry within the department, and renaming the department Trade and Industry. Thus McEwen incorporated industry policy within his powerful trade bailiwick, thwarting attempts to have a separate Department of Manufacturing Industry established.[95] This move extended the political base of McEwen and the Country Party to factory owners and workers in the growing urban centres.[96]

The general import quotas imposed by the Menzies Liberal coalition government in 1952 to ease a chronic shortage of foreign exchange were retained until 1960. These sweeping measures, which covered 98 per cent by value of Australian imports, actually increased the effective rate of protection.[97] Thus, having become more dependent on protection than ever before, Australian manufacturers were alarmed about the removal of import restrictions in 1960. To allay their fears, the government, on McEwen's urging, established the Special Advisory Authority (SAA) which, upon the request of any industry, could provide temporary assistance within a few months. This was far quicker than the Tariff Board procedure which required 18 months to investigate industry requests for assistance.[98] When McEwen appointed a high protectionist, Sir Frank Meere, to head the Special Advisory Authority, it became apparent that the new body would be little more than a rubber stamp for populist protectionism. In his first year as SAA chairman, Meere recommended increased protection, sometimes to double the previous level, to all 29 industries that came before him.[99] Meere's attitude to protection was best summed up by the slogan 'You make it and I'll protect it'.[100] McEwen considered Meere's advice 'an invaluable means of circumventing the delays involved in the usual Tariff Board procedures'. As 'a means of giving quick protection and a measure of security to Australian industry', establishment of the SAA was ranked by McEwen as one of his most notable achievements as a minister.[101]

Through his dominance of trade and industry portfolios during the 1950s and 1960s, McEwen was able to ensure that Australia's domestic regime of high protection for manufacturing was not disturbed by the principles of free trade espoused by the General Agreement on Tariffs and Trade (GATT). Prior to 1970, Australia was unwilling to reduce tariffs to the degree that some industries might be jeopardised. This was despite the fact that Australia had been among the 22 original signatories to the GATT, established in 1947 to achieve global trade liberalisation. The GATT established a comprehensive set of rules to govern state behaviour in setting trade barriers and it provided a framework for multilateral negotiations designed to reduce tariff and non-tariff barriers to trade. At the heart of the GATT was the principle of non-discrimination, expressed in the unconditional most-favoured-nation rule which states that any advantage granted by one member to another 'shall be accorded immediately and unconditionally' to all other GATT members.[102]

Although Australia has strongly supported the GATT in principle, that support has been tempered by domestic considerations. From the outset, Australia benefited from Great Britain's successful struggle to retain the British preferential system, a trading arrangement which clearly defied the spirit of the GATT. As well, there was marked resistance to tariff reductions which would have a substantial impact on protected industries. Australia refused to take part in any of the GATT multilateral tariff reductions negotiated in the 1950s and 1960s and made only minor reductions in the margin of preference for British imports. As a result, by 1970, Australia had the dubious distinction of sharing with New Zealand the highest manufacturing tariff rates in the industrialised world.[103]

CRACKS IN THE EDIFICE

McEwen ensured that Australia did not participate in the GATT Kennedy Round of negotiations (1964–67) which resulted in significant global reductions in tariff barriers. With South Africa and Canada, Australia claimed that its heavy reliance on staple exports, its relatively weak manufacturing sector, and the failure of the GATT to address agricultural protectionism, prevented it from implementing linear across-the-board tariff cuts. In recognition of these disadvantages, the GATT made concessions which allowed Australia (and Canada) to move more slowly in dropping their trade barriers.[104] But the growing movement towards world trade liberalisation had its supporters in Australia. Moreover, the British government's determination to join the European Common Market cast doubt on the future of the special trade relationship between Australia and Great Britain.[105] As a result of these international trends, Australian tariff policy came under scrutiny for the first time since the 1920s.

In 1963, the Menzies government commissioned Sir James Vernon to conduct a general inquiry into the effects of the tariff, the first such investigation in over 30 years. The Vernon Report, tabled in 1965, slaughtered several sacred cows of protectionism. Among its recommendations, the report suggested that the government should seek other economic policies to secure full employment, that the mere presence of an industry should no longer be sufficient cause for tariff protection, and that a general 'benchmark' tariff should be set which could not be exceeded.[106] Response to the Vernon Report varied. The Liberal-Country Party government, which had courted manufacturers' support on the basis of its high-tariff policies, found it politically unpalatable. The government's independent advisory body, the Tariff Board, welcomed the spirit of the report but opposed a uniform benchmark tariff. And predictably, manufacturers opposed any hint of tariff reductions. As a result, the Vernon Report, like the Brigden Report of 1929, was shelved.

Although the Australian government tried to bury the Vernon Report, Tariff Board chairman, G.A. Rattigan, did not. The Tariff Board had become little more than an instrument of McEwenism, but that began to change in 1963 when McEwen made a terrible blunder in appointing Rattigan, the Comptroller-General of Customs and an apparently mild-mannered man, to head the Board. McEwen had not anticipated that, as Tariff Board chairman, Rattigan would challenge the assumptions of 'all-round' protectionism and lead the way in rationalising the tariff.[107] Rattigan was appalled by the vicious circle of protectionism created by increasing levels of protection for inefficient and uncompetitive industries. In 1967, he announced that the Tariff Board would undertake a systematic review of all heavily protected industries with a view to reallocating resources away from those sectors which would not survive without substantial protection and towards more efficient industries.[108] Such a review was in keeping with the Tariff Board's responsibilities as set out in its original legislation but that part of the Act had never before been implemented. Although the tariff review did not begin for another four years, Rattigan's announcement struck the death knell for unbridled protectionism in Australia.

The election of the Whitlam Labor government in 1972 paved the way for the first real tariff reform since the New Protection. Favourable economic conditions and public support for trade liberalisation enabled Prime Minister Gough Whitlam to break with Labor Party tradition and radically alter the course of tariff policies. Whitlam and his advisers believed that the Labor Party's cherished socio-economic aims could best be achieved through micro-economic reforms such as tariff reductions and industry restructuring. Within the Labor Party, opposition to Whitlam's reforms was spearheaded by the Minister for Secondary Industry, Dr Jim Cairns, who maintained a populist view of tariff protection as the best means to create jobs, redistribute income, and preserve national self-sufficiency. Cairns was supported by trade unionists, and by nationalists alarmed by the movement into Australia of US multinational corporations.[109]

Whitlam's views prevailed. He transformed the Tariff Board into the Industries Assistance Commission (IAC), and gave it a new mandate to scrutinise all sectors of Australian industry, including manufacturing, rural production, mining and services. And he moved the IAC out of the Secondary Industry portfolio and into his own Department to prevent Cairns from blocking IAC recommendations to cut tariff protection.[110] This move symbolised a historic breach in the government's attitude to protection. It would no longer be assumed that the mere existence of an industry entitled it to tariff protection at the level needed to sustain it. The IAC's new objective was 'to encourage those economic activities in Australia, and the producers of the goods and services concerned, which contribute to improving the efficiency with which the community's productive resources are used' – a polite way of saying that manufacturers would not be able to rely on tariff protection to maintain unviable industries.[111] That implication led manufacturers to dub the new-look tariff board the 'Industries Assassination Commission'.

The government's commitment to tariff reform appeared to be underlined in July 1973, when Prime Minister Whitlam cut tariffs across the board by 25 per cent. This was the biggest single tariff reduction in Australian history. Whitlam's focus, however, was not tariff policy, nor industry restructuring; rather, the tariff reduction was a macro-economic measure designed to reduce inflation by increasing the flow of imports. While this was compatible with the IAC's intention of achieving significant tariff reductions, it was not the government's first intent. In fact, the government recognised that the tariff cut, which reduced the average effective tariff rate from 36 to 27 per cent, would have a detrimental effect on heavily protected industries such as textiles, clothing and footwear (TCF). Thus it was accompanied by a package of $25 million to assist employees and firms adversely affected by the action.[112]

A year after the 25 per cent cut, the government was forced to backpedal. Rising unemployment, the highest inflation rate since the Second World War, a fall in profitability and a huge growth in the volume of imports led to pressure to have tariff rates restored and even heightened. The TCF industries in particular, which attributed over 30,000 job losses to the tariff cut, clamoured for new measures to protect their factories. However the government refused to restore the tariff to its old levels, and instead it offered other assistance in the form of import quotas to the textile, footwear, automotive, whitegoods and glass industries.[113]

In the meantime, the IAC's Tariff Review, initiated by Rattigan in 1971, continued to recommend reductions in protection on an industry-by-industry basis. The result of the review, however, was the opposite of what had been originally intended. The most efficient, lowest cost and least protected industries saw their tariff protection cut while the least efficient, most heavily protected industries gained further assistance through non-tariff barriers. This was largely because the Tariff Review had begun in 1971 when times were good and unemployment remarkably low. However, as unemployment increased through the mid-1970s, the social costs of tariff reduction became a prominent political issue. In order to prevent further job losses in the most precarious industries, the Liberal–Country Party coalition government, elected in 1975 and headed by Prime Minister Malcolm Fraser, actually increased the effective level of protection to the TCF and motor vehicle industries through additional import restrictions.[114]

Political expediency largely accounted for the increased assistance to the weakest industrial sectors. Nevertheless, there was a growing awareness in government and industry of the need to address the long-term problems of the manufacturing sector. This became more apparent as statistics showed that although manufactured products were an increasing part of global trade, the manufacturing sector in Australia was in decline, both in terms of employment and its relative contribution to gross domestic product.[115] However, the need for urgent long-term industrial restructuring had to be balanced against the short-term social and political costs.

The actions of Liberal coalition governments in the 1960s and 1970s suggested that the short-term costs of tariff reductions outweighed the long-term benefits. Like the Menzies government before, the Fraser government was willing to defy its international obligations in order to protect Australia from the vagaries of world competition. This was demonstrated by the Fraser government's decision not to participate fully in the GATT Tokyo Round (1974–79) of across-the-board tariff cuts. One reason given was Whitlam's 25 per cent unilateral reduction in 1973. But the main reason for Australia's refusal to make tariff cuts was that the GATT had repeatedly failed to deal with agricultural protectionism, a growing problem which had been especially damaging to Australia's export interests.[116]

The adage 'make haste slowly' best describes the Fraser government's approach to tariff reductions. The appearance of three major reports on industry policy in less than five years - the 1975 Green Paper on Manufacturing, and its watered-down successors, the 1977 White Paper and the 1979 Crawford Report - gave the impression of a government that was searching for politically palatable solutions to difficult problems.[117] All three reports recognised the need for tariff reductions but shied away from the IAC's sabre-rattling approach which had caused uneasiness and instability in many industries. They also emphasised the need for greater government assistance in the short term to offset the immediate effects of tariff reductions. Such aid could take the form of bounties, exchange rate tinkering, tax incentives to stimulate investment in manufacturing and export assistance. But if the tide of informed opinion had turned in favour of tariff reduction, the Fraser government remained mired in the politics of protectionism. It took a change of government and a progressive change in the policy orientation of that government before protection would be dismantled. That switch to national corrective policies during the 1980s is discussed in the next chapter.

NOTES

1. Kym Anderson & Ross Garnaut, *Australian Protectionism: Extent, Causes and Effects,* Allen & Unwin, Sydney, 1987, p. 6 and Table 2.1 on p. 7. There is an extensive literature on tariff protection by economists, including W. M. Corden, *Australian Tariff Policy* (32nd Joseph Fisher Lecture in Economics), Griffin Press, Adelaide, 1968, and *The Theory of Protection,* Clarendon Press, Oxford, 1971; R. G. Gregory & J. J. Pincus, 'Industry assistance', in *Industrial Economics: Australian Studies,* eds L. R. Webb & R. H. Allan, Allen & Unwin, Sydney, 1982; J. J. Pincus, 'Protection and structural change from a contested markets perspective', *Australian Economic Review,* 3rd Quarter, 1986.
2. ibid., p. 47.
3. Leon Glezer, *Tariff Politics: Australian Policy-making 1960–1980,* Melbourne University Press, Melbourne, 1982; John Warhurst, *Jobs or Dogma? The Industries Assistance Commission and Australian Politics,* University of Queensland Press, St Lucia, 1982.
4. Alf Rattigan, *Industry Assistance: The Inside Story,* Melbourne University Press, Melbourne, 1986.
5. Stephen Bell, Manufacturing and the State: the politics of industry policy in post-war Australia, PhD thesis, University of New England, Armidale, 1990.
6. J. B. Stewart, Australian manufacturing industry policy: 1965–85, PhD thesis, Australian National University, Canberra, 1988.
7. Bell, Manufacturing and the State, pp. 11, 12.

8. Stewart, Australian manufacturing industry policy: 1965–85, especially Ch. 4.
9. C. D. Allin, *A History of the Tariff Relations of the Australian Colonies,* University of Minnesota Press, 1918.
10. A. J. Reitsma, *Trade Protection in Australia,* Brisbane, 1960, pp. 7–9; or, better still, Ambrose Pratt, *David Syme, The Father of Protection in Australia,* Ward Lock, London, 1908.
11. Reitsma, *Trade Protection in Australia,* pp. 9–10.
12. Barry Dyster & David Meredith, *Australia in the International Economy,* Cambridge University Press, Melbourne, 1990, p. 60.
13. R. Norris, *The Emergent Commonwealth,* Melbourne University Press, Melbourne, 1975, p. 40.
14. The constitutional clause derived its name from its author, Tasmanian Premier Sir Edward Braddon, *Equality in Diversity, Fifty Years of the Commonwealth Grants Commission,* Australian Government Publishing Service, Canberra, 1983, pp. 2–4.
15. F. K. Crowley, *Australia's Western Third,* Heinemann, Melbourne, 1960, p. 150.
16. Alfred Deakin, *Federated Australia: Selections from Letters to the* Morning Post *1900–1910,* ed. J. A. La Nauze, Melbourne University Press, Melbourne, 1968, pp. 23–4, January 1901.
17. ibid., p. 71.
18. Between 1901 and 1910, eight governments were elected; of these, two were Protectionist with Labor support (1902–1904 and 1905–1908), two were Protectionist-Free-trader alliances (1904–1905 and 1909–1910), and three were Labor (1904, 1908–1909, and 1910–1913).
19. Brian Galligan, *Politics of the High Court,* University of Queensland Press, St Lucia, 1987.
20. H. V. Evatt, *Liberalism in Australia: An Historical Sketch of Australian Politics Down to the Year 1915,* Law Book Co., Sydney, 1918.
21. J. A. La Nauze, *Alfred Deakin, A Biography,* 2nd edn, Melbourne, 1979, Ch. 18; John Rickard, *Class and Politics: New South Wales, Victoria and the Early Commonwealth 1890–1910,* Australian National University Press, Canberra, 1976, Ch. 7.
22. R. C. Mills, 'The Tariff Board of Australia', *The Economic Record,* May 1927, p. 53.
23. Leon Glezer, *Tariff Politics: Australian Policy Making, 1960–1980,* Melbourne University Press, Melbourne, 1982, p. 8.
24. Ulrich Ellis, *A History of the Australian Country Party,* Melbourne University Press, Melbourne, 1963, p. 88.
25. F. A. Bland, *Shadows and Realities of Government,* Workers' Educational Association of NSW, Sydney, 1923, p. 227.
26. W. K. Hancock, *Australia,* Ernest Benn, London, 1930, p. 89.
27. Edward Shann, *An Economic History of Australia,* Cambridge University Press, Cambridge, 1948, p. 410.

28. ibid., p. 409.
29. First Annual Report of the Interstate Commission, quoted in Shann, p. 411.
30. ibid., p. 416.
31. *NSW v Commonwealth* (1915) 20 CLR 54.
32. Parliamentary Debates, Senate: 20 July 1921, Senator Russell, p. 10268.
33. ibid., Senator Pratten, p. 10273; and Senator Earle, p. 10280.
34. ibid., Senator Russell, p. 10271.
35. Tariff Board Act 1924, S.3.
36. Tariff Board, *Annual Report,* 1924, Government Printer, Victoria, p. 14.
37. See examples cited by R. C. Mills, 'The Tariff Board of Australia', pp. 76–7.
38. *Annual Report,* 1924, Tariff Board, for this and the following quotation.
39. Mills, 'The Tariff Board of Australia', p. 67–8.
40. These and the following examples are from the Tariff Board's *Annual Report,* 1924.
41. Tariff Board, *Annual Report,* 1923, p. 5; *Annual Report,* 1924, p. 13.
42. Tariff Board, *Annual Report,* 1924, p. 4.
43. Tariff Board, *Annual Report,* 1923, p. 4; and *Annual Report,* 1925, p. 20.
44. Tariff Board, *Annual Report,* 1924, p. 11.
45. Tariff Board, *Annual Report,* 1923, pp. 7–8.
46. Tariff Board, *Annual Report,* 1927, Government Printer, Canberra.
47. Tariff Board, *Annual Report,* 1927, p. 14.
48. ibid., p. 22.
49. ibid., p. 24.
50. Mills, 'The Tariff Board of Australia', p. 79.
51. Glezer, pp. 10–11.
52. J. B. Brigden, 'The Australian tariff and the standard of living', *The Economic Record,* Nov. 1925, p. 29.
53. ibid., p. 30.
54. ibid., p. 38.
55. ibid., p. 45.
56. F. C. Benham, 'The Australian tariff and the standard of living: a reply', *The Economic Record,* May 1926, pp. 20–42.
57. F. C. Benham, 'The Australian tariff and the standard of living: a restatement', *The Economic Record,* Vol. 3, Nov. 1927, pp. 239–48.
58. J. B. Brigden, 'Comment on Mr Benham's restatement', *The Economic Record,* Vol. 3, Nov. 1927, p. 249.
59. L. F. Giblin, 'Some costs of marketing control', *The Economic Record,* Vol. 4, Feb. 1928, p. 148.
60. J. B. Brigden *et al., The Australian Tariff, An Economic Enquiry,* Melbourne University Press, Melbourne, 1929, p. xi.

61. S. M. Bruce, Foreword in Brigden *et al.*, *The Australian Tariff*, p. vii.
62. Brigden *et al.*, *The Australian Tariff*, pp. 1, 5.
63. Jacob Viner, 'The Australian tariff', *The Economic Record*, Nov. 1929, p. 306.
64. Brigden *et al.*, *The Australian Tariff*, p. 70.
65. ibid., Part IV, pp. 71-87.
66. Viner, 'The Australian tariff', p. 307.
67. Brigden, *et al.*, *The Australian Tariff*, pp. 1-9.
68. Dyster & Meredith, *Australia in the International Economy*, pp. 123-35; C. B. Schedvin, *Australia and the Great Depression: A Study of Economic Development and Policy in the 1920s and 1930s*, Sydney University Press, Sydney, 1973.
69. On the Scullin tariffs see, John Robertson, *J. H. Scullin, A Political Biography*, University of Western Australia Press, Nedlands, 1974, Chs 11-12; and C. B. Schedvin, *Australia and the Great Depression*, Ch. 8.
70. Scullin was not alone in resorting to tariff increases in an attempt to combat the recession. The American and Canadian governments sharply increased tariffs in 1930. Even Great Britain, the champion of economic liberalism since the 1840s, abandoned its commitment to free trade in the vain hope of protecting its domestic economy.
71. Scullin had absorbed and popularised the lessons of the 1890s for the 1920s from the prescient observations of economist E. O. G. Shann in *The Boom of 1890 - And Now*, Cornstalk Publishing Company, Sydney, 1927. See John Robertson, *J. H. Scullin: A Political Biography*, University of Western Australia Press, Nedlands, 1974, pp. 183-5.
72. Quoted in Robertson, *J. H. Scullin*, p. 185.
73. ibid., p. 115.
74. Alf Rattigan, *Industry Assistance: the Inside Story*, Melbourne University Press, Melbourne, 1986, pp. 78-9.
75. For Scullin's speech, *Representatives*, 3 April 1930, pp. 820-31, and Gullett's reply, ibid., pp. 831 ff.
76. Gullett, ibid., p. 831.
77. Scullin, ibid., p. 824.
78. ibid., p. 126.
79. Robinson, *J. H. Scullin*, p. 104.
80. ibid., p. 193.
81. ibid., p. 195.
82. Crowley, *Australia's Western Third*, p. 273-6.
83. The best study of the Ottawa Agreements is by Ian Drummond, *Imperial Economic Policy, 1917-1939*, University of Toronto Press, Toronto, 1974.
84. J. B. Brigden, 'The new tariff policy', *Australian Quarterly*, No. 31, Sept. 1936, pp. 12, 20.
85. D. B. Copland, *Is Our Tariff A Handicap? Effects on Australia's Recovery*, Edgar H. Baillie, Melbourne, 1936, p. 3.

86. L. F. Giblin, *Some Economic Effects of the Australian Tariff*, Hassell Press, Adelaide, 1936, p. 7.
87. Brigden, *Australian Quarterly*, 1936, pp. 20–22.
88. John McEwen, *John McEwen: His Story*, no publisher or date (distributed by his wife, and based on oral history tapes), p. 6.
89. ibid.
90. Australian Parliamentary Debates, 15 November 1934, p. 375.
91. ibid., p. 17.
92. ibid.
93. John McEwen, Address to the Country Party Federal Council, Canberra, 15–16 November, 1957.
94. ibid., p. 85.
95. ibid., p. 50; for a detailed account, see Ross Deane, *The Establishment of the Department of Trade*, Australian National University Press, Canberra, 1963.
96. Kym Anderson & Ross Garnaut, *Australian Protectionism*, Allen & Unwin, Sydney, 1987, p. 48.
97. P. J. Lloyd, *Non-Tariff Distortions of Australian Trade*, Australian National University Press, Canberra, 1973, p. 11.
98. G. A. Rattigan, *Industry Assistance*, p. 5.
99. Glezer, *Tariff Politics*, p. 71.
100. ibid.; Kym Anderson & Ross Garnaut, *Australian Protectionism*, Allen & Unwin, Sydney, 1987, p. 48.
101. ibid., p. 68.
102. Gerard Curzon, *Multilateral Commercial Diplomacy: The General Agreement on Tariffs and Trade and its Impact on National Commercial Policies and Techniques*, Michael Joseph Ltd, London, 1965, Ch. 3.
103. Anderson & Garnaut, *Australian Protectionism*, pp. 6–7. According to the authors' calculations, in 1970 the average manufacturing tariff rate in Canada was 14 per cent and in Australia 23 per cent. This compares with 12 per cent in Japan, 9 per cent in the United States, and 3 per cent in Switzerland.
104. Jack A. Finlayson, 'Canadian international economic policy', in *Canada and the International Political Economic Environment*, eds D. Stairs and G. R. Winham, Research Study 28 for the Royal Commission on the Economic Union and Development Prospects for Canada, University of Toronto Press, Toronto, 1985, p. 48; R. H. Snape, 'Australia's relations with GATT', *The Economic Record*, March 1984, pp. 23–6; J. G. Crawford, *Australian Trade Policy, 1942–1966*, Australian National University Press, Canberra, 1968, pp. 169–76.
105. J. D. B. Miller, *The EEC and Australia*, Nelson, Melbourne, 1976.
106. *Report of the Committee of Economic Enquiry*, The Vernon Report, May 1965.
107. For a discussion of his early days at the helm of the Tariff Board and his relations with McEwen, see Chapter 1 of Rattigan's memoirs, *Industry Assistance*.

108. Glezer, *Tariff Politics*, pp. 92–8.
109. ibid., Chapter 11.
110. Rattigan, *Industry Assistance*, Ch. 8; and Warhurst, *Jobs or Dogma?*, Ch. 3.
111. Industries Assistance Commission Act, quoted in the IAC *Annual Report, 1973–74*, Canberra, 1975, p. 17.
112. Gough Whitlam, *The Whitlam Government, 1972–1975*, Penguin, Melbourne, 1985, pp. 191–4; Rattigan, pp. 161–71.
113. Glezer, *Tariff Politics*, pp. 125–29.
114. Kym Anderson & R. H. Snape, 'The Regulation of Import Competition and its Effects on the Environment of Australian Industry', Centre for Economic Policy Research, Discussion Paper 5, Canberra, 1980, pp. 9–16.
115. Frank Stilwell, *The Accord . . . and Beyond*, Pluto Press, Sydney, 1986, p. 91.
116. In 1954–55, the Australian government had been instrumental in pushing for a review of the GATT partly because tariff cuts against commodity exports were being effectively undone by the implementation of non-tariff barriers such as export subsidies and import quotas. The GATT Review led to some gains for Australia but the problem of agricultural protectionism remained. See J. McEwen's speech at the plenary session of the Ninth Session of the Contracting Parties of the GATT, 9 November 1954, printed in Crawford, *Australian Trade Policy*, pp. 148–57; Curzon, *Multilateral Commercial Diplomacy*, Ch. 8.
117. *Policies for the Development of Manufacturing Industry, A Green Paper*, Canberra, 1975; *White Paper on Manufacturing Industry*, Canberra, 1977; *Report of Study Group on Structural Adjustment*, The Crawford Report, Canberra, 1979.

CHAPTER 4

From Protection to Correction

The election of the Hawke Labor government in March 1983 brought to a boil the long-simmering debate between free-traders and protectionists. Initially it seemed that the protectionists had won an easy victory: an ALP policy document produced in 1982 entitled 'New Directions for Australian Industry' pointed down the well-worn path of industry protection. 'New Directions' was implicitly protectionist and sought to 'ensure that the external influences that are encouraging a process of de-industrialisation by way of intense import competition and relocation of industry overseas are brought under control'.[1] Equally, while some unions recognised in principle the need for future tariff reform, they were categorically against the prospect of tariff cuts in the middle of a recession. Thus, the ALP's election platform invoked the traditional mechanisms of defensive protectionist policy to maintain jobs within a rapidly declining manufacturing sector and pledged that a Labor government would 'support by subsidy or trade protection, industries . . . which the government determines are in the national interest'.[2]

Even the new Labor prime minister, Bob Hawke, a long-time critic of Australia's high tariff regime, refused to countenance moves to cut protection when he first came to power. As ACTU president and a member of the Jackson and Crawford committees during the 1970s, Hawke had advocated a program to reduce protection when unemployment eased to 5 per cent. In the depths of the recession with the unemployment rate peaking near 10 per cent, however, Hawke had no intention of paring protection to the detriment of manufacturing jobs - and Labor votes. In fact, if necessary, he was prepared to stem the flow of imports by raising the general levy on imports first imposed by the Fraser government in 1978.[3] It would not be stretching the point to say that on the matter of tariff policy in 1983, Hawke and the ALP appeared set to follow in Fraser's footsteps.

Certainly, there was little in Labor's 1983 tariff policy which foreshadowed the tremendous *volte-face* in the party's historic protectionist attitude to manufacturing industry, epitomised by the general tariff reductions announced in 1988 and 1991. In its industry policy in 1983, Labor was committed to traditional Labor interventionism where the state played an active and far-reaching role in promoting industrial development. Closer analysis, however, reveals that this interventionist policy was more selective than in the past. Its most important features were industry plans for specific sectors and increased government assistance to promote exports, skills training, research and development and improved access to investment and venture capital. Such selective interventionism was designed to correct the structural deficiencies in Australian manufacturing caused, in great part, by years of high protection. The sectoral plans were designed to wean the most heavily protected industries from their dependency on protection. In addition, positive assistance programs (as distinct from defensive assistance in the form of trade barriers) were developed to rectify other problems attributed to the legacy of protection: the lack of an export culture, the high penetration of transnational companies, and the lack of private sector funding for research and development. In other words, the federal Labor Party had moved to a more selective interventionism in key areas of industry policy without yet jettisoning the blanket protectionism of tariffs.

Labor's interventionist industry policy was generally supported by trade unions and manufacturers as well as those who believed that responsibility for industrial development was better left to the state than the 'invisible hand'. Ironically, in attempting to correct for the worst excesses of protectionism, this interventionist policy sowed the seeds of its own destruction. With corrective industry plans and programs in place, the government was free to proceed with a program to slash protection for Australian manufacturing at a time when economic liberalism was the ascendant orthodoxy. Thus, the economic 'dries', including those in the Labor government itself, argued that, following tariff reductions, the next logical step was to scale down the state's role in developing and implementing industry policy in order to allow the market place to determine the 'allocation of resources' - and the winners and losers. Embraced as it was by Labor's opponents in the Liberal Party, this view of a less interventionist or 'weakened' state appears to have considerable bipartisan support at the political level. Nevertheless, selective interventionism retains considerable support within the Labor Party, and particularly within the trade unions, as well as with industry groups and the public at large. A *laissez-faire* view of the state has not received universal acclaim, and now appears less viable politically for a country experiencing severe recession with fairly bleak prospects for recovery. As Australia moves further into the 1990s, the debate over when and how the state should provide industry assistance remains keenly contested. Such issues are taken up in the concluding chapter.

This chapter charts the historic change in Labor's strategy for industry assistance and development from its past reliance on a unified national policy of tariff protection to a patchwork of policies across all three levels of economic activity - macro or national, meso or sectoral, and micro or firm. In particular, it examines the most important industry plans and programs implemented during the 1980s and attempts to plot their development against economic and electoral cross-currents. Through this discussion, it will become clear that the federal Labor government dismantled Australia's traditional industry policy of protection in favour of a more selective policy of corrective intervention designed to nurture new and innovative industries, rehabilitate ageing industries, and 'smooth the dying pillow' of those which could not survive without the crutch of protection.

SETTING THE SCENE

Labor came to power on 5 March 1983 in the midst of a shattered economy. A wages break-out in 1981-82, fuelled by the illusion that the minerals boom would last forever, was followed by the collapse of the boom and a severe recession in 1982-83. The figures that year told a grim story: unemployment averaged 9 per cent, the annual inflation rate 11.5 per cent, and the gross domestic product experienced a negative growth rate of 2 per cent in real terms. And as bad as the recession seemed then, there were ominous signs that worse was still to come, especially in the manufacturing sector.

It was also a period of profound frustration, anger and despair. The union movement's antagonism towards the Liberal-National coalition government was to be expected, especially given Fraser's supporting role in the 1975 dismissal of the Whitlam government. What was remarkable, however, was the estrangement which had also occurred between the Fraser government and business leaders. This was due in part to their perception that Fraser had wasted opportunities for reform and deregulation; had hectored business groups and generally taken them for granted; and had exploited industrial conflict for electoral purposes.[4] By contrast, during the same period, the heir apparent to the ALP leadership, ACTU president Bob Hawke, had earned a reputation as a consensus-builder and a potential friend to big business. Thus, when Hawke succeeded Bill Hayden in the Labor leadership in February 1983, business leaders had cause to be confident of his professed goal to foster a new era of goodwill and his shared sense of purpose among government, business and labour. In stark contrast to the stormy reception given to previous Labor governments by business leaders, the election of the Hawke government was viewed rather benignly and, in some cases, even welcomed.

During the election campaign, Hawke promised that an ALP government would bring about a period of 'national reconciliation, national recovery and national reconstruction'. The vehicle for reconciliation was the highly orchestrated National Economic Summit Conference which Hawke convened in Parliament House six weeks after the election. The Summit's primary purpose was to bring together the leaders of government, business and labour to secure consensus on the government's economic strategy and to strike a bargain between unions and employers in which the unions agreed to wage restraint in return for the continuing acceptance by business of centralised wage-fixing. In an atmosphere of goodwill and euphoria, the consensus was achieved and the bargain struck. With only one exception (Queensland Premier Sir Joh Bjelke-Petersen) summit delegates voiced their support for Treasurer Paul Keating's economic strategy of fiscal expansion to restore economic growth and reduce inflation and unemployment.[5]

Although the National Economic Summit heralded a period of reconciliation among business, labour and government, it did not produce a tripartite working agreement similar to the corporatist arrangements found in small open European states such as Austria and Switzerland. This was not due to hostility from the business sector to the notion of corporatism as such but rather to internal dissension and fragmentation. This prevented business leaders from forming a single peak association which could act with the same degree of cohesion and authority as the ACTU. Thus, the cornerstone of the Labor government's economic strategy was limited to the Prices and Incomes Accord, a bilateral agreement negotiated by the federal parliamentary Labor Party and the ACTU prior to the 1983 election. Gwyn Singleton describes the Accord as both a 'prescription for a comprehensive prices and incomes policy . . . to facilitate economic recovery and to reduce unemployment and inflation' and 'a philosophical statement, a programme for social reform'.[6] Hawke's corporatist vision was not fulfilled in the Accord itself nor in the host of tripartite advisory bodies established in the wake of the Summit: the Advisory Council on Prices and Incomes (ACPI), the Australian Manufacturing Council (AMC), the Trade Development Council (TDC), and the Economic Planning Advisory Council (EPAC). These tripartite councils were rather pale imitations of corporatism: they were purely advisory; the partners often retained their conflicting group interests; and they soon became captive to their dominant constituents (EPAC by Treasury, the AMC by business and the TDC by the unions). Although the experience of the Accord and the tripartite councils suggested that corporatism was unworkable at the national level in Australia, they were emblems of a new era of consensual politics.

Shortly after Labor came to power, the economy began to recover. This improvement owed less perhaps to the change of government than to the fact that Labor's victory coincided with the nadir of the recession. Nevertheless, the Accord, which traded off wage restraint in return for tax cuts and social welfare measures, facilitated a speedier recovery than might otherwise have been expected. In essence, the Accord removed the threat of another wages explosion and allowed the government to proceed with a strategy of fiscal expansionism without fear of sending inflation spiralling. The Accord also underpinned Treasurer Keating's fiscal program which was designed to restore profitability and investment in the manufacturing sector in order to provide the basis for strong employment growth. In general terms, the expansionary fiscal policy worked and, in 1984 and 1985, Australia's real GDP growth surpassed the OECD average. However, this overall improvement was achieved primarily through employment growth in the public and service sectors while the ailing manufacturing sector continued to perform poorly both in terms of investment and employment.[7] Thus, while Keating's fiscal policy contributed to a rapid recovery, it masked the serious problems which continued to plague Australia's highly protected manufacturing sector.

This provided an even greater challenge for Hawke to proceed with his third goal which was to commence a program of national reconstruction. The strategy adopted to achieve industrial renewal was lifted from the 1979 Crawford Report and sketched out in 1982 in an ALP policy document by the shadow minister for industry, John Dawkins. The strategy sought to achieve the following aims: the provision of government support for the development of technologically advanced sunrise industries, that is, ones with highest potential for growth and technological innovation; the facilitation of manufacturing exports; improved corporate access to finance for equity and debt by extending the role of the Australian Industry Development Corporation (AIDC) and the Commonwealth Development Bank (CDB); development of an employment and education policy designed to raise the skill level of the workforce; and the reduction of protective tariffs *when unemployment eased.*[8] The ultimate goal of this strategy was to create an efficient and competitive manufacturing sector - that is, one whose viability was not dependent on trade barriers and other forms of government protection. The Fraser government had espoused a similar long-term strategy but had failed to carry it through. Whether the Hawke government could succeed where its predecessor failed depended to a great extent on its unity of purpose, the courage of its conviction and its capacity to compensate those who suffered through the process.

The first indication that the Hawke government was not as blithely protectionist as its campaign promises had suggested was the rescue package designed for the steel industry and announced by Industry Minister Senator John Button in August 1983. The steel plan was a brilliant compromise which saved jobs and promoted massive investment in Australia's steel industry without increasing protection, and is examined in detail in the following chapter. Then, four months later, in December 1983, the government floated the Australian dollar. This heralded the advent of Australian financial deregulation, a two-year process which radically altered the rules under which banks and other financial institutions could operate, thus opening the Australian economy to greater international competition.[9]

Financial deregulation, which involved loosening the restrictions on non-bank financial institutions, removing the controls on lending rates, and allowing foreign banks to operate in Australia, was undertaken in order to deal with long term changes in the domestic and international financial environment. In theory, deregulation was supposed to strengthen the links between the domestic and international capital markets and provide wider access to investment capital for Australian industry. Instead, it triggered an orgy of ill-fated speculative corporate take-overs and a series of disastrous adventures into merchant banking which brought grief to thousands of Australians. With the benefit of hindsight, the Labor government should not have moved so quickly or radically to loosen state control over the financial markets. Nevertheless, financial deregulation can be properly viewed as the first major initiative in dismantling the apparatus of the protective state. From then on, economic liberalism tempered by corrective policies was ascendant while the advocates of government intervention and industry protection became the new 'despised sect'.

There are many theories as to why the Hawke government adopted the mantle of economic liberalism; one proposition is based on the influence wielded by senior bureaucrats while others reflect economic, political, electoral and international considerations. The theory commonly espoused in newspaper columns is that the government has been 'captured' by a cohort of bureaucrats, trained in economics, and working in central agencies such as Treasury and Finance and in authorities such as the Industry Commission (IC) and the Bureau of Industry Economics (BIE). This argument is sustained by the fact of Treasury's predominant role in setting macroeconomic policy. Moreover, Treasury has no 'client base' and can operate in a purely ideological realm whereas departments such as Industry, Technology and Commerce (DITAC) and Primary Industries and Energy (DPIE) represent the vested interests of their clients. There is obvious truth in the claim that econocrats exercise considerable control over the political agenda in Canberra, but the claim does not provide sufficient explanation for how it came to be that way.

Another theory suggests that Labor's shift to the right under Hawke was driven by a desperate desire to cling to office after the bitter experience of opposition during the Menzies years and the dismissal of the Whitlam government in 1975. This view is tantalising to many Labor supporters, especially those on the left who believe that the Hawke government has betrayed the venerable tradition of Curtin and Chifley. But its romantic idealism would sow the seeds for the Labor Party's irrelevancy in implying that it would be better for Labor to languish in opposition with its traditions intact rather than moving forward to reflect and shape the changing political culture.

Others look beyond Australia to suggest that the impetus for smaller government, deregulation, privatisation and other 'market solutions' came from overseas and that the Hawke government's economic policies simply reflect those implemented by other OECD nations. Thus 'restructuring' and 'micro-economic reform' were simply the Australian variants of Thatcherism, Reaganomics, Rogernomics, perestroika and similar reforms which were taking place in Sweden, Japan and Canada.[10] While there is much truth in this observation, it cannot explain why the Hawke government moved in step with governments in other industrialised nations when, in the past, Australia has so often stood alone, especially in terms of its tariff policies.

The most plausible explanation of the Hawke government's move to embrace economic liberalism lies in Cliff Walsh's analysis of the government's shifting economic strategies since 1983. Walsh argued that the Hawke government did not come to power with an ambitious agenda for economic liberalism. Instead, the current strategy of wide-ranging economic reform was the cumulative result of four successive policy phases, each shaped by pragmatic responses to changing economic and political circumstances. The first phase involved the National Economic Summit Conference and the establishment of the Accord and the various tripartite advisory bodies. The second phase, from 1984 to early 1986, was characterised by attempts at modest reforms such as changes to the tax structure and the genesis of corrective industry plans for the most heavily protected sectors. The third phase, from 1985 to 1988, was driven by concerns about the balance of payments and the alarming growth in Australia's overseas indebtedness. Policy-makers forced a depreciation in the value of the Australian dollar in order to reduce imports and increase exports. Fiscal policy was tightened and the government began to undertake sweeping reforms in areas under its direct control: taxation, tariffs, the public service, federal government business enterprises (GBEs) and telecommunications. However, these changes were insufficient to force a shift of resources into the traded goods sector (Australia's export and import-competing industries). Furthermore, strong domestic demand fuelled a sharp increase in imports and led to a blow-out in the current account. By 1989, it was apparent that a longer term strategy was necessary to relieve the balance-of-payments constraint on economic growth. This shifted the focus of micro-economic reform into more difficult areas such as transport, the labour market, state GBEs and state economic policies. Walsh argues that it was only in this fourth phase that the government fully embraced economic liberalism.[11]

The way in which Australian industry policy evolved during the 1980s does not conform entirely to the four distinct phases described by Walsh; in fact, analysts have more commonly divided the Labor government's industry policy into two broad phases, the first from 1983 to 1986, and the second from 1986 to the present. Randal Stewart has characterised the 1983–86 period as 'Phase 1' industry policy where the focus was on tariff protection and selective assistance plans. Stewart described this form of industry policy as vertical assistance which aided the firm to produce a product rather than encouraging improvement in production processes through investment, new technology, and research and development. Stewart claimed that, in 1986, 'Phase 1' policy was supplanted by 'Phase 2' industry policy which provided horizontal assistance in areas such as product development and commercialisation, production and marketing. This type of assistance, in areas such as export facilitation and research and development, is designed to help companies develop innovative processes which will lift their overall efficiency and competitiveness. Stewart characterised this 'Phase 2' policy as government intervention in cases of market failure.[12] Stewart's argument suffers because it imposes a logic, refuted by the historical evidence, that DITAC methodically implemented progressive stages of a preconceived policy. Furthermore, the analysis presented here suggests that DITAC's role in developing industry policy was somewhat marginal since the department was rather divorced from its minister, Senator Button, who developed direct and extensive contacts with industry and relied heavily on his personal staff. Compared with the work undertaken by the AMC and its sectoral industry councils, moreover, DITAC's role was secondary.

Stephen Bell's analysis is similar to Stewart's in that Labor's industry policy is seen as interventionist from the outset but swinging towards non-interventionism and a preference for 'letting the market decide' by the mid-1980s.[13] Bell was dismayed by the government's move to economic rationalism, but again there are enough examples of government intervention in the late 1980s – albeit in the form of corrective policies – to argue that the government has not sacrificed the manufacturing sector on the altar of free market ideology. Bell also insisted that:

> the virulence of economic liberal, anti-statist ideologies and the support given to such sentiments by key state institutions, by political leaders, and by powerful sectors of the economy and society, have constrained the capacity of the state in Australia to initiate or promote new departures in manufacturing development.[14]

Our depiction of the policy changes in the 1980s refutes this notion that the state's capacity has somehow been 'weakened' in the process of dismantling protection. We depict the state as moving decisively to tailor strategies specific to the needs of various industry sectors, strategies which are statist in conception and implementation. And, when restructuring has not occurred at a rate deemed appropriate by the state – as in the case of the textile, clothing and footwear industries – the state has moved unilaterally to hasten the pace of restructuring. Invariably there have been conflicts within the state apparatus: for example, the Industry Commission has criticised the government's part in attempting to direct the restructuring of the automotive industry.[15] But, even now in the 1990s, economic rationalists still expect the state to act as the catalyst for implementing a vast array of micro-economic reforms. When the pace of reform is not to their liking, it is invariably the government which has to take the blame. Far from indicating that the state's capacity has been weakened by the process of dismantling its protective policies, the evidence suggests that the state continues to play the most important role in the restructuring process. The rest of this chapter traces the key developments in the shift of the state's policy for manufacturing industry from protection to correction.

JOHN BUTTON AND SECTORAL CORPORATISM

The principal architect of corrective industry policy is Senator John Button, the minister of the Department of Industry, Trade and Commerce (DITAC) since 1983. Button has been one of Labor's most important ministers: government leader in the Senate, a member of the Expenditure Review Committee and, in early 1991 during the Gulf War, one of five ministers in the war cabinet. He was also one of a handful of senior cabinet members to retain his ministry in the 1987 shuffle. Energetic and outspoken, Senator Button was consistently one of the government's most popular ministers, a darling of the media and, through his work as industry minister, respected by unions and manufacturers alike. However, the characteristics which endeared him to the public, namely his sardonic wit and tendency to speak frankly, often rankled his cabinet colleagues. More importantly, his support for an interventionist industry policy led him into ritual conflict with the disciples of the free market such as Treasurer Paul Keating and, until 1990, Finance Minister, Peter Walsh. Although the press dwelt on these recurring skirmishes, the ideological differences between Button and the Treasurer should not be overemphasised. Like the majority of his cabinet colleagues, Button was one of the new breed of Labor ministers, a rationalist rather than a populist and committed to overhauling the Australian economy despite the short-term costs. Thus, he had far more in common with his contemporaries than he did with his predecessors in the industry portfolio.

Button's greatest achievement has been to shift the focus of Australian industry policy from a defensive orientation to a forward-looking approach based on fostering the development of innovative, export-oriented industries. This has been an enormous task, achieved by gradually reducing assistance to the least efficient industries in order to force their withdrawal from uncompetitive activities; by promoting industry expansion into areas where Australia has a comparative advantage such as raw material processing; and by removing impediments to competitiveness through changes to the tax system and industry infrastructure reform. Changing the focus of industry policy, however, is not the same as changing the entrenched protectionist views of manufacturing labour and capital. Heavily protected industries were initially reluctant to embrace the changes but, by the late 1980s, most had come to accept Button's 1983 warning that protection could not be viewed as 'a panacea for industrial reconstruction'.[16]

Button's own thinking on industry policy developed as he grappled with the job. While applying his considerable intellectual and political skills to dealing with the immediate problems of troubled industries such as steel, motor vehicles and textiles, clothing and footwear, he simultaneously worked towards a longer term, coherent national strategy. Button was given the industry portfolio in the first place because he wanted it, and he chose it rather than others because of the challenge that it presented for changing the whole orientation of Australian manufacturing industry.[17] He had visited a number of manufacturing plants over the years and had always come away with the conviction that things needed to be improved.

In early 1984, Button made an extensive tour of European, and particularly Swedish, industrial concerns which proved to be an important formative influence on his own (and the Hawke government's) thinking on industry policy.[18] He visited, or had discussions with senior executives from leading European enterprises - Philips Industries of Holland, British Leyland, Westland Helicopters and British Aerospace from the United Kingdom, France's Airbus Industries, Nestles in Switzerland, Daimler Benz in Germany, and Sweden's Volvo, Saab Scania and Swedish Space Corporation - and with government ministers and officials from the OECD, GATT, ILO and UNCTAD. Button found that all the major European countries were tackling enormous structural problems with varying degrees of success, and that, except for Sweden, they were largely pre-occupied with European problems. Sweden in particular impressed Button because he found there not only a genuine interest and 'fraternal relationship' in government circles, but a model for Australia of a comparable country with an industry policy that was successful.

Button's reflections on Swedish industry policy helped develop and crystallise his thinking on Australia.[19] Sweden was an obvious model because, besides having a congenial social democratic government, it had a similar macro-economic profile at the time, a higher deficit than Australia, a similarly high inflation rate and relatively high unemployment. The government had negotiated with the unions a moderate wage increase of 10 per cent over two years and was tackling the deficit slowly but firmly. Sweden was unique, however, in having been through its major restructuring, most notably in steel, shipbuilding and mining. Button was particularly impressed by the tough-minded and forward-looking approach of its Social Democratic government: on coming back into power, it had 'cancelled all hand-outs to ailing industries, and diverted all the funds into research and development, industry development, venture capital activities, etc'. This change in policy direction had been discussed in detail with the trade union movement. In 1984, $1 billion was to be spent on its industry development program, and all the major Swedish companies were on their feet and making good profits. Button was impressed by the Swedes' immense skills in commercialising and adapting technology quickly; their belief in the market and hence their refusal to bail out weak industries, as Australian governments were prone to do; and yet their ability to determine the area of the market they wanted to be in and direct government resources in terms of education, research and export incentives. Button noted there were some one thousand PhD students pursuing studies related to particular aspects of Swedish industry.

From the Swedish comparison, Button drew some perceptive conclusions for Australian industry policy. First, he diagnosed that Australia was reaping 'the horrible consequences' of import replacement that had been adopted after the Second World War and was totally unsuited to a rapidly changing world. Furthermore, because of Australia's unsophisticated capital structure and weak technological base, market forces alone could not sort out the problem, and nor could governments determine precisely industry priorities. Second, the government needed to adopt a measured approach, first establishing 'broad guidelines in our minds about what areas of industry will have most comparative advantage (actual or created) in the 1980s and beyond, and what areas should be left to basically market solutions'. Button insisted that the tariff was inappropriate for supporting even the chosen industries, but that the government should encourage research and workforce training, the development of expertise and better marketing. Third, there was the added difficulty of having to deal with such fundamental restructuring during very difficult economic conditions. Button noted the Australian penchant for looking to panaceas such as the recent mining boom, or talk of sunrise industries as an easy way out. He found no such loose talk of sunrise industries in Europe and was confirmed in his view that the relevance of new technologies was for improving existing industries. Fourth, there was a three-stage paradigm for industry policy: getting the macro-economic policies right; preparing structural adjustment programs, including social safety net provisions ('the hard mattress'); and proceeding with the restructuring. By early 1984, Australia had got the first of these stages right, not adequately addressed the second, and only given some attention to the third. Fifth, the offsets policy as followed by the Australian government to achieve technology transfer was considered by the Swedes as appropriate only for underdeveloped countries to earn foreign exchange. Technology transfers in aircraft offsets only made sense if Australia planned eventually to build aeroplanes – there was no point if Australia was going to go on forever making wingtips for others, Button mused. Finally, Button concluded, the dynamics of technology and international trade dictated specialisation, and government must be more selective in what it supported in industry policy.

Button's thinking was to be honed and severely tested through the 1980s as he battled to wean public thinking from protection and implement a corrective national policy. The historic shift in attitude that he achieved was the result of a long process of tripartite consultations and negotiations in which the government sought to foster a sense of shared purpose among capital and labour. The most formal of these negotiations occurred under the auspices of the Australian Manufacturing Council (AMC) and its constituent Industry Councils. The AMC had first been established by the Fraser government in mid-1977 as one outcome of the White Paper on manufacturing industry. Its role was to provide a forum in which representatives of business, unions and government, together with academics and consumers, could discuss industry development issues and advise the government on industry policy. Despite its influential membership (which included Sir Peter Abeles, head of Thomas Nationwide Transport (TNT), Brian Loton, Chief General Manager of BHP, and ACTU president, Bob Hawke) the AMC did not play a prominent role in industry policy-making largely because its role was superseded by the formation of the Crawford Study Group on Structural Adjustment in 1978.[20] By 1980, the AMC had lapsed into inactivity.

When Labor came to power in 1983, part of its much vaunted commitment to consensus-seeking through tripartism included the restructuring of the AMC and the establishment of sectoral industry councils under its aegis. On 26 March and 27 March 1984, Button announced the appointments to the revitalised AMC and its industry councils. The membership of the new AMC reflected the spirit of tripartism although its membership was weighted towards the business community: of its thirty members, thirteen were drawn from business, eight from trade unions, six from government and three from academe. Button also provided the AMC with a secretariat to provide administrative, clerical and research support for itself and the sectoral industry councils. The secretariat was located in Melbourne, the heartland of manufacturing, and was funded by, but independent of, DITAC.

Through its seminars and publications, the AMC played a significant role in fostering public awareness of deficiencies in the manufacturing sector and the need for fundamental structural change. In particular, its 1986 policy document, 'Future Directions for Australian Manufacturing', warned that Australians could no longer proclaim with confidence 'no worries' and 'she'll be right'[21] – typically laconic expressions of optimism which masked a deeper sense of apathy and insecurity. However, the AMC's most important work has been undertaken at the sectoral level by its industry councils. While the AMC was required to 'consult, advise and communicate' on matters of general concern to manufacturing industry, the industry councils focused on issues particular to their sector. Modelled on the AMC, they are also tripartite and each reports directly to the industry minister. At the peak of their influence in 1988, there were eleven industry councils in operation: Textiles, Clothing and Footwear; Processed Food; Machinery and Metal Engineering; Basic Metals; Metal Fabrication; Forestry and Forest Products; Paper Conversion, Printing and Publishing; Chemical and Plastics; Electrical, Electronics and Information Industries; Aerospace; and Automotive.[22]

Each industry council commenced its work by preparing an inventory to allow the government to identify the strengths, weaknesses and opportunities in its particular sector. Generally the industry councils identified more weaknesses than strengths; nearly all of them cited the small and scattered domestic market, poor marketing skills, and high labour costs as major impediments to efficiency. In addition, many of them sought to externalise their own shortcomings instead of looking at issues such as restrictive work practices, poor managerial skills, and outdated technology. For instance, the Automotive Industry Council complained of the poor image of Australian-built vehicles implying that the onus was on consumers to alter their perceptions rather than on the manufacturers to improve their cars.[23] This is an apt illustration of the tremendous change in industry attitudes which was yet to come.

Some critics have argued that the AMC and the industry councils, which are limited to an advisory role and are forced to contend with an established and hostile bureaucracy, lack the resources and authority to implement sectoral strategies.[24] But to suggest that they are nothing more than window-dressing to disguise the government's primary goal of phasing out industry assistance is to deny their importance in establishing a genuine dialogue among the industry participants whose past relations were often frosty if not hostile. To a large extent, this hostility was a legacy of protective statism where the compulsory arbitration system of awards perpetuated an occupational basis for union membership. This occupational or craft bias in the industrial relations system inhibited the development of 'a strong union identity with the fortunes of a particular industry or employer'.[25] The industry councils provided a unique and unprecedented forum in which conflicting interests could work together in a non-adversarial situation to undertake a frank assessment of their industry's prospects. In many cases, unions and employers realised that it was in their mutual interest to abandon previously held positions and explore ways to achieve the survival and prosperity of their industries. This marked the genesis of an attitudinal change among unions and manufacturers alike, the prerequisite for the development of a viable manufacturing sector.

The emphasis on sectoral negotiations stemmed in part from Labor's commitment to its traditional party base, the blue collar unions, to develop industry plans 'through a process of consultation and negotiation with trade unions and employers'.[26] This was particularly the case for the mature industries – steel, heavy engineering and shipbuilding, cars, and textiles, clothing and footwear – which were large employers of labour, either regionally or nationally. These are industries which are intensive in their use of capital, energy and labour, and which are in decline in many parts of the developed world as comparative advantage shifts to the newly industrialised countries. The challenge for Button was to develop industry plans which were compatible with the government's overall objective to reduce protection and foster efficient industries but which also minimised disruptions to the workforce in order to keep the faith of the trade unions. It was here that the industry councils played an important role in minimising the potential for political backlash against a government that aimed to reduce protection in the long run.

There is nothing uniquely Australian about the industry plans – they have already been adopted in various guises throughout Europe and North America. The shift to sectoral planning was a manifestation of the OECD's reorientation to structural adjustment during the 1970s when it became apparent that macro-economic policy alone could not bring about lasting improvements in the performance of industry and service sectors. In most cases, however, sectoral plans overseas have effectively *increased* protection in the short term in order to give industries time to adjust in the long term.[27] By contrast, Button's industry plans are novel in providing adjustment assistance to troubled sectors while at the same time reducing tariff and non-tariff protection. To a great extent, Button's industry plans were designed to take account of the fact that protectionist policies of the past had contributed to the malaise of Australian manufacturing. Just as the state had implemented protection in all its guises in the past, now, given Australia's changed economic circumstances and relative decline in comparative terms, the state had a responsibility to implement corrective programs to eliminate protection and its consequences. However, withdrawing protection altogether was not an option for a government that was committed to restoring profitability and encouraging new investment in the manufacturing sector. This required a stable, predictable macroeconomic environment in the medium term, so industry restructuring was initially limited to weaning the least efficient industries gradually from the milch cow of protection.

Button's industry plans were based on a carrot-and-stick approach to restructuring. The carrots included bounties, industry modernisation schemes, support for labour and management training and skills upgrading, special research and development (R&D) grants, export market development programs, and labour adjustment assistance designed to compensate and retrain those who lost their jobs through the restructuring process. The sticks included the reduction of barrier protection through the abolition of import quotas and substantial tariff cuts, and, in some cases, penalties for non-compliance. The most important of these plans - the steel plan, the car plan and the textiles, clothing and footwear plan - are analysed in Chapters 5, 6 and 7 respectively.

In essence, the sectoral plans for steel, heavy engineering, cars, and textiles, clothing and footwear, served to place in isolation those industries which required special treatment for political, regional and social reasons. In addition to the plans for declining sectors, the government also designed specific packages to improve the competitiveness of relatively healthy sectors such as chemicals and plastics, fertilisers, processed food, non-ferrous metals, and pulp, paper and printing. These plans and assistance packages for mature industry sectors epitomise the corrective industry programs developed between 1983 and 1986.

With most of the sectoral plans for Australia's mature industries in place by 1986, the focus of industry policy shifted to the sunrise industries: biotechnology, communications equipment, medical, dental and veterinary equipment and the information and aerospace industries. Unlike traditional manufacturing industries, these industries generally operate in a global market, are involved in high value-added activities and are characterised by a high degree of research and technology. The Hawke government introduced a range of assistance measures for the 'brain-based' industries beginning with a 150 per cent tax concession for business R&D.

SECTORAL STRATEGIES FOR NEW INDUSTRIES

Following the October 1984 general election, the Department of Industry acquired responsibility for the technology section of the former Department of Science and Technology. This was a clear signal that, having established corrective programs for Australia's ageing industries, the government now intended to focus on making the manufacturing sector far more technologically oriented. Like Button's previous industry reforms, this initiative also required state action to correct for past neglect and malpractice, especially in the area of Australia's expenditure on industrial R&D. Here the problem lies not with the public sector, whose expenditure on R&D in Australia compares favourably with other OECD nations, but with the business sector whose contributions have traditionally been low. Thus, in terms of total expenditure on R&D, the OECD ranks Australia at the bottom of the group of middle performers which includes Canada, Italy, and Switzerland.[28]

To a large extent, Australia's potential for economic growth depends on its performance in technological development in the manufacturing and service sectors. Throughout the world, industries with the highest growth rates are those which spend relatively more on R&D as a proportion of value-added (mainly pharmaceuticals, computers, electronics and scientific instruments). Expenditure on R&D is also an important factor in a nation's export performance especially in the high-technology product sectors where there is a strong correlation between R&D expenditure and trade performance. In addition to its role in developing innovative products, R&D can also be directed to the production process in order to increase productivity and lift competitiveness.[29] Thus, the private sector's poor commitment to R&D in Australia has serious implications for the nation's capacity to become internationally competitive.

Nowhere is this problem more apparent than in the manufacturing sector where private sector R&D is 'strikingly low' by international comparisons.[30] Industry's reluctance to spend on R&D can be attributed to a number of causes including poor management skills, an opportunistic business tradition which limits its horizons to short-term profits, a lack of venture capital, and the absence of economies of scale. In addition, certain structural characteristics of Australian manufacturing such as the small and fragmented nature of local manufacturing, the preponderance of mature industries, and the high level of foreign ownership in R&D-intensive industries also contributes to the low level of business spending on research and development in Australian manufacturing. Most if not all of these factors were caused by protectionist policies; so it can be said that the poor record of business expenditure on R&D for Australian manufacturing is itself a legacy of protection.

The Hawke government's approach to improving the level of R&D expenditure in Australia was compatible with other elements of its corrective industry policy. Rather than increasing the public sector's share of total R&D spending, the government introduced policies designed to encourage the private sector to take more responsibility for funding and carrying out R&D. The most important of these policies was the 150 per cent tax concession for R&D which was announced by Hawke during the 1984 election campaign and introduced on 1 July 1985.[31] Although there are difficulties in isolating the effect of other factors, expenditure on industry R&D grew dramatically after the concession was announced; in 1986–87, it had increased by 85 per cent in real terms since 1981–82 and had almost doubled as a percentage of GDP.[32] The concession was originally set to expire after six years but in the March 1991 industry policy statement, the prime minister announced that it would be reduced to 125 per cent in 1993 and retained as a permanent feature of the Income Tax Act.

In the case of certain high-technology and scientific industry sectors, the R&D tax concession alone was insufficient assistance to ensure the development of a viable industry. In these cases, DITAC devised and implemented sectoral industry strategies which were developed in consultation with the appropriate industry councils and administered by DITAC. These strategies are designed to increase

Australian local content, research and development, and export activities in industries which are often dominated by foreign multinationals. In a sense they have been developed in accordance with the Labor government's policy of 1983 to control the 'external influences . . . encouraging a process of de-industrialisation' - but with an important difference. Whereas in the past this would have involved the use of tariff and non-tariff protection or restrictions on foreign investment, the industry strategies of the late 1980s rely on non-distorting forms of assistance. Thus, even the hard-liners at the Industry Commission can scarcely find cause for complaint. By 1987, industry strategies were in place for metal-working machines and robots, communications equipment, medical and scientific equipment, biotechnology, space technology, pharmaceutical products, and the information industries.[33]

Pharmaceutical Products Industry Strategy

Since 1950, the Commonwealth government has subsidised drug consumers through the Pharmaceutical Benefits Scheme (PBS). Under the PBS, the government buys many types of prescription drugs which are then distributed through pharmacies to the public. The government has been able to keep the cost of these drugs relatively low because of its monopsony position as the sole buyer of drugs in Australia; and, as a result, the prices paid to drug companies in Australia have been about 50 per cent of the world average. In response to this relatively low return on their Australian operations, however, the multinational drug companies pulled out of R&D in Australia, and confined their operations to formulation and packaging only. As a result, drug exports fell while imports rose and Australia began to run a trade deficit in pharmaceuticals which amounted to $460 million in 1989–90.[34] The Labor government could not abolish the PBS, which had become an important social benefit for millions of Australians, and so the challenge was to reverse the trade deficit in pharmaceuticals while still retaining the scheme.

In September 1987, Senator Button and Health Minister Dr Neal Blewett announced the introduction of a five-year sectoral plan which was designed to revive the Australian pharmaceutical industry by encouraging R&D, strengthening employment opportunities, and increasing investment, production and export performance.

The principal element of the plan is the payment of higher PBS prices to companies who commit themselves to increasing exports from Australia as well as raising spending on R&D in Australia.[35] At the same time, the government did not wish to increase the total cost of drugs under the PBS; cost-reducing measures were therefore introduced to the scheme which have subsequently provoked a backlash among pharmacists and consumers, especially pensioners.[36]

The IAC and its successor, the Industry Commission (IC), have been generally critical of the various industry plans and strategies on the grounds that these forms of assistance distort the market and, more specifically, are less transparent than tariffs. In the case of the pharmaceutical industry, however, the IC concedes that past pricing practices under the PBS 'may have created a bias against investment or undertaking local research and development' and hence Labor's new five-year plan could be seen as 'enhancing efficiency rather than providing assistance'.[37] The early indications suggest that the plan is working very well; by mid-1990, five companies had committed themselves to spending $68 million on R&D over five years and to increasing exports by $266 million by 1993. If the export target is achieved, three of these drug companies will ascend into Australia's top twelve manufacturing exporters.[38]

Information Industries Strategy

Like the Pharmaceutical Products Industry Strategy, the Information Industries Strategy (IIS) aims to exert a measure of control over the activities of transnational corporations operating in Australia. Compared with the Whitlam government's cant against transnationals during the 1970s and the subsequent establishment of the Foreign Investment Review Board, the IIS is a far more sophisticated attempt to direct the nature of foreign investment and activities in Australia.

Australia's prosperity in the 1990s will depend largely on its ability to tap into the rapidly growing global market for information products and services. This market, which includes computer hardware and software, communications equipment and information and communication services, accounted for 19 per cent of world trade in 1988. In the same year, Australia ran a trade deficit of nearly $4 billion in the information industries sector.[39] To a great extent, this trade imbalance reflected the domination by transnational corporations of the international market for information products and services. For instance, the manufacturing of computer hardware in Australia has generally consisted of low value-added, assembly-only operations, the legacy of past industry policy which forced transnationals to incorporate a local element into their productions in order to fulfil contract requirements. The transient nature of this type of production has neither contributed to skills formation nor enhanced Australia's indigenous technological capacity.[40]

A second problem is the nature of Australia's computer software industry. Although hundreds of small Australian-owned companies have developed world class products in communications and software applications, their export potential has been limited by the lack of resources for overseas marketing. Thus, successful product commercialisation has rested on their capacity to enter into joint ventures with larger overseas corporations.[41]

In order to overcome these problems, DITAC developed the Information Industries Strategy (IIS), which has become the centrepiece of DITAC's overall program for industry development. The Information Industries Strategy was announced by Button in September 1987 after 18 months of tripartite consultation and study. The IIS is designed to rectify Australia's growing trade deficit in the information industries sector by encouraging firms to link into world markets through alliances with foreign companies and to develop specialised products which are internationally competitive in terms of quality, design, delivery and price. Like other industry plans, the IIS has specific initiatives aimed at product R&D, increased exports, and skills formation and development. An Information Industries Board has been established to advise the industry minister and monitor the effectiveness of the Strategy.

The key element of the Information Industries Strategy is the Partnerships for Development scheme introduced in September 1988. The Partnerships scheme, which waives offsets requirements for transnational corporations that have entered into joint ventures with Australian companies, was a deliberate attempt to move away from market-distorting assistance mechanisms, such as offsets, which have a sorry legacy in Australia.

The offsets program was introduced in 1970 to expand the technological capacity of Australian manufacturing industry and provide new opportunities for employment. Under the terms of the offsets program, foreign companies who win government contracts in Australia are required to involve Australian manufacturing industry in high technology or export-oriented activities.[42] The program was the target of considerable criticism during the 1980s. The Industry Commission, in particular, claimed that the program distorts market outcomes and tends to reinforce a dependent mentality in which industry looks first to the government for assistance. There is little doubt that the offsets program incorporates some of the most undesirable elements of industry assistance; it lacks transparency and its cost effectiveness is difficult to gauge.[43] There is also evidence to suggest that overseas suppliers often increase contract prices in order to meet offsets obligations.[44] Worst of all, many foreign companies simply fail to comply with their offsets obligations in Australia. Despite changes to the offsets policy in March 1986, the program remained the target of continuing criticism.[45] In March 1987, the Joint Committee of Public Accounts found that the offsets program was still poorly administered and open to abuse, lacked accountability, and, worst of all, failed to achieve its primary purpose, the transfer of technology.[46]

The Partnerships for Development scheme has been designed to circumvent the shortcomings of the offsets program. Under the terms of the scheme, transnational companies which enter into partnership agreements with either private or public enterprises are required to increase their local R&D expenditure to 5 per cent of total sales turnover in Australia and achieve a 50 per cent export to import ratio within seven years. In return, the Commonwealth and state governments exempt these companies from civil offsets obligations. In addition, the Commonwealth government has undertaken an infrastructure program designed to ensure an adequate supply of skilled people through tertiary training and a 'fast track' immigration scheme. Early reports indicate that the Partnerships scheme has been embraced by the transnationals; in the first eighteen months of the scheme, twenty Partnership Agreements were signed.[47] The success of the program to date provides plenty of ammunition for the supporters of an interventionist industry strategy.

While praising the Partnerships for Development scheme for its innovative approach to developing indigenous high-technology industries, Winton Higgins has argued that, because it is not tripartite (unions have no access to negotiations for Partnerships Agreements), 'the government wants to disenfranchise organised labour in hi-tech industries'.[48] This is highly unlikely. Higgins forgets that the scheme was developed after months of tripartite negotiations; if the unions are unhappy with the result, they have not said so publicly. Furthermore, corporatist plans have been implemented only in the case of mature industry sectors where unions and management have needed to work together to improve work practices and increase productivity, and where restructuring involved some contraction in the sector, inevitably leading to job losses. In these cases, the precondition for successful restructuring was tripartite agreement. By contrast, strategies for sunrise industries were not meant to focus on shopfloor and factory issues (nor did they need to) and were designed to promote the growth, rather than the contraction, of these sectors.

DISMANTLING THE PROTECTIVE STATE

In 1985–86, Australia's terms of trade collapsed. In the past, a similar situation would have triggered a defensive reaction in the form of import quotas or higher tariffs. Instead, apart from 'talking down' the value of the Australian dollar, the Hawke government did not erect barriers to shield manufacturing industry from import pressure. Rather, the government signalled its commitment to improving Australia's competitiveness by hastening the pace of structural reform and proceeded to announce changes designed to strengthen industry infrastructure. The government continued to scale down or eliminate defensive forms of industry assistance including assistance for agricultural producers. These changes were all implemented as part of the Hawke government's goal to make the economy more open, flexible and responsive so that in the future it could adapt more quickly and easily to external pressures. With many of these reforms in place by 1988, the government was free to tackle the most important bastion of protective statism – the protective tariff.

In May 1986 the Treasurer warned that Australia risked becoming a 'banana republic'. While Keating's blunt statement shocked those who cherished the myth of the lucky country, it did not surprise those familiar with long-term trends showing that Australia's terms of trade had been in gradual decline since the early 1960s. In the past, favourable commodity prices had come to the rescue enabling the economy to accommodate the decline and giving governments the pretext for inaction. However, the end of the resource boom and a collapse in world commodity prices in the early 1980s triggered a dramatic depreciation in the Australian dollar and a sharp decline in Australia's terms of trade in early 1985. Together, these developments contributed to a massive increase in the foreign debt while the cost of debt-servicing increased due to the fall of the dollar. As a result, Australia's current account deficit, which averaged 2.4 per cent of GDP between financial years 1959/60 and 1979/80, more than doubled to 5.2 per cent in 1984/85.[49]

This crisis forced the government to back-pedal on its strategy to promote growth through fiscal expansion and abandon its commitment to maintain real wages. As the government only had moral suasion over the income settings for executives and professionals, the axe fell on unionised workers; the Accord was renegotiated and full wage-indexation was abandoned. For such short-term pain, the government hoped that there would be long-term gain. In particular, the depreciation of the Australian dollar immediately gave a competitive edge to export and import-competing sectors. To enhance that benefit, in an address to the nation in June 1986, Prime Minister Hawke announced the beginning of an export drive to increase Australian business commitment to exporting and to improve export investment, production and marketing.[50] Similar strategies had been launched by previous governments with little overall effect, but this time the Hawke government had a single body, AUSTRADE, to give institutional support and direction to its export campaign.

AUSTRADE and the national export drive

Years of industry protection had contributed to the development of a manufacturing sector which was content to produce almost exclusively for the home market. In 1984, exports from Australia's manufacturing industries accounted for a mere 14 per cent of their total output compared with 27 per cent for Canada and 29 per cent for New Zealand.[51] While manufactures are the fastest-growing sector of world trade, Australia was the only industrial country which had not increased its proportion of merchandise exports to GDP since the 1950s. Even when these figures are adjusted to account for Australia's small population and distance from markets, its performance has still lagged relative to other industrial nations.[52]

The deterioration in Australia's terms of trade in 1985/86 highlighted the need to improve Australia's export performance in the manufacturing and service sectors. In addition to relieving the current account deficit, an improvement in the export orientation of manufacturers would contribute to employment growth and a more efficient manufacturing sector based on economies of scale. To that end, in April 1985, Trade Minister John Dawkins announced the formation of the Australian Trade Commission (AUSTRADE), an amalgamation of a host of Commonwealth government trade-related agencies: the Trade Commissioner Service, the Export Development Grants Board, the Export Finance Insurance Commission and the Australian Overseas Projects Corporation. AUSTRADE was designed to function as a 'one-stop trade shop' and its primary role was to assist exporters to develop existing and new markets.[53]

Like the sectoral plans for industry restructuring, the establishment of AUSTRADE and the emphasis on export promotion is a clear example of corrective statism. This defies the trend in many other industrial countries where governments have shifted responsibility for export facilitation to industry associations and export consortia. In 1987, Australia topped the list of industrial countries for expenditure on export promotion per $1000 of exports. Significantly, after Australia, the second biggest spender on export promotion was Canada, where the government was also struggling to overcome the legacy of protection which had resulted in an obsession with home markets to the detriment of manufacturing exports.[54]

AUSTRADE's principal assistance scheme is the Export Market Development Grants Scheme (EMDG) which provides financial support to small and medium-sized exporters to develop or enhance foreign markets for goods and services. The EMDG program is directed at export promotion, especially for profitable companies with high Australian value added products, or to stimulate joint activities by firms which could benefit from generic product promotion. But the critics of interventionist industry policy have been critical even of this selective approach. For instance, the IAC claimed that programs like the EMDG 'can unduly bias exporting firms' investment decisions toward export market development activity'.[55] However, that is precisely what the interventionists believe that government should be doing. In particular, the AMC urges manufacturers to abandon their typically opportunistic approach which is focused on marginal, short-term export activities. Instead, they should view export market development as a long-term proposition based on investment in 'product design, packaging, foreign distribution, marketing, developing brand image and other activities'.[56]

Clearly, Dawkins' original notion to combine and reorganise the patchwork of export facilitation programs into a central agency was an appropriate way to make the various programs more accessible to potential exporters. However, considerable doubts have been raised about AUSTRADE's effectiveness. In December 1990, a consultant's report on AUSTRADE by McKinsey & Company found that 45 per cent of its resources were directed into administrative and support activities; that many of AUSTRADE's services were duplicated by programs at the state level; and that the organisation was dominated by 'a risk-averse culture which constrains initiative taking'.[57] While these are characteristics symptomatic of most federal bureaucracies, in AUSTRADE's case it reflected a far more serious failure to channel resources where they were most needed. For instance, in 1987–88, only 37.2 per cent of AUSTRADE's staff were located overseas.[58] And of these, a disproportionate number were located in Western, English-speaking countries rather than in the more difficult markets of Asia and the Middle East. The McKinsey report revealed that AUSTRADE dedicated more resources to the US market than it did to India, Indonesia, Korea, Taiwan and Thailand combined. Problems such as these led the McKinsey report to conclude that: 'While AUSTRADE can point to many examples of exports they have helped happen, in our judgement these do not add up enough to be confident that the country is clearly receiving adequate return for its investment in AUSTRADE'.[59]

While the poor performance of AUSTRADE is not an indictment of export assistance schemes *per se*, it does suggest that the government has yet to develop and implement a coherent export strategy for Australian manufacturing industry. In the March 1991 Industry Statement, the government announced that responsibility for AUSTRADE would be shifted from DITAC to the Department of Foreign Affairs and Trade. In addition, AUSTRADE's headquarters were to be relocated from Canberra to Sydney. Two months later, in late May, AUSTRADE announced the closing of several North American posts in order to redirect resources to more difficult markets. A year after its restructuring, however, AUSTRADE is still under criticism from industry groups and the opposition for being too bureaucratic and complacent. According to the opposition's ambitious 'Fightback' package (Dr Hewson's radical prospectus for more efficient government by the Liberal coalition), AUSTRADE's budget of $130 million would be slashed in half under a Liberal government with many of its services contracted out to the private sector.[60]

More encouraging was the initiative by Dr Neal Blewett, when minister for trade and overseas development, for developing a coordinated strategy with the states for lifting Australia's trade performance and improving investment activities. As a first step, the Commonwealth, in consultation with state governments and industry groups, made an extensive review of existing practices which revealed a plethora of uncoordinated policies and programs at Commonwealth and state level. An extensive report documenting this mishmash of practices and canvassing proposals for improved coordination and information flow was prepared and circulated in draft form in November 1991.[61] This was quickly followed by the inaugural meeting of federal, state and territory ministers responsible for international trade and business development. In the spirit of 'closer partnership with the states', the catchcry of New Federalism, this intergovernmental forum agreed on a number of strategies for improving the coordination of trade and investment development activities. These included the establishment of Export Centres around Australia by AUSTRADE and of state coordinating committees to oversee state involvement in such centres, co-location of AUSTRADE and state government overseas trade and investment offices, and various joint measures for exploring and promoting trade opportunities.[62] The ministerial council agreed to meet annually to review progress.

Education and industry training

The tariff reductions were an important signal of the Hawke government's intention to continue the process of dismantling protectionism and, when necessary, introducing corrective policies to facilitate structural adjustment. An important part of this process was the restructuring of the education system in order to provide the basis for a more educated and skilled workforce. These reforms commenced with the 'machinery of government' changes in July 1987 when Hawke announced the establishment of the Department of Employment, Education and Training (DEET), to be headed by former trade minister, John Dawkins.

In his White Paper of July 1988, Dawkins reaffirmed the government's intention to direct an 'increasing share of total higher education resources . . . to those fields of study of greatest relevance to the national goals of industrial development and economic restructuring'.[63] The White Paper identified these fields as engineering, science and technology, and business and management studies.[64] This shift in funding priorities provoked a hostile response from academics, particularly in the humanities and social sciences, who argued that the social and cultural relevance of their disciplines was equally important. Their complaints may be well-founded: in several Canadian provinces during the 1970s and early 1980s, similar attempts to channel students into specific vocational programs produced the reverse effect. As the much touted jobs in areas such as computer science failed to materialise, enrolments in the arts surged disproportionately to other disciplines. There are signs of a similar mismatch in Australia between government priorities for education and actual job opportunities, with very high levels of unemployment among engineering graduates.

In September 1989, as part of the ongoing process of shifting responsibility for industrial development from the state to the private sector, the federal government announced the introduction of the Training Guarantee Scheme, a training levy which was proposed by the ACTU in *Australia Reconstructed*.[65] Under the terms of the scheme, companies with an annual payroll exceeding $200,000 were required to spend an amount equal to 1 per cent of their payroll on a government approved training scheme in 1990–91 (the figure rose to 1.5 per cent in 1991–92). Industries could provide their own training or contribute to approved training funds. Results to date have been mixed. Predictably, there has been some rorting of the system and, with some companies designating South Pacific holidays as training schemes, DEET will have to tighten its monitoring and administration of the training scheme.

Defence policy

One of the earliest arguments for protection, espoused in the late nineteenth century by David Syme, was the need for Australia to be self-sufficient in the event of war. This view was reinforced during the two World Wars when Australia, cut off from its traditional sources of supply, was forced to develop considerable industrial capacity for import replacement and the war effort. Although defence production was retooled for peacetime, governments continued to promote a policy of import replacement, partly to ensure national self-reliance in the event of a future war but also because the needs of the Defence Department played an important role in the development of Australian industry. In addition to plant and equipment required for specific defence projects, the armed services have relied on Australian sources for most of their everyday supplies. Australian industry also benefits from defence requirements for high technology items and facilities. Thus, protecting Australia's defence industries has always been considered as serving the national interest. This protection was delivered by tariff and non-tariff barriers as well as other forms of assistance such as procurement policies, which favoured Australian manufacturers, and offsets which guaranteed certain levels of local content in defence projects.

Australia's defence production has been traditionally carried out by a combination of government and privately owned factories. The strategic implications of certain defence purchases require orders to be placed with Australian companies regardless of cost. Without cost as a factor, there has been little pressure on these establishments to improve productivity, efficiency and competitiveness. Moreover, past practice tended to establish defence production in certain companies and then allocate work exclusively to them. Subsequently, these monopolies lapsed into poor performance and high costs. The extra cost incurred in securing the involvement of Australian industry in defence contracts was essentially assistance by any other name and was at odds with the Hawke government's objective to foster industries which are export-oriented and internationally competitive.

Years of defence industry protection had created government defence factories which were in a decrepit state and ill-matched to the nation's strategic needs. If the Labor government was serious in its desire to restructure industry to lift overall competitiveness, its own defence factories could not be exempted from the process. In 1985, Defence Minister Kim Beazley commenced a program to rationalise, corporatise and privatise most of its defence plants. Munitions factories - some a hundred years old - were closed; ammunition, heavy engineering and naval engineering plants were rationalised; government aircraft factories were corporatised; and the Commonwealth Aircraft Corporation and the Williamstown Naval Dockyard were sold to private interests.[66]

The Hawke government also acted to reduce protection for private companies with defence contracts. In June 1984, Hawke announced that Australian participation in certain defence contracts could no longer be taken for granted and that in some cases Australian companies would have to compete with foreign companies for defence contracts. While acknowledging that strategic priorities 'often involve cost premiums above those associated with the Government's general policies', Hawke stated that the Departments of Defence and Defence Support had to become far more selective in judging the potential benefits and penalties of Australian participation in defence contracts.[67] This was underscored in 1989 when the government's purchasing policy, which gave a 20 per cent preference to Australian and New Zealand goods and services, was abolished.

The government's willingness to reduce protection to the defence industries was recognition that, despite the importance of defence requirements to local industry, defence procurement could not in itself counter the relative decline of industries such as shipbuilding and heavy engineering. The peacetime requirements of the defence forces are generally too small, too infrequent and too limited in duration to provide a viable long term base for industries. In a 1986 report to the defence minister, Paul Dibb noted that 'even if all defence capital equipment expenditure could be directed to Australian industry, this would represent a very small increment to our industrial sector'.[68] Thus, industries with defence implications such as heavy engineering, steel, shipbuilding, aerospace, electronics and telecommunications have not been exempted from policies designed to reduce assistance and lift competitiveness. Nevertheless, the strategic implications of many defence contracts inevitably allow a certain measure of industry assistance for defence production in Australia. Just how much assistance is hard to quantify: the complex set of arrangements, such as offsets and industry assistance programs administered by the Defence Department, means that even the IAC has found it 'extremely difficult to measure its extent and assess its economic impact'.[69]

Government purchasing policy

The dismantling of protective practices continued throughout the late 1980s, as the Hawke government began to scrutinise government practices such as offsets and purchasing policy. Prior to 1954, the Commonwealth government's policy on purchasing required the acceptance of the lowest tender. Since then, the party in power has been increasingly inclined to use procurement policy as a mechanism to achieve broader political, economic and industrial goals. During the late 1950s and 1960s, the Menzies government progressively implemented guidelines which allowed departmental ministers to give preference to Australian goods which had strategic importance (primarily defence-related). In 1972, concern over the role of foreign multinationals in Australia led the Whitlam government to change purchasing policy in order to strengthen Australian control and ownership of industry. Under those rules, in the event of equally acceptable tenders for any government contract, preference would be given to Australian-owned companies. Then, in 1977, faced with a severe slump in manufacturing industry, the Fraser government proclaimed that government purchasing policy should assist industrial recovery.[70] Over a six-year period, the government tinkered with various procurement policies designed to give tariff preference to Australian goods and services.

When first elected, the Hawke government continued the tradition of using purchasing policy to address a broader economic agenda. In December 1983, new guidelines were introduced which gave an automatic 20 per cent margin of preference to all Australasian goods and services and allowed departmental ministers to grant discretionary preferences of up to 30 per cent where employment effects, defence or high technology industries were concerned.[71] However, several government reports cast considerable doubt on the overall effectiveness of procurement policies in contributing to industrial development. In particular, a study by the Bureau of Industry Economics (BIE) in 1988 argued that the procurement policy was at odds with the general direction of the government's industry development objectives. The BIE report observed that procurement policy was protective, selective and discriminated in favour of those businesses which happened to sell to the government. It also noted that the government's ability to use procurements as a tool for industry development was being eroded by the privatisation of government business enterprises and the decentralisation of purchasing responsibility. The study concluded that, overall, 'the benefits of the program are likely to be exceeded by the costs'.[72] The government accepted the thrust of the BIE report and, in November 1989, the Commonwealth purchasing preference was abolished. In effect, this signalled a return to the policy which had operated prior to 1954 when the Commonwealth government sought the best value for money in its purchasing.

Traditionally, the states' purchasing policy, which discriminated in favour of local firms and against Australian firms located in other states, was more detrimental to the development of national economic efficiency. 'State preferencing' had existed since colonial times and, despite the constitutional requirement of absolutely *free* trade, commerce and intercourse among the states mandated by section 92, it flourished until the 1980s. Since Australian business was 'decentralised and state-oriented', as John Wanna points out, 'preferencing was not problematic except for large or expanding enterprises'.[73] State preferencing reinforced the localism of business and was jealously guarded by state governments and professional groups.

By the 1980s, however, state preferencing was coming under increasing pressure from the Commonwealth government, economic rationalists and business groups and large corporations with national perspectives. The policy was criticised in a series of special inquiry reports through the 1970s and early 1980s, and by the Bureau of Industry Economics in a report in 1985 on heavy engineering.[74] A further catalyst for change was the agreement for Closer Economic Relations (CER) with New Zealand, signed in 1980 and coming into effect in 1983, which was antithetical to such restraints on access to trade. After extensive intergovernmental negotiation, the council of Commonwealth and state industry ministers agreed in principle in late 1984 to phase out state preferences, a draft agreement was prepared the following year, and an agreement signed in 1986. This National Preference Agreement (NPA) imposed on the states the obligation to extend the margin of preference applied by each state to products from throughout Australia and, after New Zealand joined the NPA, to New Zealand as well.[75]

The NPA did not standardise preference rates, however. Four of the states, New South Wales, Victoria, Queensland and South Australia joined the Commonwealth in applying a 20 per cent margin while Western Australia and Tasmania applied only a 10 per cent preference. After the Commonwealth abolished its preferences, only Victoria followed suit. Of the other parties to the agreement, New Zealand and the Australian Capital Territory have never had preferences, while the other states retain their earlier 20 and 10 per cent rates. The continuation of such preferences makes little sense, but so far at least efforts to have them abolished in Queensland and South Australia have been aborted.

The 1988 general tariff reductions

The 1986 economic crisis highlighted the need to shift resources into the traded goods sector (export and import-competing industries). However, macro-economic policy proved to be too crude an instrument to effect that change, as Button had anticipated back in early 1984. In June 1987, Button announced his intention to focus on tariff reform if the Hawke government was elected to a third term. In particular, Button stated that he would push for across-the-board tariff cuts if the economy improved.[76] This was a daring proposal; hitherto, the Hawke government had cautiously implemented tariff reductions on an industry-by-industry basis and only in conjunction with specific sectoral assistance arrangements. Fearing a repeat of the huge political backlash triggered by Whitlam's across-the-board cut in 1973, Button's advisers quickly cooled down his public enthusiasm for such an action. Nevertheless, Button had put the prospect of a general tariff reduction on the table, thus signalling a major turning point in the Hawke government's previous practice of targeted industry-by-industry reductions in protection.

A sharp decline in the value of the Australian dollar gave the government an opportunity to introduce a program of general tariff reductions which would bring Australia's tariff structure more in line with other OECD nations. The timing was significant; a depreciated dollar effectively raised the price of imports, thus minimising the immediate economic impact of the cuts. In April 1988, Button took his proposals for a general tariff reduction to the cabinet's Structural Adjustment Committee. He had abandoned the notion of an across-the-board cut in favour of a top-down approach to bring the maximum tariff rate down to 15 per cent over several years. The advantage of the top-down approach was that it targeted only the most heavily protected industries and helped to reduce the disparities in protection levels between various industries.[77]

While the Confederation of Australian Industry endorsed the tariff reductions, the union movement was less favourable. Armed with statistics which predicted 9,000 manufacturing job losses within two years of the proposed cuts, the ACTU strongly opposed Button's proposal. The ACTU's opposition helped to strengthen his hand against the combined forces of Treasury and the Department of Prime Minister and Cabinet which favoured reductions to 10 per cent.[78] Ultimately a compromise was reached; tariffs above 15 per cent would be reduced to 15 per cent over four years while tariffs between 10 and 15 per cent would be gradually cut to 10 per cent. The tariff reductions were announced in Treasurer Keating's May Economic Statement which introduced a package of structural reforms including changes in the business tax structure, a reduction in assistance to rural industries, and deregulation of telecommunications.[79] The trade-off for the tariff cuts was the abolition of the 2 per cent import revenue duty, a tax which had been paid principally by manufacturers on the purchase of imported intermediate and capital goods.

This was the most ambitious tariff reform undertaken since the 1973 cut and was calculated to result in a reduction of the average effective rate of assistance from 19 to 14 per cent by 1992–93. However these cuts did not extend to the most heavily protected industry sectors - cars and textiles, clothing and footwear. Although Button did tinker with the sectoral plans for these industries in order to increase the pace of restructuring, one of the basic goals of the plans was to provide a stable investment climate in the short term. Thus, economic as well as political considerations prevented him from applying the general tariff reductions to these special case industries. As a result, the general tariff reductions actually served to increase the gap between assistance rates for these troubled industries and the rest of the manufacturing sector. And by leaving high levels of assistance for the motor vehicle and TCF industries, Australia's tariff rates in 1992 will still be higher on average than were those of Canada, the United States, Japan and the EEC in the late 1980s. While economic 'dries' might deplore the Hawke government's failure to push for greater reductions in 1988, the prospect of further tariff cuts was a potentially useful bargaining chip to secure access for Australia's primary exports in the event that the GATT Uruguay Round collapsed before reaching an agreement to reduce agricultural protection.

Industry policy in the late 1980s

The aftermath of the 1985–86 economic crisis laid bare the fundamental conflict over industry policy within the Hawke government.

Treasurer Keating believed that the depreciation of the Australian dollar would result in the necessary adjustments by reducing imports and increasing exports; in effect, transferring resources into more competitive parts of the economy. By contrast, Button was sceptical of Keating's 'J-curve optimism' believing that macro-economic policy alone could not achieve these adjustments because it did not deal with impediments to industry efficiency at the micro-economic level. In addition, Button identified an attitudinal problem on the part of Australian managers and workers whose 'variety of cultural cringes' were preventing the development of a less restrictive, more outward-looking manufacturing sector despite the dollar devaluation.[80] The best evidence in support of Button's pessimism was the continuing lack of business investment in the manufacturing sector. Thus, it was no small victory for Button when Prime Minister Hawke announced during the 1987 election campaign that, if re-elected, his government would focus on reducing barriers to industry efficiency through micro-economic reform in key areas such as the labour market and transport and communications.

After winning the July 1987 election, Hawke moved quickly to demonstrate his new commitment to micro-economic reform by restructuring the Commonwealth public service. As part of the changes, responsibility for AUSTRADE was moved from the former Department of Trade to DITAC, together with the science portfolio and the Commonwealth Scientific and Industrial Research Organisation (CSIRO). This new super-ministry now had responsibility for exports, science, technology and small business, thus giving the industry minister scope for greater program coordination in designing industry policy. At the same time, the Industries Assistance Commission was shifted to Treasury, a move widely interpreted as a 'clash of the Titans' resulting in a personal victory for Keating over Button and a triumph for economic rationalism.[81] Neither view can be sustained under analysis. For his part, Button, who had frequently been frustrated by his failure to get references under way, notably on the mining industry, was not unhappy to lose control of the IAC.[82] Nor is there any evidence that Keating played a machiavellian role in the move. Rather, the initiative came from senior officials within the IAC who proposed it to Treasury secretary, Bernie Fraser, and the proposal was cleared with Button by Keating before it was made public.[83]

The IAC's restlessness is best understood as an act of self-preservation. By 1987 it had completed the general review of tariff assistance begun by the Tariff Board in 1971 under Rattigan's direction. With the IAC's original mandate fulfilled, the Treasurer announced cutbacks to its funding and staff in May 1987.[84] This was an ominous development for the future of the IAC and, in order to justify its continuing existence, it wanted to sketch out a new role for itself in the area of micro-economic reform. In particular, IAC officials wanted to undertake a rolling review of all non-tariff forms of assistance. The IAC's identity crisis mirrored a less obvious change in Treasury where one consequence of Keating's macro-economic reforms was a reduction in the government's scope for controlling the economy. Thus, it was equally important for Treasury to stake out new areas of responsibility, hence its developing interest in micro-economic reform. With their shared opposition to sectoral and interventionist approaches to industry policy, Treasury and the IAC had become ideal bedmates although it took some time for Treasury to work out just what the revamped Industry Commission might do. However, despite their combined power and influence, the transfer of the IAC to Treasury did not weaken Button's industry policy. If anything, the Hawke government's commitment to a corrective policy for manufacturing industry emerged even more clearly during the next two years. The best evidence for that is to be seen in the bailout of Kodak Australasia in 1989.

To intervene or not to intervene?: the Kodak bailout

In early September 1989, Kodak Australasia told Button that it would close the film-manufacturing section of its Melbourne factory, at the cost of 500 jobs, unless it was bailed out by the Commonwealth government.[85] The threatened closure was part of a world-wide rationalisation by its US parent company, Eastman Kodak, which was trying to prevent a takeover bid. The Coburg factory was the next in line for a streamlining process which had already occurred in Kodak's Canadian, British and European subsidiaries. Some of the reasons behind Kodak's decision to shut down part of its Australian operations were evident in a Bureau of Industry Economics report issued in draft form just prior to Kodak's announcement. The BIE report compared the production of Ektacolor paper at Kodak plants in Australia, Brazil, Canada and the United Kingdom, and found that even though the Australian operation was efficient and profitable, production could be undertaken more cheaply at its other plants. In particular, top-heavy management and restrictive work practices led to lower productivity and higher unit costs at the Coburg plant than elsewhere.[86]

Kodak's demand for government assistance put the cabinet in a considerable quandary. On one hand, the threatened closure was part of the parent company's international strategy to increase its overall competitiveness, something which was completely in tune with the Hawke government's industry policy. Thus, a bailout – of an efficient company no less – would make an utter sham of the government's policy to 'level the playing field'. On the other hand, Kodak was Australia's second largest exporter of value-added manufactures, with exports to Asia and the Middle East worth almost $170 million a year. This was exactly the kind of company activity that the government's industry policy was designed to promote. A decision either way would be politically painful.

In this case, pragmatism and interventionism triumphed over economic rationalism. Button initially suggested that the government pay Kodak a $60 million bounty over five years, but adverse press reaction, accusing Kodak of industrial blackmail and castigating the government for reneging on its commitment to reduce protection, forced him to cut the amount.[87] On 31 October, he announced that Kodak would receive bounty payments totalling $36 million over three years. The payment was conditional on Kodak maintaining its exports commitments for five years, otherwise the bounty would have to be repaid in full.[88]

Subsequent to the Kodak decision, a bounty was introduced on citric acid production to support the continued development and commercialisation of fermentation technology in Australia.[89] Critics of this sort of intervention point out that it allows incredible scope for arbitrary decisions. For instance, Winton Higgins wonders why the government did not offer similar assistance to Labtam, 'an Australian fast-growth computer hardware and spectrometer exporter with $28 million in export sales in 1988/89', which was forced out of business in July 1990 after the USSR defaulted on its debts to the company.[90] Furthermore, there is no guarantee that government intervention to assist a specific product or company will succeed, a point underlined by Swedish industrial relations experts Rut and Olle Hammarstrom who declared: 'Government intervention seems to delay – but not stop – the impact of market forces'.[91] The argument over selective intervention of the Kodak variety and others is highly topical in Australia and is considered in the concluding chapter.

THE LAST NAIL IN THE COFFIN

With most of the Hawke government's corrective policies in place by the late 1980s, the manufacturing sector had begun to show definite signs of improvement. Business investment grew at unprecedented rates: by 16.4 and 14.5 per cent in 1987/88 and 1988/89 respectively. Manufacturing exports also surged ahead in 1989/90 especially in higher value-added manufactures.[92] Although these were considerable achievements overall, much of the improvement was limited to high performance sectors, such as the steel industry, while many other manufacturing sectors continued to perform poorly. Furthermore, improvements in the manufacturing sector, and the economy overall, had to be measured against growth in other countries, not against Australia's past record. International comparisons suggested that Australia still had far to go: on the World Economic Forum's measure of competitiveness in 1990, Australia ranked only thirteenth out of twenty-three nations, lagging well behind comparable nations such as Canada (fifth) and New Zealand (ninth). By the Forum's estimations, Australia rated very well in its use of natural and human resources but was very poor in its industrial efficiency and international orientation.[93]

Protectionism had been the industry policy for decades; no-one expected the restructuring of the manufacturing sector to occur overnight. However, there were indications that industry had not adjusted as quickly as the government had hoped. For instance, a survey by the Australian Bureau of Statistics in 1988 indicated that only one-third of Australia's manufacturing plants used advanced technologies commonly employed in other countries. Of even greater concern was that few manufacturers planned to acquire new technologies in the future.[94] The apparent reluctance of Australian manufacturing industry to capitalise on the opportunities created by the government's corrective assistance policies dismayed Industry Minister Senator John Button. In July 1989, he lashed out at the manufacturing sector, claiming that the government had done 'all the right things' to boost industry but had 'grossly overestimated' the response from a 'narrowly-based and somnambulant industry sector'.[95]

Despite the slow and often disappointing pace of restructuring in the manufacturing sector, there was, by the end of the 1980s, a broad consensus on the need to phase out the remnants of the protective tariff. Within this consensus, the most extreme view was embodied in a report commissioned by the prime minister to assess the implications for Australia of economic change in Northeast Asia in which Professor Ross Garnaut recommended the complete phasing out of tariffs by the year 2000.[96] Garnaut based his recommendations on the belief that the complete removal of protection would 'cause Australian producers to see themselves as operating in a world market, like those in the small, high-wage economies of Europe'.[97] In July 1990, the Australian Manufacturing Council released its own report which explicitly rejected Garnaut's recommendations, proposing instead that tariffs for all industries except motor vehicles fall to a maximum of 10 per cent by the year 2000 while car manufacturing would be protected by a 25 per cent tariff.[98] Although public debate focused on the differences between the Garnaut and AMC recommendations, the contrast was overdrawn and tended to disguise the emerging consensus that protection had outlived its usefulness. The AMC Report declared:

> High protection may well have been an appropriate strategy for Australia when it was adopted, but it is no longer appropriate as the main pillar of Australian industry policy. It tends to make industry focus inwards, it concentrates resources in the wrong areas and it creates a burden for the rest of the economy.[99]

Table 4.1 *Assistance to manufacturing, 1987–88, 1989–90 and end of March 1991 program, at current prices ($ million)*

Industry	1987–88	1989–90	March 1991 program
Assistance to outputs			
Tariffs	11,284	10,521	3,842
Quantitative import restrictions	764	551	—
Bounties	198	139	6
Export incentives	159	190	162
Assistance to materials			
Tariffs	4,467	4,429	1,769
Quantitative import restrictions	292	131	—
Export incentives	111	105	104

Source: Industry Commission, *Annual Report 1990–91*, p. 237.

Figure 4.1 *Average effective rates of assistance for the manufacturing sector, 1968–69 to 2000–01*

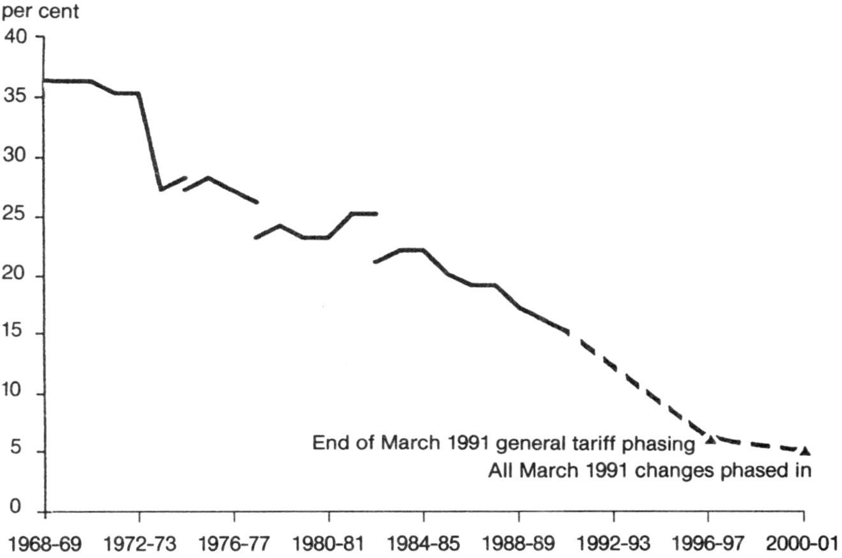

Note: The discontinuities in the series reflect the periodic rebasing of the estimates to account for changes in the structure of the manufacturing sector.

Source: Industry Commission, *Annual Report 1990–91*, p. 2.

On 12 March 1991, the Hawke government announced a program of phased reductions which would cut the general tariff rate to 5 per cent by 1996[100]. Figure 4.1 and Table 4.1 show the overall effect of the March 1991 changes in reducing protective assistance through to the year 2000. These reductions were designed to follow on from the four-year program introduced in 1988 which phased tariff rates down to 10 or 15 per cent by 1992. The scheduled reductions were dramatic proof of the government's commitment to deliver Australia from the legacy of protectionism. But it was not a complete victory

Table 4.2 *Average effective rates of assistance to manufacturing industries (per cent)*

Industry	1987–88	1989–90	March 1991 program
Food and beverages	7	3	2
Textiles	65	72	22
Clothing and footwear	174	173	50
Wood	18	15	4
Paper	9	5	1
Chemicals	12	11	4
Non-metallic minerals	4	3	1
Basic minerals	8	8	4
Fabricated metals	22	18	5
Transport equipment	46	35	12
Other machinery and equipment	22	17	4
Miscellaneous	26	22	6
Total manufacturing	19	16	5

Source: Industry Commission, *Annual Report 1990–91*, pp. 252–9.

for the advocates of trade liberalisation because the government continued to exempt the car and textile, clothing and footwear industries from the general tariff rates. The special plans are currently keeping tariff protection higher for these sectors and even by the year 2000, they will still have special protective rates, as indicated in Table 4.2.

The tariff reductions were announced as part of the government's Industry Statement which blended the economic liberalism of the Garnaut Report with the practical realities sketched out by the AMC Report. On one hand, with the exception of the car and TCF industries, the government effectively adopted Garnaut's recommendation to phase out tariffs – after all, a 5 per cent general tariff will not protect Australian industry from foreign competition. On the other hand, the government recognised the claims made by the AMC and the ACTU that tariff reductions should be linked to other factors affecting industry's competitiveness; for example, taxation, transport and labour market reforms, and the implementation of positive assistance measures to facilitate industry adjustment. Accordingly the government moved to lower input costs for business by expanding sales tax exemptions and simplifying depreciation measures while strengthening the various positive assistance programs. This involved extending indefinitely the 125 per cent tax deduction for R&D expenditure; increased spending on education, work experience programs, apprenticeship training places, and management skills training; increased funding for labour adjustment assistance programs for workers retrenched from the car and TCF industries; and increased funding for export services and the 'Australian made' campaign.

It is a measure of how discredited protective statism had become that the Hawke government was able to announce a program of tariff cuts in the midst of the worst recession since the 1930s. There were some critics: South Australian premier and federal president of the ALP, John Bannon, revealed his fears for the future of the car industry in South Australia when he criticised the federal government for ignoring the regional impact of reduced protection;[101] and the TCF industry's peak association, the Textiles, Clothing and Footwear Council of Australia, bitterly opposed the cuts which pre-empted the 1992 mid-term review of the TCF plan.[102] But opponents of the tariff cuts formed a distinct minority; the bulk of the criticism accused the government of avoiding the hard issues of structural reform in areas such as the waterfront, transport, telecommunications, the public sector and the labour market. The underlying implication was that the Labor government was hamstrung by its association with the union movement. In particular, the federal opposition leader, Dr John Hewson, suggested that micro-economic reforms in these areas 'have been effectively vetoed by the union leadership'.[103]

The prime minister had anticipated these accusations. In the Industry Statement he commented on the paradox that:

> Those who for more than a generation in office entrenched the inadequacies of the past and themselves effected no change whatsoever, now with an hypocrisy that is truly breathtaking, clamour for even faster change.
>
> They bear an onus . . . of showing how in a practical way this could be achieved without poisoning the better industrial relations and investment environment we have created - without, in short, bringing the whole process to a grinding halt.[104]

Despite this defence, critics of the Industry Statement had a valid point. With the walls of protection coming down, industry and unions had the right to expect the government to move quickly to remove remaining impediments to competitiveness, especially in the area of industry infrastructure which also suffered the legacy of protection. Although the Labor government initiated major programs of micro-economic reform and 'New Federalism' to improve the efficiency of public services and the effectiveness of intergovernmental arrangements and processes, progress has been slow on the former and, with Keating's accession to the prime ministership in late 1991, has stalled on the latter. These issues are taken up in the final chapter.

NOTES

1. John Dawkins MP, Shadow Minister for Industry and Commerce, 'New Directions for Australian Industry: ALP Policy for Manufacturing Industry', no date [late 1982].
2. Australian Labor Party, *Australian Labor Party Platform, Constitution and Rules as Approved by the 35th National Conference*, Canberra, 1982, p. 118.
3. John Langmore, 'The Labor government in a de-regulatory era', in *Business and Government Under Labor*, eds Brian Galligan & Gwynneth Singleton, Longman Cheshire, Melbourne, 1991, pp. 75-91.
4. Peter A. McLaughlin, 'How business relates to the Hawke government: the captains of industry', in *Business and Government Under Labor*, eds Galligan & Singleton, pp. 146-67.
5. National Economic Summit Conference, 11-14 April 1983, *Record of Proceedings*, Vol. 2, Australian Government Publishing Service, Canberra, p. 3. The choice of venue was significant and marked the momentous nature of the occasion; this was the first time ever that the Parliament had been used for a non-parliamentary gathering.
6. Gwynneth Singleton, *The Accord and the Australian Labour Movement*, Melbourne University Press, Melbourne, 1990, p. 154.
7. Michael Keating & Geoff Dixon, *Making Economic Policy in Australia, 1983-1988*, Longman Cheshire, Melbourne, 1989, pp. 11-13; Cliff Walsh, 'The national economy and management strategies', in *Business and Government Under Labor*, eds Galligan & Singleton, pp. 35-46.
8. Dawkins, 'New Directions for Australian Industry: ALP Policy for Manufacturing Industry'.
9. See Jon Perkins, *The Deregulation of the Australian Financial System: the Experience of the 1980s*, Melbourne University Press, Melbourne, 1989.
10. Rick Kuhn, 'The Accord and business: the distinctiveness of the Hawke government's approach to capital accumulation', in *Business and Government Under Labor*, eds Galligan & Singleton, pp. 47-74.
11. Cliff Walsh, 'The national economy and management strategies', in *Business and Government Under Labor*, eds Galligan & Singleton, pp. 35-46.
12. Randal Stewart, 'Industrial policy', paper delivered at the Australasian Political Studies Association Conference, Hobart, 23-26 September 1990.

13. Stephen Bell, Manufacturing and the State: the politics of industry policy in postwar Australia, PhD thesis, University of New England, 1991, p. 190.
14. ibid., p. 284.
15. Industry Commission, *Draft Report on the Automotive Industry,* September 1990, p. xv.
16. Speech by Senator John Button, Minister for Industry and Commerce, 14 April 1983, National Economic Summit Conference, 11-14 April 1983, *Record of Proceedings,* Vol. 2, Australian Government Publishing Service, Canberra, 1983.
17. Interview with Button, 29 July 1991.
18. Button interview, and Button's report to Hawke, 11 February 1984.
19. The following is based on Button's report in a long letter to Hawke, 11 February 1984.
20. Australian Manufacturing Council (AMC), *Annual Report.* During this period, the AMC was primarily a forum for business. In 1980, 19 of its 36 members were business leaders while only five were unionists.
21. AMC, *Future Directions for Australian Manufacturing Industry,* Canberra, 1986, p. 54.
22. AMC, *Annual Report, 1985-86,* Canberra, 1986, pp. 2-11.
23. *Australian Financial Review,* 2 December 1985.
24. Peter Ewer, Winton Higgins & Annette Stevens, *Unions and the Future of Australian Manufacturing,* Allen & Unwin, Sydney, 1987, pp. 123-6.
25. Richard Curtain, 'Emergence of Workplace Bargaining within a Centralised Wages System: The New Industrial Relations in Australia', National Key Centre in Industrial Relations, Working Paper No. 2, Monash University, Clayton, Victoria, August 1990, p. 2.
26. Australian Labor Party Platform, *Constitution and Rules as approved by the 35th National Conference,* Canberra 1982, p. 117. A cross-factional deal between unions in the manufacturing sector resulted in the resolution concerning the role of the industry councils.
27. For a comparative study of government plans to restructure mature industries, see Michael Trebilcock, *The Political Economy of Economic Adjustment: The Case of Declining Sectors,* University of Toronto Press, Toronto, 1986.
28. Economic Planning and Advisory Council (EPAC), *Technology and Innovation,* Council Paper 19, Canberra, 1986, pp. 5-9.
29. *Improving Australia's Competitiveness Through Industrial Research and Development,* A report to the Prime Minister by the Australian Science and Technology Council (ASTEC), Canberra, 1987, p. 16.
30. *Public Investment in Research and Development in Australia,* A report to the Prime Minister by ASTEC (Canberra, 1985), p. 11.
31. The tax concession was reportedly inspired by Button who convinced Hawke to support it despite opposition from Finance and Treasury; *The Australian,* 9 January 1985.

32. DITAC Backgrounder to the May Economic Statement, 1988.
33. For details about the various strategies see, DITAC, *Annual Report 1986–87*, Canberra, 1987, pp. 28–32.
34. Peter Roberts, *Australian Financial Review*, 11 April 1990.
35. Ministers for Industry, Technology & Commerce, and Community Services & Health, Joint Media Statement, 115/87, 13 September 1987.
36. In 1989, the Pharmaceutical Benefits Remuneration Tribunal announced changes to the structure of payments to pharmacists under the PBS. The pharmacists successfully fought a rear-guard action against some of the changes although it is inevitable that many small chemists will eventually be forced out of business. In the August 1990 Budget, the Commonwealth government restructured the PBS in an effort to save $2 billion over two years. In part, these savings were to be achieved by reducing the subsidy available to drug consumers. See James Bruce, *The Bulletin*, 14 August 1990; and *Australian Financial Review*, 25 July, 22 August & 12 September 1990.
37. Industry Commission *Annual Report 1989–90*, Australian Government Publishing Service, Canberra, 1990, p. 102.
38. Peter Roberts, *Australian Financial Review*, 1 May 1990. DITAC, *Annual Report 1989–90*, pp. 28-9. Companies participating in the industry plan include ICI Australia Ltd, Glaxo Australia Pty Ltd, Sigma Company Ltd, F. H. Faulding and Company Ltd, Beecham (Australia) Pty Ltd, Cyanamid Australia Ltd, and Merck, Sharp & Dohme (Australia) Ltd.
39. OECD statistics in 1985 showed that Australia's trade performance in information, computer and communications products was ahead only of Turkey and Iceland. Figures given in Senator John N. Button, 'Ministerial Statement on the Partnerships for Development Program', 27 September 1988, p. 4.
40. AMC, *The Global Challenge: Australian Manufacturing in the 1990s: Final Report of the Pappas Carter Evans & Koop-Telesis Study*, July 1990, p. 195.
41. Randal G. Stewart, 'Industrial policy', in *Hawke and Australian Public Policy – Consensus and Restructuring*, eds C. Jennett & R. G. Stewart, Macmillan, Melbourne, 1990, pp. 121–2.
42. In Australia, offsets obligations equal to 30 per cent of the imported content are incurred in Commonwealth government contracts valued above $2.5 million ($1 million for most State contracts) and where the imported content exceeds 30 per cent. This limits offsets to a few companies involved primarily in the aerospace, information and defence industries.
43. DITAC, Australian Civil Offsets Program, *Annual Report 1988–89*, Australian Government Publishing Service, Canberra, 1989, p. 3. Offsets policies are common throughout the world; according to a 1989 report by the US Foreign Commercial Service, 102 countries use

some form of offsets or countertrade policy in their aerospace and defence purchases. DITAC notes, however, that the Australian offsets program is one of the most transparent in the world.

44. QANTAS, Ansett and Australian Airlines have all claimed that offsets increase the purchase price of aircraft and, in the case of QANTAS, reduce their competitiveness compared with other international airlines. Evidence cited in the IAC, *Annual Report 1988–89*, Australian Government Publishing Service, Canberra, 1989, p. 66.
45. The new program was developed in response to the recommendations of the Inglis Committee in 1984. The most important features of the new policy announced by Button and Defence Minister Kim Beazley were the emphasis on technology transfer (by multiplying the value of offsets for R&D and training) and the tightening of administrative and review procedures. See the *Report of the (Inglis) Committee of Review on Offsets*, Australian Government Publishing Service, Canberra, 1984.
46. The government has been very slow to address systematically the problems raised by the Public Accounts Committee in 1987. Thus, in November 1989, two and half years after its initial review, the Public Accounts Committee revealed that many of its recommendations had still not been acted on. Parliament of the Commonwealth of Australia, Joint Committee of Public Accounts, Report 270, 'Implementation of the Offsets Program', March 1987 and Report 305, 'Review of the Finance Minute on Report 270 - 'Implementation of the Offsets Program', November, 1989.
47. DITAC, *Annual Report, 1989–90*, p. 27.
48. Winton Higgins, 'Missing the boat: Labor and industry in the eighties', in *Business and Government Under Labor*, eds Galligan & Singleton, pp. 102–117.
49. Bureau of Industry Economics (BIE), *Trade Performance of Australian Manufacturing*, Information Bulletin 15, Australian Government Publishing Service, Canberra, 1989, p. 1; Keating & Dixon, *Making Economic Policy in Australia*, pp. 14–17.
50. The Hon. R. J. L. Hawke, 'Supporting statement to the address to the nation on the economic situation', 11 June 1986, *Commonwealth Record*, Vol. 11, No. 22.
51. Report of the National Export Marketing Strategy Panel (the Ferris Report), *Lifting Australia's Performance as an Exporter of Manufacturing and Services*, January 1985, p. 6.
52. Report of the Committee for Review of Export Market Development Assistance (the Hughes Report), *Australian Exports: Performances, Obstacles and Issues of Assistance*, Australian Government Publishing Service, Canberra, 1989, p. xiv.
53. The Hon. John Dawkins, 23 April 1985, *Commonwealth Record*, Vol. 10, No. 16.

54. Statistics based on evidence provided in the Hughes Report, p. xxiv. For a provocative study of the Canadian state's role in promoting an 'import substitution industrialization psyche' see Glen Williams, *Not for Export: Towards a Political Economy of Canada's Arrested Industrialization*, McClelland & Stewart, Toronto, 1983.
55. IAC submission to the Committee for Review of Financial Support for Export Market Development, quoted in IAC, *Annual Report 1988–89*, p. 78.
56. AMC, *The Global Challenge: Australian Manufacturing in the 1990s: Final Report of the Pappas Carter Evans & Koop-Telesis Study*, July 1990, pp. 132–3.
57. McKinsey & Company, 'Organising to Deliver Export Impact,' 20 December 1990, p. 5.
58. AUSTRADE, *Annual Report 1987–88*, p. 45.
59. McKinsey report, p. 2.
60. Guy McKenna, 'More time needed for Austrade's ills', *Australian Financial Review*, 21 January 1992, p. 10.
61. Australian Trade and Investment Development, 15 November 1991.
62. 'Towards a National Trade Strategy', Joint Communique by Commonwealth, state and territory ministers with responsibilities for international trade and business development, 28 November 1991.
63. 'Higher Education – a policy statement', circulated by J. S. Dawkins, Minister for Employment, Education & Training, July 1988 (Canberra, 1988), p. 8.
64. ibid., p. 17.
65. ACTU, *Australia Reconstructed: ACTU/TDC Mission to Western Europe*, Australian Government Publishing Service, Canberra, 1987, p. 123–6.
66. Department of Defence, 'The Defence of Australia 1987' (The White Paper), presented to Parliament by the Minister for Defence, Kim Beazley, M.P., March 1987, Canberra, 1987, pp. 82–4.
67. Statement by the Minister of Defence, Gordon Scholes and the Minister for Defence Support, Brian Howe, 3 June 1984 in *Commonwealth Record*, Vol. 9, No. 22.
68. Paul Dibb, *Review of Australia's Defence Capabilities*, Canberra, 1986, p. 108.
69. IAC, *Annual Report, 1987–88*, Australian Government Publishing Service, Canberra, 1988, p. 78.
70. Fraser, 26 October 1977 in *Commonwealth Record*, Vol. 2, No. 42, pp. 1504–5.
71. Button and Minister for Administrative Services, John Brown, in *Commonwealth Record*, December 1983, Vol. 8, No. 49, p. 2177.
72. These studies are the Lusher Report, House of Representatives Standing Committee on Expenditure, *Commonwealth Government Purchasing*, Australian Government Publishing Service, Canberra,

1981; Report of the (Inglis) Committee of Review on Government High Technology Purchasing Arrangements, Australian Government Publishing Service, Canberra 1987; and the Bureau of Industry Economics, *The Commonwealth Purchasing Preference Margin as an Industry Development Mechanism*, Australian Government Publishing Service, Canberra, 1988, p. xiii.

73. John Wanna, 'Business' in B. Galligan, O. Hughes & C. Walsh, eds, *Intergovernmental Relations and Public Policy*, Allen & Unwin, Sydney, 1991, p. 325. This account draws on Wanna's work.
74. Bureau of Industry Economics, *Heavy Engineering in Australia: Problems and Prospects*, Australian Government Publishing Service, Canberra, 1985.
75. See discussion by Bureau of Industry Economics, The Commonwealth Purchasing Preference Margin as an Industry Development Mechanism.
76. *Australian Financial Review*, 30 June 1987.
77. *Australian Financial Review*, 6 April 1988.
78. *Age*, 15 April 1988; *Australian*, 20 April 1988 and *Australian Financial Review*, 22 April 1988.
79. Minister for Industry, Technology and Commerce, 'Government moves to cut industry costs and boost exports', *News Release* 78/88, 25 May 1988.
80. *Australian Financial Review*, 10 April 1986.
81. See for instance, Ian Davis in the *Canberra Times*, 5 August 1987.
82. *Age*, 9 October 1987.
83. Button Interview, 29 July 1991, *Sydney Morning Herald*, 17 July 1987; *National Times on Sunday*, 6 September 1987.
84. Mini-Budget, May 1987, *Australian Financial Review*, 27 May 1987.
85. *Age*, 16 September 1989.
86. Bureau of Industry Economics, *International productivity differences in manufacturing – photographic paper*, Discussion Paper 6, Australian Government Publishing Service, Canberra, 1990.
87. For samples of hostile press reaction see editorials in the *Australian Financial Review*, 20 September 1989; the *Mercury* (Hobart), 20 September 1989, the *Herald* (Melbourne), 21 September 1989, and the *Australian*, 26 September 1989. Several journalists mentioned that the Kodak factory was in Prime Minister Hawke's electorate of Wills implying that electoral considerations were also a factor in the decision. The government was to lose this blue-ribbon Labor seat in an April 1992 by-election after Hawke retired from politics.
88. Senator John Button, Minister for Industry, Technology & Commerce, News Release, 31 October 1989.
89. Department of the Prime Minister & Cabinet, *Building a Competitive Australia*, Statement by the Minister for Industry, Technology & Commerce, Senator the Honourable John N. Button, Canberra, 1991, Section 3, p. 16.

90. Winton Higgins, 'Missing the boat: Labor and industry in the 1980s', in *Government and Business Under Labor*, eds Galligan & Singleton, pp. 75–91.
91. Rut & Olle Hammarstrom, 'Blend of co-operation and competition key to Sweden's industry policy example,' *Australian Financial Review*, 7 March 1991.
92. AUSTRADE, *Annual Report, 1989–90*, pp. 21–5.
93. World Economic Forum measures are quoted in DITAC's *Annual Report, 1989–90*, pp. 12–14. On a scale with 22 other nations, Australia's rankings were as follows: natural endowment utilisation 3; human resources 7; future orientation 12; socio-political stability 12; impact of the state 12; market orientation 13; dynamism of the economy 13; financial dynamism 14; industrial efficiency 15; and international orientation 19.
94. Australian Bureau of Statistics, *Manufacturing Technology Statistics, Australia 30 June 1988, Summary*, Commonwealth Government Printer, Canberra, 1989.
95. *Sydney Morning Herald*, 15 July 1989.
96. Ross Garnaut, *Australia and the Northeast Asian Ascendancy*, Australian Government Publishing Service, Canberra, 1989.
97. Professor Garnaut quoted in an extract from his Shann Memorial Lecture published in the *Australian Financial Review*, 16 August 1990.
98. AMC, *The Global Challenge: Australian Manufacturing in the 1990s, Final Report of the Pappas Carter Evans & Koop-Telesis Study*, July 1990, Chapter 3.
99. ibid., p. 47.
100. The Department of Prime Minister & Cabinet, *Building a Competitive Australia*, Statements by Prime Minister Bob Hawke, Treasurer Paul Keating and Industry Minister John Button, 12 March 1991, Australian Government Publishing Service, Canberra, 1991.
101. *Australian Financial Review*, 13 March 1991.
102. The Textiles, Clothing and Footwear Council of Australia Limited, Press Release, 12 March 1991.
103. Hewson quoted in the *Australian Financial Review*, 13 March 1991.
104. *Building a Competitive Australia*, Statement by the Prime Minister, Bob Hawke, Section 1, p. 12.

CHAPTER 5
The Steel Industry

> For industrialized or industrializing countries of the world, steel is more than an industry; it is a state of mind . . . Steel is economic strength, the symbol of burgeoning industrialization; it is the material of which bridges, cities and manufacturing industries are built. Steel abounds in dramatic industrial imagery: billowing smokestacks, sinewy workers, plants and equipment of Brobdingnagian proportions.[1]

In most industrialised countries the steel industry sector is composed of several large firms with most of these being private enterprises. In the United Kingdom, France, Italy, Sweden, South Africa and Brazil, however, national governments used to have majority ownership of steel capacity, although that has been changing in a number of countries. The United Kingdom and South Africa have recently privatised their steel industries, while Brazil is in the early stages of privatisation which is scheduled to be completed by 1996. Australia has always been somewhat unusual among industrialised countries because its steel industry has been dominated by a single private firm, the Broken Hill Proprietary Company Ltd. This virtual monopoly has allowed BHP to exercise considerable leverage over government policy towards the steel industry. In addition, a sectoral policy for steel, unlike such policies for other Australian manufacturing sectors such as the motor vehicle and textile, clothing and footwear industries, is essentially firm-specific. Thus, in providing assistance to the steel industry, the state runs the risk of appearing to be the captive of a single company. It was in this context that the Hawke government in 1983 sought to resolve the steel industry's crisis with a solution that fell short of a corporate bailout.

A PROFILE OF BHP

BHP was not the first company to make steel in Australia; that distinction belongs to the Eskbanks Ironworks which was formed in Lithgow, New South Wales in 1900. However, persistent difficulties with land transport and raw material supplies forced Eskbanks to move its operations to Port Kembla, New South Wales where iron ore and coal could be brought in by ship. The Port Kembla steelworks were recommissioned in 1928 and operated under the company name, Australian Iron and Steel.[2]

In the meantime BHP, a mining company formed in 1885 to extract and process lead, silver and zinc, also ventured into steelmaking. In 1915 the town of Newcastle, New South Wales, ideally placed with its harbour and its proximity to coal deposits and the Sydney market, became the site of BHP's first steelworks.[3] Under the ambitious leadership of Essington Lewis who was keen to see BHP control all the auxiliary and finishing industries related to steel, BHP expanded its operations through a series of takeovers and mergers. Between 1929 and 1935 the company purchased majority interests in Lysaght Brothers in Sydney, the nail and barbed-wire section of the Titan Manufacturing Company, the Commonwealth Steel Company and the Australian Wire Rope Works Pty Ltd at Newcastle. This expansion was capped in 1935 by the purchase of its only competitor in steelmaking, the Australian Iron and Steel Company (AIS), which had been suffering from sliding profits and technical difficulties since the beginning of the Depression.[4] The acquisition of AIS and its Port Kembla steelworks meant that from then on BHP enjoyed a virtual monopoly in Australian steel production.[5]

Over the next forty years BHP continued to expand its operations. Upstream development included the establishment of a shipbuilding industry at Whyalla, South Australia in 1940 in order to provide BHP with its own fleet to carry coal, iron ore and finished steel. The company also acquired titles to iron ore deposits in South Australia and Western Australia through agreements with the state governments which required it to establish steel plants in those states. Those bargains resulted in BHP opening an ironworks at Whyalla in 1941, a steel rolling mill at Kwinana, Western Australia in 1952, an integrated steelworks at Whyalla in 1958, and a blast furnace at Kwinana in 1968.[6]

BHP also acquired interests in downstream manufacturers of steel products such as pipes, wires, and cold rolled sheets. By 1980 BHP owned John Lysaght (Australia) Ltd (makers of cold rolled steel products such as office furniture and sheet steel), Australian Wire

Industries Pty Ltd (wire and wire rope), Titan Manufacturing Company Pty Ltd (mining equipment and machine tools), Rheem Australia Ltd (containers and water heaters), Commonwealth Steel Company Ltd (stainless steel and special alloys) and dozens of other companies which finished BHP's steel products. In addition, BHP held large shareholdings in many other companies including a 49.8 per cent share in Tubemakers of Australia Ltd.[7]

Almost all of BHP's steel production occurs at its three integrated steelworks where iron and steel making is combined with subsequent rolling and finishing. Port Kembla, the largest, specialises in hot and cold flat-rolled products. Newcastle produces shapes, 'merchant' bar, light structurals and rods, and Whyalla, the smallest, produces mainly heavy structurals and rails. In 1980 BHP's other steel plants included a rod rolling mill at Geelong, a fencepost plant at Brisbane, a blast furnace and steel rolling mill at Kwinana, and a hot and cold rolled strip processing plant at Westernport, Victoria. BHP's Steel Division also encompassed the mines which supply raw materials for steel making: dolomite and limestone quarries, coal mines adjacent to the steelworks at Newcastle and Port Kembla, and iron ore mines in Western Australia and South Australia.

BHP's access to cheap coal and iron ore and its ability to run its plants near capacity has historically made it a low-cost producer among the world's steelmakers. Thus, the steel industry has been one of Australia's most efficient and least-protected manufacturing sectors. Unlike many other Australian industries, BHP was also a successful exporter; by the late 1970s, at least one-third of the company's output was destined for overseas markets. While manufacturers of passenger motor vehicles, whitegoods, and textiles, clothing and footwear were forced to appeal for more protection against imports during the 1970s, BHP remained viable under relatively low rates of tariff protection.

THE CRISIS IN WORLD STEEL

Steel markets are particularly sensitive to business cycles because demand for steel is based on demand for steel products such as capital goods and consumer durables - purchases which are postponed during recessions. Because steel production involves a very high fixed capital cost, a business downturn encourages producers to use the export market to maintain output. This inevitably results in a glut on the steel market which then forces prices even lower. Such was the state of the industry following the 1974 energy crisis. The glut in the world market was worsened by the growing use of steel-replacing products such as concrete and aluminium, and the coming on-stream of increased capacity which had been planned and under construction before the downturn. As a result, between 1979 and 1983 world productive capacity in steel grew significantly while consumption fell steadily.[8] Hardest hit of all were the 'mature' steel industries in North America and Western Europe. Their relative efficiency had been declining prior to the oil shock and, by the late 1970s, they were increasingly displaced in markets at home and abroad by high quality, low cost steel from Japan and newly industrialised countries such as Taiwan, Korea and Brazil.

During the crisis, governments around the world moved to rescue their ailing steel companies. The nature of state intervention varied among nations depending on a host of factors including state tradition, the prevailing political culture and economic conditions, the party in office, and the structure of interest groups. Broadly speaking, the types of state intervention seen in the steel industry can be characterised as either protective or corrective. Protective assistance involves the *ad hoc* adoption of laws and policies that protect incomes and jobs from market changes. The instruments of such protective assistance include corporate bailouts, state acquisition, and market protection by means of tariffs and quotas, and by non-tariff barriers such as voluntary export restraint agreements. In effect, protective assistance props up inefficient companies and retards economic growth at the expense of taxpayers, consumers, and efficient producers overseas.

In Great Britain the political imperative to protect jobs typically resulted in governments of both stripes resorting to protective assistance policies to aid the ailing steel industry. Labour governments twice resorted to nationalisation, and only in recent years has a more determined Conservative government been able to put the British steel industry on a more efficient and profitable footing. Payment of operating subsidies, the traditional fall-back of concerned British governments, did not serve to improve industry productivity, although the rationale for them was quite clear. In 1982, it was estimated that the removal of the subsidies to British Steel would cost 75,000 jobs, mostly in economically depressed cities and towns.[9] The Thatcher government finally bit the bullet and, through a combination of operating subsidies to improve productivity and wholesale privatisation, the British steel industry has become one of the world's most profitable producers. This has been achieved at some considerable cost to employment with job losses of some 200,000 in the last couple of decades.[10]

In the United States the strength of narrow interest groups has resulted in the same sort of protective policies designed to restore the steel industry's short-run profitability at the expense of long-term competitiveness. Costs were reduced by exempting steel companies from compliance with environmental controls. Domestic market shares were protected through a trigger price mechanism which established minimum prices for imported steel, with imports below the set price automatically triggering an anti-dumping investigation. The trigger price was replaced after 1982 by so-called voluntary export restraint agreements with other steel exporting nations such as Japan and Australia.[11]

In contrast to the protective assistance policies which impeded structural adjustment in the British and American steel industries, governments in West Germany and Japan have deliberately shaped their institutions and economic policies to encourage labour and capital to adjust to changing conditions and world markets. Industry restructuring has been brought about through policies of corrective assistance which offer investment incentives and subsidies to the companies and compensation to retrenched employees through short-term income support and retraining programs. The West German government resisted intervention until 1982 when the heart of the European steel industry in the Saar and Ruhr Valleys was threatened. A plan for restructuring was developed through tripartite negotiations with the companies and unions and resulted in government subsidies to promote investment. These loans were administered on a commercial basis by national banks. The government also funded a 'social plan' devised by the steelworkers' union, IG-Metall, to minimise social dislocation through early retirement plans and wage level maintenance for workers transferred to lower-paid jobs.[12]

Like the small, open West European economies, Japan has used adjustment policies designed to help labour and capital adapt to world market conditions. The Ministry of International Trade and Industry (MITI) has developed stabilisation plans for declining industries such as steel, formulated through advisory councils consisting of the unions, the companies and their creditors. The industry plans are generally designed to scrap excess capacity and channel investment into new product lines. In addition, workers laid off from structurally depressed industries are eligible for retraining allowances in addition to unemployment insurance benefits. The government also subsidises retraining for workers who are shifted to another job within a firm.[13]

AUSTRALIAN STEEL IN TROUBLE

During the global steel crisis of the 1970s, the Australian steel industry continued to prosper, largely due to the capital equipment requirements of the massive mineral resource extraction projects being undertaken in Australia. As a result, while other OECD countries reported a drop in steel consumption between 1979 and 1981, Australian steel consumption actually increased in that period.[14] Such was BHP's optimism during the minerals boom that, in 1978, the company based its forward plans on the premise that it would market 9.9 million tonnes of steel in 1983.

The abrupt end to the boom in mid-1981 had a dramatic effect on Australian steel usage. Large construction projects were deferred or cancelled and domestic consumption fell almost immediately. The problem was compounded by declining world demand for steel and the global recession of 1981–82. In the past, BHP had relied on increased exports to counter shortfalls in domestic consumption, but the international steel surplus had contributed to a steady decline in BHP's steel exports, from 30 to 40 per cent of its total production in the mid-1970s to about 15 per cent in 1981. The sharp drop in domestic demand together with the decline in exports meant that, by 1982, BHP's expected output in the year to May 1983 was only 5.71 million tonnes - well below the 9.9 million tonnes predicted during the heady days of the minerals boom.[15]

The crisis in the Australian steel industry made headlines in July 1982 when BHP's Steel Division reported its first loss since 1923.[16] BHP blamed this loss on a number of factors: severe deterioration in the international and Australian steel markets, with a fall of 20 per cent in domestic consumption; rapid increases in state government taxes and charges; low productivity and rising input costs, especially in terms of wages combined with an excessive number of work-hours lost through strikes at the steelworks.[17]

In addition to the industry's internal difficulties, BHP's directors apportioned a major part of the blame to import penetration, citing a 36 per cent increase in steel imports during 1981 as a major cause of the industry's problems.[18] BHP's decline in international competitiveness was reflected in a net loss of $144 million for the Steel Division for the financial year 1982/83.[19]

The tendency to blame the steel industry's crisis on imports is a phenomenon which has been noted elsewhere, especially in the United States during the late 1970s. As Kent Jones observed:

> Even if the industry's problems lie largely in domestic market shifts, technological change, or mismanagement, imports provide a highly visible, politically expedient scapegoat on which to shunt the blame . . . In times of adversity, economic or otherwise, it is not uncommon to perceive foreign influences as the cause of the problem. Thus, steel imports emerge as the culprit in the decline of the domestic industry.[20]

This was not only true of the steel industry in Australia but also of the car industry and textiles, clothing and footwear companies and other industry sectors whose international competitiveness declined dramatically during the 1970s. Rather than addressing their internal problems, these industries blamed their woes on imports.

There was little doubt that BHP was partly responsible for its predicament in 1982. BHP managing director, Brian Loton, acknowledged the company's culpability in taking for granted continual rising demand.[21] Perhaps more serious was BHP's failure to invest sufficiently in new technology to keep its Steel Division at the leading edge of world production. During the minerals boom, BHP directed its investment into its most profitable divisions - Minerals, Oil and Gas - while their poor cousin, the Steel Division, was relatively neglected. There had been substantial investment in the Steel Division - in fact $1.8 billion between 1974 and 1983 - but that was designed to upgrade existing facilities rather than adopt new technology. Between 1975 and 1980, BHP's capital expenditure per tonne of raw steel lagged behind that of comparable countries, and it was only in 1980-82 that it shot ahead, only to plunge again in 1982-83 (see Figure 5.1). Most notably, BHP's continuous casting ratio was low with production still relying mainly on the traditional method of casting molten steel into ingots which were then cooled, reheated and rolled into various semi-finished shapes for further processing. By contrast, 45 per cent of steel produced in the EEC and 71 per cent of Japanese production used the more efficient

Figure 5.1 *Comparison of investment intensity in crude steel production: Australia, Japan, USA and EEC, 1973–83 (US$ per tonne)*

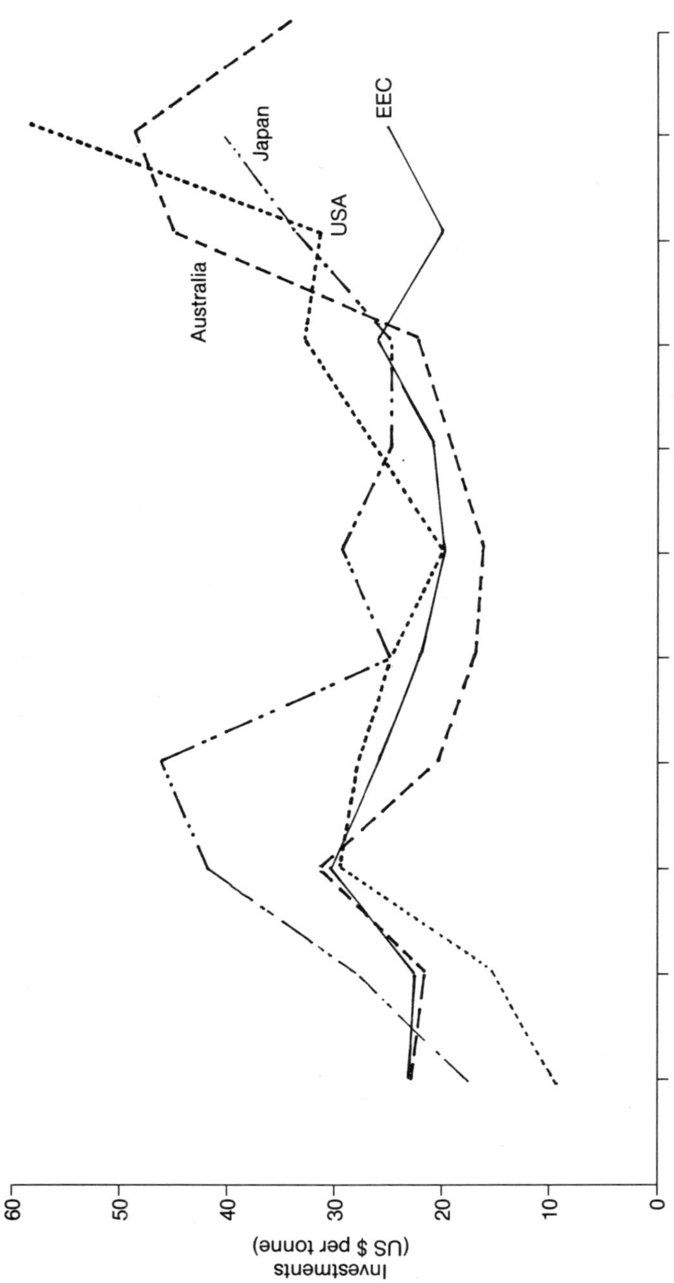

Source: Figures supplied by BHP.

method of continuous casting. This process by-passes the ingot stage by directing the molten steel into a water-cooled mould where the steel is formed into slabs which can then be cut and shaped for further processing. Only 20 per cent of BHP's steel output was produced through continuous casters, with this technology lag making BHP less efficient, less productive and less profitable than its foreign competitors.[22]

THE SEARCH FOR PROTECTION

In BHP's 1982 *Annual Report*, the company directors declared that while the Steel Division continued to lose money, BHP would continue to reduce production, cut jobs, and postpone investment.[23] Underlying this claim was the implication that BHP would not attempt to 'lift its game' until the government acted to curtail imports. The first cuts involved the closure of old and inefficient plant: 400 workers at Kwinana were involuntarily retrenched when the blast furnace there was closed. A few months later, BHP announced further closures that would cost 1,700 jobs in Newcastle - about 18 per cent of the city's workforce - and 1,000 jobs at Port Kembla.[24]

The crisis in Australian steel posed a difficult political dilemma for Prime Minister Malcolm Fraser. Following the completion of a seven-year Industries Assistance Commission study of the steel industry in 1981, the Fraser government decided to reduce tariff rates to 15 per cent (with concessions for some developing countries). These reductions reflected the relative health of the domestic steel industry and were consistent with Fraser's renewed conviction of the necessity for world trade liberalisation. Now BHP was demanding an increase in protection through the imposition of import quotas to ensure an 85 to 90 per cent market share for local steel.[25]

No government could afford to ignore BHP's claims because its troubles had the potential to cause tremendous economic and social dislocation. Plant closures, retrenchments and job shedding were already taking their toll in Kwinana and the cities of Whyalla, Newcastle and Wollongong where hundreds of steelworkers had already lost their jobs. Further plant closures had the potential to devastate South Australia where BHP was the second largest employer in the state. There were also political considerations: job losses of this magnitude could trigger an enormous electoral backlash. Thus, with the strong backing of the other affected interests, particularly unions and local communities, BHP convinced the government to reconsider the issue of assistance to the steel industry. On 21 May 1982, industry minister, Sir Phillip Lynch, referred the steel industry to the Temporary Assistance Authority (TAA) which was empowered to recommend emergency assistance for the industry, and to the Industries Assistance Commission to review the issue of long-term assistance for Australian steel producers.

At both the TAA and IAC inquiries, BHP underlined its claim for a guaranteed market share. This request was not unusual given that manufacturers of motor vehicles and textiles, clothing and footwear had guaranteed market shares through import restrictions. Whether BHP would be granted similar treatment, however, was another issue. Within the cabinet, those who supported BHP included the industry minister, Sir Phillip Lynch (whose electorate was the site of BHP's subsidiary, John Lysaght (Australia) Ltd), the acting industry minister, Wal Fife, and his assisting minister, Michael Hodgman. On the other side, the prime minister and several key cabinet ministers including Treasurer John Howard and the Country Party leader, Doug Anthony, were opposed to BHP's demands.[26]

The opponents of guaranteed market protection for BHP based their arguments on commercial, economic and moral claims. Anthony's position reflected the concerns of his rural constituents who opposed increased assistance to the steel industry at a time when farmers were suffering from drought, inflation, rising interest rates and a higher value Australian dollar.[27] Other steel users lobbied against any increase in protection which would raise the price of steel, thereby further eroding their own competitiveness and leading to higher unemployment. They argued that it was vital to have access to alternative suppliers for products not manufactured locally, or when products did not meet the required quality standards, and when industrial disputes and poor company performance threatened to halt deliveries.[28]

The demands of the rural sector and downstream steel users had to be balanced against the government's desire to prevent further job losses within the steel industry. This resulted in a compromise on the issue of short-term protection: short-term quotas were introduced, but at a lower level than BHP had requested.[29] According to BHP's calculations, the quotas would fix the domestic market shares at 70 per cent for BHP and John Lysaght (Australia) Ltd, well below the level BHP had sought. Moreover, the decision to set quotas at fixed levels meant that as domestic demand continued to contract, BHP's market share would decline even further. Claiming that it showed 'no support for the steel industry', the company angrily rejected the government's decision.[30]

Having failed in its bid to obtain the level of short-term protection it had requested, BHP mounted an aggressive campaign to secure a favourable outcome from the IAC inquiry. Initially, BHP chief executive Brian Loton had been optimistic that the government would meet BHP's demands.[31] That confidence must have been shaken by the public hostility which surfaced against the 'Big Australian' during the course of the IAC hearings. Submissions to the inquiry attacked BHP for its low productivity levels, sub-standard products, poor delivery times, and outmoded plant and technology. BHP's productivity levels, which indicated that an Australian steelworker produced 200 tonnes of steel per year compared with his Korean counterpart who produced 400 tonnes, suggested also that BHP was relatively inefficient. And steel users such as Toyota and Ford Motors complained of sub-standard products and unreliable delivery times. BHP was also rebuked for failing to make use of an accelerated depreciation scheme which had been announced especially for the iron and steel industry in the August 1981 Budget. Even Malcolm Fraser entered the fray and, on 23 August 1982, publicly criticised BHP for failing to rationalise and reorganise its steel operations during the past decade.[32] Comments like these from a prime minister whose government had traditionally been a friend of big business revealed the extent to which BHP had alienated even its closest supporters.

In its submission to the IAC in December 1982, BHP requested a ten-year package of government assistance consisting of tariff quotas to guarantee an 85 per cent share of the domestic market for Australian steelmakers and special tax concessions to allow BHP to write-off capital expenditure in the year when that would occur. In return, BHP said it planned, but *did not promise* to invest $2,800 million into its steelworks during the period of government assistance. But BHP also warned that even with a guaranteed market share and tax write offs, 8,300 workers were destined to lose their jobs over the next few years. On the other hand, if government assistance was not forthcoming, the company claimed that it would close its steelworks at Newcastle, Port Kembla and Whyalla within four years. Effectively, BHP would pull out of steel production altogether, leaving the Melbourne mini-mill operated by Smorgons Consolidated Ltd as the only steel producer in the country.[33] Even after discounting rhetorical bluster, there was genuine apprehension among senior trade union officials that BHP was serious about phasing out its massive investment in steel making.[34]

BHP's threats and its refusal to commit itself fully to an investment plan led to considerable public cynicism about its claims. The opposition's industry spokesman, Chris Hurford, described BHP's threats as 'shadow boxing' while the chairman of the IAC inquiry, W. A. McKinnon, suggested that the company's submission was tantamount to asking for a 'blank cheque'.[35] Comments like these, coming after six months of bad press, led BHP to try to counter its poor public image with a public relations campaign in January and February 1983.[36] But it was too late to influence the IAC and in the draft report released in March 1983, the Commission recommended against any new protective arrangements for the iron and steel industry.

The draft report was a split decision which represented three different views in the debate over protectionist policy in Australia. In one of the two dissenting reports, commissioner John Sheaffer supported BHP's request with only a few minor changes. By contrast, David McBride's report, which more closely resembled the usual IAC approach to government assistance, advocated the replacement of quotas with bounties. The majority report, by McKinnon and G. F. Johnson, expressed support for the retention of a more efficient domestic steel industry but opposed any new barrier assistance which would perpetuate inefficiencies and raise costs for user industries and the community in general. Instead, the report recommended the withdrawal of the developing country preference for steel imports from Korea and a five-year plan of value-based quotas. Above-quota imports would attract a 50 per cent tariff which would be reduced to 25 per cent over the duration of the plan. The IAC believed that the plan would encourage the steel industry to restructure and specialise in the products in which it was most efficient.[37]

The draft report was criticised from all quarters. The *Australian Financial Review* complained that in 'having a bob each way,' the IAC had 'virtually guaranteed the worst possible outcome' for the steel industry.[38] BHP's reaction was predictable. David Rice, executive general manager of the Steel Division, described the IAC plan as 'little more than a holding operation for five years . . . which would not provide a satisfactory climate for any significant investment'.[39] Steelworkers were also bitterly disappointed. Their dismay was voiced by the national president of the Federated Ironworkers Association (FIA), Harry Hurrell, who denounced the report as 'a band aid solution to an industry that is bleeding to death'.[40]

THE STEEL PLAN

The Australian Labor Party had been committed to market-driven sectoral adjustment since the release of the Jackson Report in 1975 which had urged the nation to embark on the long-term process of industrial structural adjustment. In particular, the adjustment process envisaged by ALP policy-makers included phased tariff reductions, the abolition of quotas, export facilitation, increased productivity and other improvements to enhance international competitiveness. It was understood that there would be painful short-term disruptions; hence the restructuring process was to be planned and gradual with provision for regional assistance and retraining programs. Tariff reductions and industrial restructuring were already on the agenda for the passenger motor vehicle and textiles, clothing and footwear sectors. Few, however, could have predicted that the relatively healthy steel industry would be the guinea-pig for the ALP's first experiment in corrective government intervention at the sectoral level.

There was little doubt that a Labor government would offer assistance to BHP; throughout 1982 ALP politicians reiterated the Party's commitment to maintain a viable and efficient steel industry in Australia. However, the Party's industry policy implicitly rejected policies of protective assistance. Tariff increases were seen as counter-productive to structural adjustment, a burden to the community at large and a violation of the Party's commitment to ease global trade restrictions. Nationalisation was also rejected; when opposition industry spokesman Chris Hurford raised the spectre of an ALP government buying equity in BHP's troubled Steel Division, Party members quickly and firmly rejected the prospect.[41] Rather, Labor politicians promised some form of positive adjustment assistance to be negotiated through tripartite consultations among government, unions and the companies. In addition, Labor shadow ministers stated that government assistance to the steel industry would be contingent on guarantees that BHP would prevent further retrenchments.[42]

This pledge to protect jobs was seemingly incompatible with corrective adjustment assistance policy; after all, employment reductions were a major feature of Japanese and West German policies for structural adjustment in the steel industry sector. However, BHP had already cut thousands of jobs since 1982, and a party which pegged its electoral fortunes to a great degree on its union base could not hope to win support on a platform which promoted the need for further job losses. This political reality was underlined three weeks before the March 1983 election when the new Labor leader, R. J. L. Hawke, reiterated the Labor party's commitment to maintain the jobs of all workers currently employed in the steel industry.

In a speech to the Federated Ironworkers Association in February, Hawke announced that within one hundred days of coming to power his government would introduce a ten-year development plan which would provide tariff quotas and/or bounties in order to guarantee an unspecified market share for the local steelmakers. Hawke's promise closely approximated BHP's demands in its submission to the IAC inquiry three months earlier. This perhaps was the most obvious evidence that an ALP government was serious in its commitment to maintain the steel industry and was willing partly to meet BHP on its own terms. But Hawke also made it clear that the government expected pledges from BHP in return.[43] Thus, on 22 February, Hawke met with BHP executives Brian Loton and David Rice to discuss future plans for the industry.[44]

When the ALP came to power in March 1983, the steel industry was high on the new government's list of priorities. An early success in achieving a consensus on a plan to restructure the steel industry could consolidate public support for the government's industry policy and pave the way for future restructuring in other troubled sectors. On 18 March, just prior to the public release of the IAC's draft report on the steel industry, the new industry minister, Senator John Button, asked BHP if it could implement a voluntary early retirement scheme in order to avoid further retrenchments. This would buy the new government time to hold tripartite negotiations to devise and implement an assistance plan while at the same time avoiding further politically damaging job losses. However, three days after Button's request and less than 24 hours after the release of the IAC's draft report, BHP sacked 641 workers at its Steel Division collieries in Newcastle and Wollongong. Button responded angrily and in a characteristic understatement observed that BHP's directors were not 'the most politically and socially sensitive board in Australia'.[45] BHP was unmoved and on 11 April 1983, the opening day of the government's National Economic Summit, the company reiterated its claim that it would not commit itself to the steel industry in the long term if the IAC's recommendations were adopted.[46]

While the IAC was roundly criticised for failing to achieve a consensus on its recommendations for the steel industry, at least it gave the government plenty of flexibility for determining a long-term strategy. Given the diversity of views on the steel industry, however, any decision was bound to please some more than others. Moreover, the climate of public and private opinion seemed to militate against a rational debate. Most Australians supported BHP's view that it was vital to maintain a steel industry because of its contribution, both directly and indirectly, to total employment, its technological capacity and its role in the nation's defence capability. The ACTU leadership was vitally concerned about job losses in the industry; it also considered steel to be Australia's most important industry because of its downstream effects on other key manufacturing sectors such as motor vehicles.[47] But the company's demands and threats had not endeared the 'Big Australian' to ordinary Australians and, as retrenchments continued, hostility mounted.[48]

On 31 March 1983 Button convened a meeting of the Steel Industry Advisory Council (SIAC) which had been established in September 1982 under the auspices of the Australian Manufacturing Council. This was a tripartite body that had been set up in 1978 by the Liberals to advise the government on industry policy, but had operated only as a 'talkfest'.[49] The SIAC was chaired by the industry minister and had fifteen members including five industry officials, five union officials, two representatives from downstream industries, a steel importer and two parliamentarians, one from the government and one from the opposition.[50] Naturally, members of the SIAC, who included David Rice from BHP and Harry Hurrell from the Federated Ironworkers Association, held the same views which they had espoused during the IAC inquiry. BHP and the unions desired quota restrictions while steel users and importers claimed that that would result in higher steel prices. Instead, steel users proposed bounty payments to assist the purchase of domestic steel but parliamentarians argued that bounties imposed a direct cost on the national budget.[51]

Although the views of the Council members remained polarised, the SIAC discussions revealed that the participants were all willing to make firm commitments to a steel industry plan. This was a dramatic departure from the year long stand-off between the government and BHP and could be explained by several events since the election of the new government. Undoubtedly, the release of the final IAC report was a significant factor behind the apparently sudden willingness of steel companies, unions and government to negotiate and compromise. In the final report released in May 1983, the IAC confirmed its view that the steel industry's problems were largely of a cyclical nature stemming from the economy-wide recession. It argued that, under these circumstances, short-term assistance was not warranted and that long-term assistance would be an inefficient allocation of resources which would be prejudicial to steel users and the community in general. In short, no further short-term or long-term assistance was recommended after the quota arrangements expired on 31 December 1983.[52] This left the steel industry in an extremely vulnerable position and if the major players could not come to an agreement among themselves, the future of industry assistance would be left entirely for the government to determine.

The climate of fear and uncertainty surrounding the IAC report was at least partly offset by the spirit of consensus and conciliation generated by the new Labor government, and in particular, by Prime Minister Hawke at the National Economic Summit Conference in April 1983. And, despite divergent views within the Steel Industry Advisory Council itself, the IAC's unwelcome verdict herded the council members into agreement on one crucial point: the need for government assistance to restructure the steel industry. In its own report on the steel industry, the SIAC rejected the IAC's view that the industry would recover when the recession lifted. By contrast, the SIAC believed that other factors including excess world steel capacity, declining productivity and government intervention in the industry overseas also contributed to Australian steel producers' difficulties. Far from being the result of normal market fluctuations, the Australian steel industry faced 'severe problems' which required government assistance in order to reach a long-term solution.[53]

The SIAC proposed several different possible assistant packages including market assistance in the form of quotas, tariffs, bounties and anti-dumping procedures and investment assistance through accelerated depreciation, group taxation, concessional loans, interest rebates, cash grants or government equity. Other options involved bilateral agreements such as the granting of import restraints in return for investment commitments from BHP, or tax concessions in return for the company's commitment to productivity improvements. However, one option was markedly different from the others because it proposed a kind of sectoral corporatism involving commitments from the federal government, the steel companies and the unions.

Together, the IAC recommendations, the Steel Industry Advisory Council Report and private consultations with industry and the unions formed the basis for the government's assistance package for the steel industry, announced by Senator Button on 11 August 1983. The steel plan was a well-crafted sectoral plan which tied government intervention in the form of a guaranteed market share and bounties to corresponding corporate commitments and union undertakings for industrial harmony. Government assistance was a compromise which rejected increased market protection in favour of production bounties. Tariff increases and quotas had been ruled out because of their adverse impact on steel users; instead, a safety mechanism was set which would allow for a review of the assistance measures if the local producers' domestic market share in certain product categories fell below 80 per cent or rose above 90 per cent. The government also promised to establish a fast-track anti-dumping mechanism to deal quickly with any dumping complaints. To encourage BHP to invest in the medium term, the government promised bounties of up to $71.6 million a year for five years for steel used in the production of certain cold rolled products, pipes, tubes, quenched and tempered steel, high alloy steel bar products and stainless steel flat products.[54] Button also asked the state governments in South Australia and New South Wales to contribute to the plan by containing state charges such as power and freight costs and pay-roll tax.[55]

In return for bounty assistance, BHP promised to continue the operation of its three integrated steel plants and provide employment security during the life of the plan. This was similar to the West German Social Plan which was designed to minimise job losses over five years of restructuring in the steel industry. BHP also made an undertaking to invest $800 million over four years for capital improvements to increase labour productivity and energy efficiency. In return for job security, the unions agreed to negotiate any wage increases in line with the Prices and Incomes Accord negotiated between the Australian Council of Trade Unions (ACTU) and the federal government. And, in a separate accord between the unions and BHP, the two parties agreed to set productivity targets and promised to adhere to the procedure for the settlement of disputes which had been established in the 1982 steel award for a 38-hour week.[56] Although the assistance package ran for five years, not ten, and provided bounties, not quotas, the steel industry was delighted, with BHP's Steel Division chief, David Rice, describing it as 'the best obtainable under the circumstances'.[57] For their part, trade union leaders, Bill Kelty from the ACTU and Harry Hurrell from the Federated Ironworkers, supported the plan because it guaranteed no further job retrenchments.[58]

Like Japanese policy for troubled sectors, the steel plan was statist in conception and administration. The government appointed a three-member Steel Industry Authority (SIA), an independent body which implemented and monitored the progress of the steel plan. Under the terms of the safety mechanism, the SIA could also recommend action to the minister in the event that the industry's local market share deviated from the 80 to 90 per cent range. The SIA was also given the broader task of advising the industry minister on most aspects of the industry including 'steel industry investment, local production, imports, employment levels, productivity changes, wage settlements, steel prices, standards of product quality and customer service, levels of state government taxes and charges, assistance provided and to be provided to the steel industry' and any other matters deemed relevant by the industry minister.[59] Membership of the SIA included a senior trade union official, a position which was initially held by Charlie Fitzgibbon, senior vice-president of the ACTU and secretary of the Waterside Workers Federation who had served on the earlier Steel Industry Advisory Council, and from October 1984 by Cliff Dolan, the President of the ACTU.

THE STEEL PLAN IN ACTION, 1983–88

In the first six months of the steel plan the industry made a remarkable recovery. By June 1984, BHP was running at close to its operating capacity of 6.2 million tonnes, productivity levels had nearly reached the target of 250 tonnes per employee per annum, and the steel industry enjoyed on average an 88 per cent share of the domestic market.[60] This sudden resurgence, however, had very little to do with the steel plan. The Australian economy had recovered very strongly in mid-1983 leading to an increase in demand for steel, especially in the consumer durables, housing construction and rural sectors. Equally important was the steep depreciation of the Australian dollar which had helped BHP's exports to recover while keeping the cost of imports high.[61] BHP's recovery was also assisted by improved productivity resulting from massive job shedding prior to the commencement of the plan. The combination of strong domestic demand, the falling dollar and rising productivity resulted in the Steel Division's return to profitability in late 1983.[62] The rapid turn-around in the steel industry appeared to confirm the IAC's unpopular view that the prime cause of the steel industry's troubles was not so much import pressure nor the crisis in world steel, but a short-term fluctuation in the business cycle. Such a diagnosis, however, ignores the deep-seated problems faced by the Australian steel industry in the early 1980s, some of which have persisted: namely, the level of industrial disputation, stalled labour productivity improvements, low financial returns on capital and a volatile exchange rate.[63]

The industry's recovery continued through 1985, and by 1986, BHP had become one of the most profitable steel companies in the world. As the Australian dollar continued to fall, the price of imported steel remained high and the local industry's average market share remained strong at 89 per cent. Productivity levels had surpassed the initial target set in the BHP–union accord and were raised to 350 tonnes per employee per annum. By November 1988, productivity had reached 360 tonnes per employee per annum,[64] and in 1988/89 and 1989/90 BHP's level of profitability on the basis of a dollar per tonne shipped was third after China Steel and Nisshin, a Japanese steel company.[65]

The steel plan, however, was not an unqualified success and the degree to which the participants adhered to the plan varied. BHP generally held up its end of the agreement by keeping its three integrated steelworks in operation and making only one involuntary retrenchment in five years. In addition, BHP greatly exceeded its commitment to invest $800 million to improve cost structure, quality and service and, by the end of the plan, expenditure on capital investment approximated $2 billion, more than double BHP's initial pledge. Furthermore, increases in steel prices overall remained in line with the Consumer Price Index. But in some aspects, especially in the area of customer service and delivery schedules, BHP's performance showed alarmingly little improvement.[66]

In contrast to BHP, the federal government failed in many of its commitments to the plan. In the 1986 Budget, bounties to the steel industry were cut by 20 per cent across the board. Although this reduction could be justified in light of the industry's rapid recovery in 1983, the industry was still critical and one steel user likened it to 'moving the goal posts during the game'.[67] The government also failed to introduce an effective fast-track anti-dumping mechanism.[68]

The worst breakdown in the steel plan occurred in the area of industrial relations. Steelworkers, like the iron ore and coal miners who supply the steel mills, have traditionally been among the most militant industrial workers in the community. This historic militancy coupled with BHP's notorious record in management practices has meant that the steel industry has been especially strike-prone. Industrial relations were relatively harmonious during the first two years of the plan, but by 1986, they had soured again. At the heart of the difficulties was a lack of communication between union leaders and their membership which was exacerbated at Port Kembla by longstanding antagonism between the left-dominated local branch of the Federated Ironworkers Association and the right-dominated federal leadership of the union.[69] On the eve of publicly announcing the steel plan, Senator Button was astonished to find, on phoning a Port Kembla shop-floor steward, that local unionists knew little about the plan. So he hastily called a public meeting at Wollongong to explain and defend the proposal.[70]

Some half-hearted attempts were made to inform workers on the shop floor about the steel plan after it came into effect but a publicity campaign with posters and pamphlets enclosed in pay packets fell far short of rectifying the problem.[71] This was a matter of grave concern to the Steel Industry Authority yet, despite repeated warnings, slow progress was made in addressing steelworkers' indifference to the plan. This resulted in a continuing lack of shop-floor compliance to commitments made by union representatives at the national level. Some of the blame could also be apportioned to BHP's managers who failed to engender a common objective of company prosperity among their employees.

The apparent indifference to the goals of the plan was manifested in an increase in industrial disputes in 1986. Most of the strikes occurred at Port Kembla and Newcastle and involved blatant breaches of grievance procedures, usually on the part of the unions. As might have been expected, Port Kembla was the worst affected site. In June 1986, 700 members of the Federated Ironworkers Association defied a return-to-work order issued by the NSW Industrial Commission and walked out for a week in support of striking crane drivers.[72] In 1987, Port Kembla was again affected by a strike in protest against new workers' compensation legislation introduced in New South Wales. Although that strike was not a direct outcome of union–management conflict at Port Kembla but rather reflected tensions between the South Coast and NSW Labor Councils, it did raise for the Steel Industry Authority 'grave doubts as to the commitment by some of the parties to the security and development of the steel industry'.[73] As a result of this and other strikes across the steel industry, the number of working hours lost due to industrial disputes in the steel industry in 1986–87 increased steeply over the previous year (Table 5.1).[74]

In its final report on the steel plan, the SIA concluded that the lack of regional and shop-floor level support to commitments made by the unions' national representatives was the principal reason behind the unions' failure to comply with the dispute settlement procedures negotiated between BHP and the ACTU. The union leadership accepted some responsibility for the problem, but also apportioned part of the blame to the long history of bitter industrial relations in the steel industry as well as to individual union leaders at various plants.[75] BHP management also identified the area of industrial relations as a serious weakness of the plan; in particular, the failure 'to concentrate the attention of both management and unions on workplace change rather than on the traditional debate about global industrial relations forms and prescriptions'. The steel plan had been 'negotiated at national level without local involvement and commitment to or understanding of the objects and processes'.[76]

But even if the achievements of the steel plan in the area of industrial relations fell short of plan expectations, it was a considerable improvement on past performance which, admittedly, was poor. This is clearly shown by the statistics in Table 5.1. Working hours lost as a percentage of total possible working hours worked in three steel mills, including the troublesome Port Kembla plant,

Table 5.1 *Time lost as a percentage of total hours worked at three BHP steel works[a], 1970–90*

	WHL[b]	TPWHW	WHL/ TPWHW(%)
1970	462,964	58,409,512	0.79
1971	473,796	60,739,298	0.78
1972	219,110	55,646,198	0.39
1973	1,589,876	54,884,737	2.90
1974	821,866	58,082,269	1.42
1975	540,534	51,350,261	1.05
1976	783,782	51,121,030	1.53
1977	517,021	49,034,390	1.05
1978	1,045,040	50,315,623	2.08
1979	1,029,821	56,780,436	1.81
1980	894,707	51,954,768	1.72
1981	845,161	51,645,416	1.64
1982	555,059	44,810,753	1.24
1983	235,574	30,601,279	0.77
1984	115,934	29,813,120	0.39
1985	107,264	27,989,648	0.38
1986	217,203	30,130,801	0.72
1987	389,809	29,836,205	1.31
1988	75,461	27,992,518	0.27
1989	74,018	26,100,465	0.28
1990	60,789	25,170,087	0.24

Notes: [a] The three BHP steel works are Port Kembla, Newcastle and Whyalla.
[b] WHL = working hours lost; TPWHW = total possible working hours worked.

Source: Figures provided by BHP.

were more than halved during each year of the plan except 1987. And this had been achieved during a period of intense industry restructuring in which both work culture and practices had to be substantially changed. The old union culture, bred on relatively stable technology and steady expansion of employment, was confronted with new technology, shrinking employment levels and streamlined work practices in which old skills, customary work practices and established career patterns were affected.

The extent of restructuring, and the consequent dislocation of traditional labour practices, can be illustrated from a couple of examples.[77] The first is the size of the workforce at the three main steel works, Port Kembla, Newcastle and Whyalla, which was reduced by a quarter, from 24,500 at the beginning of the plan to

18,500 in early 1989 shortly after the plan ended. The second is the sheer scale of changes at Port Kembla which provide the context for its relatively poor industrial relations. Included in the above aggregate figures are reductions from the commissioning of new plant and job reorganisation at Port Kembla between February 1988 and February 1989 which sliced off 21 per cent of employees or 2,774 positions in a period when steel production increased 18 per cent from 2.8 million to 3.3 million tonnes. At Port Kembla's hot steel mill, during the life of the plan, the number of employees required to produce 2 million tonnes of product per annum was reduced from 126 to 60 and the number of job classifications from 7 to 2. This was achieved through a combination of capital investment, job restructuring and training in which the basis for selection was switched from seniority to ability assessed through aptitude testing and past training examination.

Nevertheless, industrial unrest during the life of the plan pointed to the need for BHP and the unions to come to some continuing working arrangement after the expiry of the steel plan in 1988. Thus, in October 1987, the Steel Industry Authority facilitated initial discussions between BHP management and the ACTU to discuss means of enhancing worker participation in BHP's plant operations. Together, BHP and the unions hammered out out a three-year agreement which promised job security and retraining in return for the unions' commitment to further productivity improvements, adherence to dispute-settling procedures and award restructuring.[78]

Clearly the participants had learned from the steel plan as the new accord was structured to address the difficulties encountered during the steel plan. Unlike the previous accord, the new BHP-union agreement was enterprise-based and operated on three tiers. At the national level, the ACTU, the steel industry union heads and BHP executives would monitor BHP's overall development program as well as industrial relations, award restructuring, and employee training. At the second tier, union officials and company representatives would monitor plant-level performance including productivity. Underpinning these were shop-floor committees in each plant where workers would be involved in regular consultations to discuss all aspects of their section's operations.[79] The proof of incorporating shop-floor unionists in the setting of more detailed performance targets has been further improvement in industrial relations, as shown in Table 5.1, for the years 1988–90.

THE STEEL PLAN IN RETROSPECT

As the steel plan neared its conclusion, there was a considerable degree of scepticism about its effectiveness and a great deal of pessimism about the future competitiveness of the Australian steel industry. In its 1987 Annual Report, the Industries Assistance Commission dismissed the notion that the plan itself had contributed to the recovery of the steel industry. It noted that steel production and consumption had already begun to recover in 1983 and that BHP had returned to profitability before the plan commenced. The IAC believed that the end of the recession followed by the sustained depreciation of the Australian dollar beginning in late 1984 were the significant factors in the improved competitive position of the industry. Nor did the IAC believe that the productivity improvements were due to the plan. Rather, increased productivity during the plan reflected previous investments, the shedding of excess labour and the closure of old plant during the recession, and the return to a higher production capacity when the recession lifted. Moreover, the IAC ominously noted that over a half of OECD steel production between 1983 and 1985 achieved labour productivity improvements equal to or better than those in Australia.[80]

The Bureau of Industry Economics agreed with the IAC on all counts. In its May 1988 report on the steel plan, the BIE suggested that the plan had established an initial climate of confidence for investment but otherwise had very little impact. The BIE believed that BHP's investment was not stimulated by the plan per se but by increased competitiveness resulting from the devaluation of the Australian dollar as well as the 18 per cent investment allowance and accelerated depreciation provisions. The BIE also dampened enthusiasm for BHP's program of capital expenditure during the plan and emphasised that 'overall investment in BHP's Steel Division appears to have been no more than that necessary to cover the real replacement cost of economic decay of its existing assets'.[81]

The House of Representatives Standing Committee on Finance and Public Administration also conducted a lengthy review of the plan, inviting submissions from BHP and other producers, unions, steel users and other interested parties. In its report the standing committee concurred with the IAC's view that macro-economic factors including the depreciation of the dollar and tax concessions were largely responsible for the steel industry's sustained recovery.[82]

However, the committee believed that the plan provided a climate of confidence which was vital to BHP's capital investment program. The committee also stated that without the plan, BHP probably would have closed at least one of its integrated steel works.[83]

The parliamentarians hailed the industry's recovery as a 'remarkable achievement'. No doubt this reflected their immense relief that all three steelworks had remained in operation, thereby preventing further unemployment and sustaining the regional economies of Whyalla, Newcastle and Wollongong. Elsewhere, in Canberra, a radically different opinion was held. The IAC believed that the plan had failed to meet its objective in 'the creation of a long-term viable steel industry providing job security for its employees and inputs to a wide range of metal and engineering industries at internationally competitive prices'.[84] Instead, the plan was merely 'an extension of temporary assistance . . . rather than an innovation in industry policy worth extending to other sectors'.[85]

The truth lies somewhere between those extremes. There is enough evidence to suggest that the macro-economic setting rather than the plan itself was largely responsible for the steel industry's speedy recovery in 1984. But that is not to say that the steel plan did not have a valuable role in the formulation and implementation of industry policy during the 1980s. Clearly, any form of government assistance was bound to dismay economic rationalists who believe that all industries should live and die by the marketplace. This view, embodied in the Garnaut Report, has gained increasing currency in political, business and academic circles in recent years. In 1983, however, the argument was largely irrelevant. The Labor government was committed to maintaining a viable steel industry in Australia and that begged the immediate question of government assistance.

The history of Australian industry policy pointed to an easier solution: a protective assistance package of tariff increases and import quotas. To the credit of Senator Button and his departmental advisers, a steel plan was devised which largely met the needs of all those affected - from the companies and unionists to importers and downstream users. At the same time, the plan fulfilled the primary goal of the Labor government's industry policy to foster international competitiveness through the reduction of protection. As an instrument of crisis management, the steel plan was far more desirable than a corporate bailout. Despite the IAC's conclusion that the steel plan was not worth extending to other sectors, it became the blueprint for subsequent plans for the passenger motor vehicle and textile, clothing and footwear sectors.

Significant also was the actual restructuring of the steel industry that was achieved during the plan and continued after its termination at the end of 1988. While it might be argued that BHP was committed to restructuring its Steel Division anyway, that could hardly have been achieved with improved industrial relations as occurred under the plan. One major lesson identified by BHP management was 'that a significant and supportive shift in both trade unions' and employers' attitudes had developed during the life of the plan and that with some difficulty, this could be translated into more positive workplace attitudes'.[86] That proved to be the case with the National Steel Industry Development Programme Agreement which was negotiated between BHP and the unions in 1988 and took effect in 1989. This program for developing the steel industry was focused primarily on improving business performance through setting targets and by identifying and implementing measures to achieve them. The Agreement was premised on better industrial relations practices learnt from the experience of the steel plan. Emphasis was placed on involvement of local union officials and employees in locally negotiated agreements that translated the broad parameters of the program into components 'owned' by shop-floor managers and workers. Such a bipartite performance agreement would have been inconceivable without the positive learning experience of the tripartite steel plan.

NOTES

1. Kent Jones, *Politics vs Economics in World Steel Trade*, Allen & Unwin, London, 1986, p. 1.
2. Industries Assistance Commission (IAC), *Report on the Iron and Steel Industry*, Report 249, 25 July 1980, Australian Government Publishing Service, Canberra, p. 27.
3. At the turn of the century, BHP ventured into mining iron ore, a vital ingredient for its lead smelter at Port Pirie, South Australia. The opening of iron mines in South Australia coincided with the depletion of silver reserves at Broken Hill and led the company to consider the viability of steelmaking. The history of mining at Broken Hill is recorded by Geoffrey Blainey in *The Rise of Broken Hill*, Macmillan, Melbourne, 1968.
4. For the story of the merger see Geoffrey Blainey, *The Steel Master: A Life of Essington Lewis*, Macmillan, Melbourne, 1971, Ch. 8.

5. The only other steel production in Australia is undertaken on a relatively small scale by the Smorgon Company Ltd which, since 1983, has operated a mini-mill in Melbourne where scrap steel is rolled into rod and merchant bar for use by the local construction industry.
6. Kosmas Tsokhas, *Beyond Dependence: Companies, Labour Processes and Australian Mining*, Oxford University Press, Melbourne, 1986, pp. 90–1.
7. The Broken Hill Proprietary Company Ltd, *Annual Report*, 1981.
8. IAC, *Report on Certain Iron and Steel Products and Certain Alloy Steel Products*, Report 321, 25 May 1983 (hereafter, May 1983 IAC Report), Australian Government Publishing Service, Canberra, p. 10.
9. Michael Trebilcock, Marsha Chandler, Morley Gunderson, Paul Halpern, Jack Quinn, *The Political Economy of Business Bailouts*, Vol. II, Ontario Economic Council, Toronto, 1985, pp. 383–6; Michael Trebilcock, *The Political Economy of Economic Adjustment: The Case of Declining Sectors*, University of Toronto Press, Toronto, 1986, pp. 175–80.
10. Information from BHP officials, 25 July 1991.
11. Michael Borrus, 'The politics of competitive erosion and the U.S. steel industry', in *American Industry in International Competition: Government Policies and Corporate Strategies*, eds John Zysman & Laura Tyson, Cornell University Press, Ithaca, 1983, pp. 60–105.
12. Martin Rhodes, 'Organized interests and industrial crisis management: restructuring the steel industry in West Germany, Italy and France', in *Organized Interests and the State: Studies in Meso-Corporatism*, ed. Alan Cawson, Sage, London, 1985, pp. 192–220.
13. Trebilcock, *et al.*, *Corporate Bailouts*, pp. 368–71.
14. May 1983 IAC *Report*, p. 7.
15. *Australian*, 17 January 1983; BHP, *Annual Report*, 1981, 'Iron and Steel Despatches', p. 6.
16. *Age*, 24 July 1982. The newspapers reported a loss of $13 million, but BHP's own accounting methods determined the loss to be $155 million.
17. According to BHP, between 1978 and 1982 hourly earnings had risen by 47 per cent, representing nearly half of the total increase in BHP's input costs. See BHP's submission to the IAC inquiry in the May 1983 IAC *Report*.
18. BHP, *Annual Report, 1982*, pp. 8-9.
19. From BHP correspondence, 25 July 1991.
20. Jones, *Politics vs Economics*, p. 2.
21. *Australian Financial Review*, 9 June 1982.
22. May 1983 IAC *Report*, pp. 22–3, 113–14. At the IAC hearing, BHP blamed its lack of investment in new technology on poor market conditions in the mid-1970s.
23. BHP, *Annual Report, 1982*, pp. 8-9.
24. Address by Dr N. R. Norman to the Institute of Steel Services Centres of Australia, *Report of Proceedings*, Australian Steel Convention 1982, Perth, 17-20 October 1982.

25. *Sydney Morning Herald,* 17 June 1982.
26. *Age,* 30 August 1982.
27. *Sydney Morning Herald,* 24 August 1982.
28. *Australian Financial Review,* 9 August 1982; May 1983 IAC Report, pp. 152–3. Car makers were the sole exception and while they supported BHP's demand for a guaranteed market share (after all, they enjoyed the same sort of protection), they claimed that BHP's demands were too broad and excessive.
29. The quotas allowed steel importers to import at their 1981–82 levels at the existing duty rates of 5 to 25 per cent, with above-quota imports dutiable at 150 per cent. Australia, House of Representatives, *Debates,* 26 August 1982, pp. 1030–1. Speech by the acting minister for industry and commerce, Mr Fife.
30. *Australian Financial Review,* 27 August 1982.
31. *Age,* 24 July 1982.
32. *Australian Financial Review,* 9 and 24 August 1982.
33. For full details of BHP's submission see, May 1983 IAC *Report,* pp. 139–49.
34. Discussions with Cliff Dolan, 23 July 1991.
35. *Australian Financial Review,* 15 December 1982.
36. *Age,* 19 February 1983.
37. IAC, *Draft Report on Certain Iron and Steel Products and Certain Alloy Steel Products,* 26 April 1983, Australian Government Publishing Service, Canberra, pp. 188–93.
38. *Australian Financial Review,* Editorial, 22 March 1983.
39. *Age,* 21 March 1983.
40. *Australian Financial Review,* 22 March 1983.
41. *Sydney Morning Herald,* 4 September 1982.
42. See for instance Stewart West's speech to the House of Representatives in the *Debates,* 26 August 1982, pp. 1032–3 and John Dawkins' comments in the *Age,* 19 February 1983.
43. Speech by R. J. L. Hawke to the Federated Ironworkers Association, *Commonwealth Record,* Vol. 8, No. 7, pp. 208–9.
44. *Australian Financial Review,* 4 March 1983.
45. *Australian Financial Review,* 28 March 1983.
46. *Commonwealth Record,* Vol. 8, No. 12, 1983, pp. 353–4; *Australian Financial Review,* 22 March and 12 April 1983.
47. From discussions with Cliff Dolan, 23 July 1991.
48. Between May 1981 and March 1983, BHP shed about 30 per cent of its workforce, or 12,936 workers. Steel Industry Advisory Council *Report,* August 1983, Australian Government Publishing Service, Canberra, 1983, pp. 4–5.
49. Cliff Dolan's description during interview 23 July 1991.
50. *Australian,* 23 March 1983.
51. SIAC *Report,* August 1983.

52. May 1983 IAC *Report*, pp. 168–81.
53. SIAC *Report*, August 1983, pp. 26–7.
54. Minister for Industry and Commerce, News Release 77/83, 11 August 1983.
55. The states refused to make specific commitments claiming that they already provided assistance to BHP in the form of concessions, subsidies and government purchasing policies. Steel Industry Authority, *Review of the Steel Plan*, June 1988, pp. 159-61.
56. Minister for Industry and Commerce, News Release, 77/83, 11 August 1983.
57. *Australian Financial Review*, 12 August 1983.
58. Cliff Dolan interview, 23 July 1991.
59. Australia, House of Representatives, *Debates*, 30 November 1983, p. 3032.
60. Steel Industry Authority (SIA), *Annual Report*, 1983–84, pp. 2–3.
61. Bureau of Industry Economics, *Australian Steel and the Steel Industry Plan 1984–1987*, Occasional Paper 5, Australian Government Publishing Service, Canberra, 1988, pp. vii.
62. BHP, *Annual Report*, 1984.
63. From BHP correspondence, 25 July 1991.
64. SIA, *Annual Report*, 1985–86, pp. 10–16; *Australian Financial Review*, 10 January 1989.
65. Supplied by BHP, correspondence, 25 July 1991.
66. SIA, *Review of the Steel Plan*, June 1988, pp. 104–9.
67. House of Representatives Standing Committee on Finance and Public Administration, *Report on the Australian Iron and Steel Industry*, November 1987, p. 22.
68. ibid., pp. 24–5.
69. We owe this point and the subsequent insight into Port Kembla's poor record to Cliff Dolan who, as a member of the SIA, was heavily involved in mediating with the unions.
70. Button interview, 27 July 1991.
71. SIA, *Annual Report*, 1983–84, p. 4 and *Quarterly Report*, December 1986, p. 7.
72. *Age*, 21 June 1986.
73. SIA, *Annual Report*, 1986–87, pp. 4–5.
74. SIA, *Annual Report*, 1986–87, p. 2.
75. House of Representatives, *Report on the Iron and Steel Industry*, p. 37.
76. John Sullivan (BHP's General Group Manager, Human Resources & External Affairs), Australian steel industry restructuring 1982–1992, unpublished paper, 20 June 1989, p. 6.
77. ibid., p. 5, for the following examples and figures.
78. J. Prescott & A. McLeod, *BHP Steel in the 1990s*, EPAC Discussion paper 90/01, Australian Government Publishing Service, Canberra, 1990.
79. *Australian Financial Review*, 22 March 1989; *Australian*, 10 July 1989.

80. IAC, *Annual Report*, 1986–87, 4 November 1987, Parliamentary Paper 288/1987, pp. 98–100.
81. Bureau of Industry Economics, *Australian Steel and the Steel Industry Plan 1984–1987*, p. 44.
82. House of Representativess, *Report on the Iron and Steel Industry*, pp. 65–66.
83. ibid., p. 77.
84. Minister for Industry and Technology, News Release, 77/83, 11 August 1983.
85. IAC, *Annual Report*, 1988–89, p. 50.
86. Sullivan, Australian steel industry restructuring 1982–1992, pp. 7–8.

CHAPTER 6

The Motor Vehicle Industry

A film clip of the first Holden rolling off the assembly line in November 1948 remains one of the most enduring images in the nation's modern memory. It was a paradoxical symbol of Australian national pride, neither a significant milestone in engineering (Australia had built aeroplane engines during the war), nor the fruit of Australian investment and ingenuity. Rather, it represented the Australianisation of the American dream, Fordism gone global. And a single act, Prime Minister Ben Chifley's opening the door of the new Holden, foreshadowed the ongoing commitment of future governments to encourage, support and protect the local manufacture of motor vehicles.

Government assistance to the motor vehicle industry began during the First World War when, to preserve foreign exchange and encourage local industrial production, the Hughes government imposed an absolute ban on the importation of car bodies. Although the quantitative restrictions were lifted after the war, the existing tariff on car bodies and body panels was doubled and new duties were levied on assembled chassis from North America. This tariff structure encouraged the proliferation of local body manufacturers and provided an incentive for North American car manufacturers to set up assembly operations in Australia. In 1925, the Ford Motor Company of Canada (a wholly-owned subsidiary of its US parent) established body-building facilities in Geelong and chassis assembly plants in Geelong, Adelaide, Brisbane, Perth and Sydney. A year later, the General Motors Corporation of the United States commenced car assembly in Melbourne using bodies manufactured by a local company, Holden Motor Body Builders. Within a few years, GM had copied Ford's example and set up assembly plants in all the mainland capital cities.[1]

While Ford and GM became important local employers, their assembly operations required neither a skilled workforce nor locally manufactured components. In 1936 the Lyons government introduced a range of measures to encourage more value-added production through the establishment of motor engine and chassis manufacturing plants in Australia. These measures included increased duties on imported engines and chassis, bounties on local engine production, import quotas on North American chassis, and by-law (i.e. duty-free) admission of imports of capital equipment and parts not available in Australia.[2] The Tariff Board, however, expressed grave reservations about the economic viability of the government's policy and, in 1938, cautioned that it was 'unwise at present to encourage or enforce the manufacture of the complete motor vehicle in Australia'.[3] Despite the Tariff Board's concerns, the government remained committed to the development of a local car manufacturing industry and, in 1940, negotiated a deal which gave Australian Consolidated Industries Ltd (ACI) sole rights to build an Australian motor vehicle with government assistance.[4]

The Second World War forced ACI to shelve its plans as industries were retooled for military production and new car registrations plummetted, but the setback was only temporary. The new Labor government was firmly committed to assisting the motor vehicle industry to become 'the keystone that will consolidate the industrial structure that we have built up during the war'.[5] The government believed an expanded automobile industry could provide the foundation for post-war reconstruction and, in 1944, invited car manufacturers to submit proposals for the local production of engines and chassis. In 1945, cabinet accepted GM-Holden's plan to manufacture a six-cylinder car with 90 per cent Australian content in return for government assistance. In January 1949, volume production of the first Holden began. In the meantime, the Australian subsidiaries of Chrysler, Ford, and International Harvester also undertook to raise the Australian content of their vehicles in return for duty-free imports of certain components.

In 1952 the young car industry received a further boost from the government when import licensing was introduced to ease a balance of payments crisis. In order to dodge the new import barriers, several foreign companies including Standard, Rootes, Rover and Volkswagen commenced local assembly and manufacturing operations in Australia while two British manufacturers, Austin and Morris, expanded their existing Australian operations.[6] The effect of import licensing was dramatic; in a three-year period from 1951/52 to

1954/55, the value of imported assembled car bodies fell by 50 per cent and the value of imported assembled chassis by 61 per cent.[7] The import restrictions also heightened demand for locally manufactured components and spare parts. This led British and West German companies to establish Australian subsidiaries to produce a wide range of parts including coils, generators, transmission assemblies and shock absorbers. At the same time, Australian-owned components manufacturers greatly expanded their activities.[8] As a result, by 1957/58, the Australian content of locally made vehicles had reached 77 per cent.

When import restrictions were lifted in 1960, local industry found itself facing stiff competition from imported cars and components. Charles McGrath, the owner of Australia's largest component manufacturer, Repco, was keen to check the flow of imports and proposed a novel form of protection: local content plans designed to increase the use of domestically produced components. Industry minister John McEwen looked favourably upon the proposal mooted by his good friend McGrath (who happened to be the president of the national Liberal Party) and, in May 1964, the Menzies Liberal coalition government established the local content plans.[9] The local content plans linked by-law concessions (i.e. duty-free entry) on imported components to the level of local content in vehicles manufactured in Australia: high-volume vehicle manufacturers were required to source 95 per cent of their components locally while low-volume manufacturers were subject to less stringent levels of local content.[10]

The original aim of the local content plans had been to protect local component producers against imports but, by any measure, the plans were an abject failure. Because a greater percentage of components for the low-volume vehicle runs could be sourced from overseas *at a lower cost,* the plans had the effect of skewing manufacturing towards low-volume vehicle production. This undermined economies of scale and led to the proliferation of models which eroded the efficiency of the vehicle manufacturing sector and fragmented the market. The increased range of models also required a more diverse array of components and thus denied the producers of components the opportunity of longer production runs. Vehicle manufacturers encouraged the existence of more than one domestic supplier; for major components there were two manufacturers and for minor components, even more. In addition, the local content plans became increasingly complicated as the federal government amended existing plans and introduced new ones in 1966, 1968 and 1971.[11] By 1971, vehicle production had become so grossly distorted as a result of the plans that the government decided to phase out the low-volume assembly plans.

In the mid-1960s Australian manufacturers began to experience increased competition in both domestic and export markets from smaller, more economical cars produced by countries such as Japan. In response to this growing import competition, the Menzies government raised the tariff on completely built-up (CBU) imports from 35 to 45 per cent in 1966. This gave Australia the ignominious distinction of having the second highest tariff rate on cars in the world (only New Zealand ranked higher). Despite the tariff hike, imports began to erode the domestic market shares of the domestic manufacturers, GMH, Ford, Chrysler and Leyland Australia and, as a result, the four companies saw their combined local market share decline steadily from 84 per cent in 1966 to 68 per cent in 1973. Two firms in particular, Chrysler and Leyland Australia, recorded losses in 1972 and, in 1974, Leyland was forced to close its manufacturing operations entirely.[12] To make matters worse for the local industry, in December 1972, two Japanese companies, Nissan and Toyota, which had been assembling vehicles under the low-volume plans, applied for government permission to manufacture in Australia under the high-volume plans requiring high local content. This sent the domestic car industry into a panic, and with the exception of GMH, the plan manufacturers began to lobby for quantitative restrictions against imports.[13]

The issue of whether the Japanese companies should be allowed to manufacture cars in Australia was a thorny one. In terms of value-added production, workforce skills and the balance of payments, manufacturing was preferable to assembly operations. It also seemed absurd in the face of growing consumer preference for Japanese cars to continue to import them when the Japanese companies were willing to set up manufacturing operations in Australia. But the perilous state of the industry rendered it unlikely, if not impossible, for the market to sustain two new manufacturers.

THE WHITLAM CAR PLAN, 1974–84

In December 1972, the newly elected Whitlam Labor government focused its attention on the troubled car industry sector and set up an interdepartmental committee in early 1973 to identify the key policy issues. The tensions which emerged within the committee reflected diverging views as to the fundamental nature of reform and the future shape of the Australian car industry. In essence, Whitlam and his department favoured an immediate Industries Assistance Commission review of assistance to car manufacturers, knowing full well that the IAC was inclined to favour substantial tariff reductions as the best means to bring about restructuring, efficiencies and economies of scale. On the other hand, the minister for secondary industry, Dr Jim Cairns, favoured ongoing government intervention and assistance through policies of 'product rationalisation, resource usage, local equity, pollution control etc. through close government supervision of the Plans'.[14] Cairns's wish to exercise direct control over the car companies was in sympathy with the climate of hostility towards the presence of multinational corporations and foreign ownership in Australia. Protracted and stormy cabinet discussions through July and August 1973 eventually resulted in a compromise favouring Whitlam. The IAC would conduct an inquiry which, in addition to taking account of the government's desire to 'improve the efficiency with which the community's productive resources are used', would also consider a broad spectrum of social, employment and environmental issues.[15]

The IAC produced a damning indictment of the car industry and of previous assistance plans. Its main recommendations were the abolition of the local content plans and phased tariff reductions to 25 per cent over seven years. The IAC predicted a number of outcomes from this policy including Japanese domination of the light vehicle sector, the rationalisation of the medium car sector to three manufacturers, and the demise of some uneconomic components manufacturers. As a result of this restructuring, the IAC estimated a net job loss of 2,000 out of a total industry workforce of 88,000.[16]

With the usual exception of a handful of newspaper editors, economists and bureaucrats who favoured tariff reductions and market-driven industrial restructuring, the IAC's report was greeted with universal hostility. Vehicle manufacturers and unions were outraged, GMH foreshadowed widespread job losses and members of the Vehicle Builders Employees Federation (VBEF) threatened work stoppages and mass protests. In South Australia, where GMH was a major employer, the premier demanded that the

Commonwealth government reject the IAC's recommendations. In Canberra, the Labor caucus was appalled, and the Department of Secondary Industry disbelieving. Together this unlikely coalition of foreign-owned companies, unionists, bureaucrats and politicians from both parties mounted what Glezer described as 'one of the most extensive exercises in industry lobbying' in twenty years.[17]

In the face of mounting hostility to the IAC report, the Standing Interdepartmental Committee on Assistance to Industry (SIDCAI) proposed an alternative to the IAC's recommendations in which the local content plans would be simplified and tariff protection increased. Under SIDCAI's plan, the existing local content plans were abolished and replaced by a single, more flexible 85 per cent local content requirement that could be averaged across the whole of a company's production. The remaining 15 per cent of components could be imported duty free under by-law concessions.[18] A trigger tariff was also introduced which raised the tariff (previously reduced to 33.75 per cent in the across-the-board tariff cut in July 1973) to 45 per cent whenever imports exceeded 20 per cent of total registrations – in effect, immediately. This was a far more protectionist plan than the IAC had proposed but, as Glezer and Warhurst have pointed out, the intense hostility towards the IAC plan, rising levels of unemployment, the ability of manufacturers to exercise their economic leverage, and the unions' political leverage through their supporters in the caucus and cabinet, all worked against the possibility of tariff reductions.[19]

The new sectoral plan commenced on 1 January 1975 and was designed to operate for ten years in order to ensure a stable environment for investment and restructuring. In dismantling the complex array of local content plans and substituting a single scheme to be applied across a company, the government aimed to encourage a return to economies of scale by reducing the range of models and bringing about greater specialisation in component production. This restructuring, it was believed, would ultimately lead to a more efficient and competitive car industry. The government accepted that the tariff increase would cause car prices to rise in the short term but believed that the cost disadvantage to consumers was outweighed by the long-term benefits of a leaner industry. And to cushion the effects of job losses which resulted from restructuring, the government also promised compensation to employees and firms through the Structural Adjustment Assistance Scheme and Non-Metropolitan Subsidy Scheme.[20]

Whitlam's road to restructuring led nowhere. First, the Fraser government's decision in 1976 to allow Nissan and Toyota-AMI to establish manufacturing facilities in Australia meant that the number of manufacturers was increased from three to five. This meant that instead of achieving economies of scale, there was an increase in the number of low-volume runs and further market fragmentation. Because car makers made no effort to standardise components, model proliferation created havoc for the components sector. For instance, every model of car manufactured in Australia required a slightly different shape of bottle to hold windscreen wiper fluid, more than twenty different types of bottles in all. Added to this was the fact that the relatively small local market could not support five manufacturers at the 85 per cent local content level and still generate a satisfactory return on investment.[21]

In addition, the Australian car industry, which was a microcosm of the US industry, was based on the manufacture of six-cylinder sedans. This became a major disability in the late 1970s when there was a major shift in consumer preference to cheaper, more fuel-efficient, and generally more reliable Japanese cars. In Detroit, Chrysler suffered the greatest losses and the US government was forced to devise a rescue package to save jobs and the company. However, bailing out Chrysler did not solve the other manufacturers' problems and, in 1981, the US government pressured Japan into a Voluntary Export Restraint Agreement to limit Japanese imports to 2.3 million vehicles a year.

Like the US administration, the Australian government adopted a defensive stance towards the industry, although one that fell short of corporate bailouts. In response to import pressure, the Fraser government had raised the tariff on CBU imports from 45 per cent to 57.5 per cent by 1978. Despite creeping protection, the local industry's market share continued to fall, plunging to 74.8 per cent in the first half of 1980.[22] Declining market shares forced companies to scale down their operations or cease production altogether. In 1980, Mitsubishi bought out the deeply troubled Chrysler company and GMH closed its Pagewood plant in Sydney. A year later, Renault closed the doors on its local assembly plant.

The failure of tariff protection alone to preserve an 80 per cent market share for local manufacturers led governments to resort to quantitative restrictions on imports. The first quotas were applied by the Whitlam government in January 1975 as a temporary expedient to prevent immediate retrenchments at GMH, Ford and

Chrysler.[23] Later, contrary to its own industry policy which sanctioned market-sharing schemes as a short-term measure only, the Fraser government entrenched quotas as an integral part of its assistance to the car industry.[24]

In 1979, the Crawford Study Group on Structural Adjustment identified the high cost of components as a major factor increasing the costs of the motor vehicle industry. The Crawford Report urged the government to consider a scheme promoted by GM International which would allow manufacturers to obtain local content credits in exchange for exports.[25] In addition to component imports allowed duty-free under the 85 per cent local content plan, the export facilitation scheme would allow a manufacturer to import duty-free components at a rate equivalent to the value of its exports. In theory, this would allow manufacturers cheaper access to high technology, specialist components and so contribute to economies of scale in both the manufacturing and local component sectors. It would also encourage the industry to become more export-oriented and lead to international competitiveness.

The scheme was predicated on the world car concept, a strategy developed in North America by Ford and General Motors in response to a deep slump in sales and production. The world car strategy was based on the assumption that if a particular model could be sold worldwide, large economies of scale could be achieved. For instance, engines produced in Australia could be used in American cars and, conversely, components made in the United States could be used in assembly plants around the world. In addition to achieving economies of scale, the world car strategy satisfied demands that cars sold in a particular country comply with local content rules.[26]

General Motors included their Australian operations in their strategy to market the 'J' car globally and, in 1979, GMH management approached the industry minister, Sir Phillip Lynch, with the export facilitation scheme proposal. The sweetener in the proposal was a guarantee that if the scheme were introduced, GMH would build an engine plant in Australia capable of producing 300,000 four-cylinder engines a year, at least half of which would be exported. With Fraser's backing, Lynch sold the idea to cabinet and, in December 1979, announced that the scheme would commence in March 1980. GMH kept its end of the bargain and commenced construction of a $300m engine plant at Fisherman's

Bend, Melbourne.[27] In January 1981, the government announced a separate export facilitation scheme for the components sector commencing in March 1982.[28]

THE LYNCH CAR PLAN

In March 1979 the Fraser government referred the issue of post-1984 assistance to the car industry to the Industries Assistance Commission. When the IAC finally reported two years later, the same competing interests and ideologies which had informed the previous debate over protection emerged once again. The IAC echoed its 1974 findings; the government and the bureaucracy were deeply divided between those who wanted to cut tariffs and force a rationalisation of the industry and those who supported the status quo; and a caucus revolt loomed. Thus, the final decision to reject the IAC report and maintain high protection was no surprise.

The IAC report, released in June 1981, observed that Australian car manufacturing was still a high cost activity due in large part to the high cost of components and the number of manufacturers and models produced in relation to the size of the market. The IAC estimated that assistance available to car makers was three to four times greater than for manufacturing industry as a whole and, in dollar terms, cost more than $1,000 million a year, or between $2,000 and $3,000 per manufactured vehicle.[29] The report urged a drastic breach with past government policy which had maintained the car industry at any cost. It recommended the dismantling of all forms of non-tariff protection including the 85 per cent local content plan, the 80:20 market-sharing policy, and quantitative restrictions on imports, and called for the return to tariff protection only in the long term.

Herein lay the paradox of Australian industry policy; due largely to spiralling protection, the car manufacturing sector had continued to occupy a significant place in the manufacturing sector in terms of employment, investment and value-added production. In 1981/82, the vehicle and component manufacturing sectors together employed 72,700 people, allocated $260 million in new fixed capital expenditure, and contributed a value-added of $1,725 million.[30] In addition, the car manufacturing industry had linkages across the manufacturing and services sectors through its reliance on painting, plastics, adhesives, textiles, aluminium and ferrous castings, tool and die making, machinery and equipment, steel and building products, automation technology, engineering, industrial design and market research.

Apart from the car industry's contribution to employment and value-added production, there were other considerations which made any decision to cut protection difficult. For instance, in Victoria and South Australia where the automotive industry accounted for 11 and 15 per cent of manufacturing employment respectively, a cut in protection would have profound social, economic and political consequences. Furthermore, the car industry, like the steel industry, was vital to Australia's defence capability; the government estimated that it provided 20 per cent of all engineering capacity for defence preparedness and 50 per cent of the existing capacity for large scale defence production.[31] In short, successive governments had achieved Chifley's wartime goal of developing the automotive industry as the keystone of Australia's industrial structure. The tremendous cost which had underwritten that achievement was sufficient alone to militate against any fundamental changes to the elaborate and highly protective arrangements shoring up the industry.

Although the IAC's recommendation to move to a tariff-only regime after 1984 was far too radical for the government to countenance, the report had nevertheless convinced the Fraser cabinet that change was vital. During cabinet discussions on post-1984 assistance in November 1981, two different options were mooted. The GMH option proposed maintaining the local content plan and quotas but expanding the credits available under the export facilitation scheme to a ceiling of 15 per cent. This plan favoured GMH, which stood to gain the most of all the car manufacturers in Australia, and was supported by Fraser and Lynch. The Mitsubishi option echoed the IAC report in proposing market-driven restructuring through a reduction in the local content requirements and relaxed import controls. The Mitsubishi option was strongly supported by the 'dry' ministers: Treasurer John Howard, Attorney-General Senator Peter Durack, and Social Security Minister Senator Fred Chaney. On 1 December 1981, Defence Minister James Killen, finally tipped the balance in favour of the GMH option on the grounds that the Mitsubishi proposal would destroy vital industry capacity and jeopardise Australia's defence capability. However, a threatened revolt from 33 caucus 'dries' who demanded the abolition of quotas by 1990 forced Lynch to amend the GMH option and scale down quota protection.[32]

The post-1984 assistance arrangements, announced in December 1981, represented a compromise between the IAC's recommendations and political considerations. The key elements of the plan were the liberalisation of imports and the expansion of the Export Facilitation Scheme. The Lynch plan retained the 57.5 per cent tariff on CBU imports but the 80:20 market sharing policy was abolished and the quantitative restrictions were replaced by a system of tariff quotas. Quotas were to be progressively expanded and imports above quota would be subject to a 150 per cent tariff to be phased down to 125 per cent by 1992. This was designed to contain model proliferation and contribute to high-volume production by encouraging producers to import certain models rather than producing them locally in small numbers.

In order to put pressure on the producers of local components and encourage exports, the Lynch plan retained the 85 per cent local content rule but raised the ceiling on export credits progressively from 7.5 per cent to 15 per cent. This meant that plan producers would be able to import up to 30 per cent by value of components (and/or cars) duty free - 15 per cent through their automatic by-law entitlements and up to 15 per cent through export credits. While the Lynch plan was patently designed for GMH, the changes were supposed to push forward further rationalisation of the components sector while allowing manufacturers easier and cheaper access to new technology being developed overseas.[33]

The Fraser government expected that, under the Lynch plan, industry restructuring would proceed at a pace which would allow it to operate under a system of tariff protection only by 1992. This objective is hard to credit; high assistance in the past had not encouraged the development of a competitive and efficient industry. Furthermore, the Lynch plan maintained assistance through tariffs and quotas at levels far higher than they had been in 1974. While expressing its hope to see a more efficient industry in ten years, the Fraser government refrained from specifying an industry objective. Instead, it hinted that a generous import quota allocation would be granted to any company which decided to pull out of manufacturing in Australia.

THE BUTTON PLAN, 1985-92

The election of the Labor government in March 1983 provided a new opportunity for all those who were dissatisfied with the Lynch plan to lobby the new government for changes to the post-1984 assistance arrangements. In opposition, the Australian Labor Party had claimed that the Lynch plan would be largely ineffective in promoting industry restructuring and resolved to alter it upon coming to government. When the ALP came to power, the car industry was sicker than ever; between March and August 1983, GMH, which had been operating at a loss for several years, retrenched hundreds of employees in Victoria and South Australia.

In October 1983, Industry Minister Senator John Button established a key tripartite body, the Car Industry Council, and charged it with the difficult task of reporting on the long-term future of the car industry within two months.[34] Button himself chaired the Car Council and appointed to it the managing directors of the five plan manufacturers, representatives of the ACTU and three unions, the president of the Federation of Automotive Parts Manufacturers and the managing director of Repco, a senior public servant from the industry department and representatives of importers, dealers and a car rental company. The terms of reference asked the council to recommend joint action to be taken by the 'stakeholders in the industry (including, as necessary, the Government)' in order to restructure the industry to become efficient and competitive at home and abroad while retaining vehicle design and manufacturing capability in Australia and maximising opportunities for long-term employment.[35]

Button believed that the best way to achieve these goals was to reduce the number of car manufacturers and models produced in Australia.[36] One crude means to achieve this would be to cut assistance to car companies selectively, thus forcing them to withdraw from Australian production. This, however, would create more problems than it solved. For instance, what criteria would be used to 'pick winners' deserving to stay in the market? Moreover, it would be an act of extreme political courage, or stupidity, to close down Mitsubishi whose operations were an important part of South Australia's manufacturing industry or to close down GMH which had pride of place in Australian car manufacturing history. Electoral considerations meant that if company closures were to take place, they should not be seen to have been forced by the government, but would have to occur voluntarily.

This left the government in a bind; the car makers agreed with the need to rationalise their production but head offices in Detroit and Tokyo were not willing to close down their Australian subsidiaries. In contrast to BHP, which had successfully exploited its monopolistic position by threatening the closure of its steelworks, the five car manufacturers resolutely underlined their intention to remain engaged in domestic production and they rejected any notion that one or more plan producers should be forced out of production.[37] Certainly, car makers were aware that the tradition of government assistance to local manufacturers has been based partly on the state's desire to maintain jobs, skills and a manufacturing capacity. This knowledge engendered the expectation that the government would continue to support uneconomic companies for the sake of other state objectives.

Conflict over the best means to restructure the car industry was worked through in the long and intensive consultative processes of the Car Council and its proposals summarised in a report released in December 1983. The report asked the government to direct the pace and nature of restructuring by setting 'a target for the industry to reach, and a strategy to reach it'.[38] In order to ensure that restructuring progressed, the Council also recommended the establishment of an Automotive Industry Authority (AIA) with statutory powers to act as a 'marriage broker' to encourage production sharing and joint use of facilities.[39] According to the industry, this was to be the extent of the government's involvement. Ultimately, it was the responsibility of the individual companies to determine how best to rationalise their production.

While the Car Council's report was replete with good intentions, it lacked incentives for restructuring. Instead of scaling down the level of assistance proposed under the Lynch plan, it merely fine-tuned the arrangements. History suggested, however, that without some sort of market-driven pressure such as tariff reductions, the car industry was unlikely to change its ways. Thus, it was left to the minister and the government to determine the level of assistance which would pressure car and component makers to restructure without destroying the whole industry. In developing his views, Button relied primarily upon his personal staff and advisers, Jeff Evans, Richard Johns and Nick Gruen, rather than his department where old-style protectionists were still ensconced in senior positions. As Button put it, the car plan was conceived and worked out in his parliamentary office.[40]

On 29 May 1984, Senator Button announced the Labor government's new plan for post-1984 assistance. Those who expected massive changes were disappointed: the individual elements of the new Button plan had much in common with the Lynch plan. The local content requirement and the export facilitation scheme were retained and tariff protection still remained very high compared with most other manufacturing sectors. But the new Passenger Motor Vehicle Plan was bold and explicit in both its objectives and the state's role in meeting them. The Button plan's principal goals were to increase all aspects of industry efficiency so that the industry would be competitive with lower levels of government assistance to provide better quality cars at less cost, and to minimise disruption to production and employment during the restructuring process. These objectives were to be achieved by reducing protection in order to increase import competition; encouraging the development of economies of scale; and facilitating improvements in quality and productivity through investment in new technology, management practices and skills training.[41] The government baldly stated that, as an outcome of this process, by the early 1990s, 'the Government expects to see no more than three vehicle manufacturing groups operating in this country'.[42]

The key features of the Button plan were the phasing out of tariff quotas by 1992, the facilitation of component standardisation and model reductions from 13 to 6 or less by 1992, and the establishment of an Automotive Industry Authority to monitor the activities and consult with the industry participants on the progress of the plan.[43] As proof of its desire to see technological skills remain in Australia, the government also promised a $150 million package of federal grants to support Australian research and development in the car industry. Finally, like their counterparts in the steel industry, car industry workers who lost their jobs as a result of restructuring would be eligible for a small retraining allowance under the Labour Adjustment Training Arrangements (LATA) scheme.[44]

The plan was applauded across the industry.[45] The plan producers committed themselves to cooperate fully with the Automotive Industry Authority to promote rationalisation and the unions agreed to keep their claims consistent with the Prices and Incomes Accord and negotiate agreements with respect to restructuring including the introduction of new technology and rationalisation.[46] Clearly the level of support and enthusiasm for the plan demonstrated the value of the industry consultation process through the Car Council's deliberations prior to the formulation of the plan.

Whether the plan would succeed in bringing about economies of scale, efficiency and restored competitiveness was another issue. Some economists had their doubts. The IAC had not wavered from its view that tariff-only protection was the most desirable way to achieve restructuring. Economists Gary Sampson and Graeme Woodbridge questioned the premise that moral suasion and tariff reductions alone would lead to efficiency improvements. They challenged the assumption that once vehicle models are abandoned, domestic demand for those models would automatically shift to the remaining models manufactured locally. A more likely outcome, particularly as protection was reduced and imports fell in price, was that some of that domestic demand would be redirected to imported cars.[47] This proved to be the case when Mitsubishi ceased production of its four-cylinder Colt in 1989.

In a 1985 report, the Bureau of Industry Economics confirmed the view that the move to greater economies of scale and high-volume production would make the Australian car industry more efficient, but was no guarantee that a high market share would be preserved. Consumer preferences for small cars, luxury vehicles, sports cars, four-wheel drives and variety in general meant that many car buyers would be willing to pay a premium for imports. The BIE concluded that 'imports will probably always have a big share of the Australian market even if the local industry continues to improve its price competitiveness'.[48] This conclusion was borne out by the 1990 figures which showed that the import share of the largest segment of the domestic market - small cars - was increasing, and that the luxury car market was overwhelmingly dominated by imports.[49]

Critics of the plan argued that the drive to achieve standardisation and high-volume production was based on the principles of Fordism which had long been superseded by flexible production, a Japanese innovation. Flexible production techniques, developed in response to fickle and rapidly changing consumer preferences, allowed for a high degree of product flexibility and differentiation at a relatively low cost. The whole system rested on a highly trained, multi-skilled workforce which worked closely with management to improve labour practices and product design. In addition, flexible production strategies minimise cost overheads through 'just-in-time' stock deliveries and the reduction of factory wastage.[50]

There is little doubt that the medium-term future of the car industry lies in flexible manufacturing. In Australia, the companies, unions and government all recognise this and urge the industry to move towards the adoption of these practices.[51] However, flexible manufacturing has only been undertaken in overseas plants where volume production exceeds 200,000 vehicles - a volume five times greater than the most successful model lines produced in Australia. This suggests that before the Australian manufacturers can fully adopt this innovative strategy, they will first have to master Fordism by dramatically increasing their production volumes.

THE BUTTON PLAN IN ACTION

The devaluation of the Australian dollar in 1985 short-circuited the Button plan by effectively cancelling out reduced import restrictions as the means to force the domestic industry to restructure its operations. As a result of the falling dollar, the increased cost of vehicles and components (particularly those from Japan) lessened the competition from imports and considerably reduced pressure on the local industry to restructure. The loss of competitive pressure combined with cost increases in the price of imported components was passed on to the consumer in the form of escalating car prices. In a two-year period from the December 1985 quarter to the December 1987 quarter, the price index of locally manufactured cars rose 34 per cent compared with an increase in the Consumer Price Index of only 17.6 per cent.[52] The rise in both imported and domestic car prices also contributed to a dramatic sales slump which resulted in declining aggregate profitability across the industry.[53]

The changes in the macro-economic setting had rendered the Button plan virtually ineffective and in April 1988, following a scheduled mid-term review of the plan, Senator Button announced several changes. In order to restore international competitive pressure on the industry, tariff quotas (which were not scheduled to end until 1992) were abolished immediately and the tariff on imported cars was cut from 57.5 to 45 per cent. Furthermore, the endpoint for phased tariff reductions was reduced to 35 per cent for 1992, which would effectively restore the industry to the same level of barrier protection it had received prior to 1965.[54] The combined effect of these changes and the appreciation of the dollar in 1989 produced significant reductions in the price of imported cars and reasserted pressure on the local industry to restructure. However, despite these changes all five plan manufacturers still remained in business and the Automotive Industry Authority found that, unless exports were dramatically increased, seven plants would soon be unsustainable.[55]

The central tenet of the government's policy for restructuring the car industry was the belief that the industry's problems were derived from the production of a large range of cars at low volumes of output. The cornerstone of the plan was the drive to increase economies of scale through high-volume production by reducing the number of models from thirteen to six and the number of manufacturing groups from five to three. Achieving volume production was also important for capacity utilisation. For instance, in 1985, of the five four-cylinder engine plants operating in Australia, only GMH's Fisherman's Bend plant operated anywhere near world scale; the rest worked collectively at less than one-third of their total capacity.[56] It was a moot point, however, as to exactly what volume constituted a sufficient economy of scale. During the halcyon days of the Australian car industry in the early 1960s, about 150,000 EH Holdens (with almost 100 per cent Australian content) were manufactured annually, many of them destined for export markets in New Zealand and Southeast Asia. By contrast, in 1984 the average production volume per model in Australia was 28,000.[57]

In the early stages of the Button plan, model reduction was left to the discretion of the manufacturers. In the first two years, however, very little progress was achieved and so, in consultation with the plan participants, the Automotive Industry Authority developed a set of sanctions to force model reduction. These measures, announced by Button in December 1986, required the producers of low-volume models (i.e. less than 15,000 per annum) to either cease production or increase the volume of output. If a producer of a low-volume model failed to make a commitment either way by December 1988, its by-law concessions for imported parts for that model could then be withdrawn. A sliding scale of penalties could be applied to models which were produced in annual volumes of less than 40,000.[58] The volumes of passenger motor vehicle model lines in 1986–89 are shown in Table 6.1.

If invoked, these 'minimum volume' penalties would have resulted in substantial cost increases in the low-selling models, effectively forcing them out of production. Although several models failed to meet the minimum production requirements, they were granted conditional exemptions from the penalties and, to date, no penalties have been invoked. This probably reflected Button's hope that the

Table 6.1 *Volume performance by passenger motor vehicle model line, 1986–89*

	Number of model lines			
Sales volumes	1986	1987	1988	1989
0–19,999	8	6	2	1
20,000–29,999	2	4	4	3
30,000–39,999	1	1	1	3
40,000+	2	2	3	2
Models manufactured in the year	13	13	10	9
Models remaining at end of year	13	10	9	8

Source: PAXUS Australia Pty Ltd, *Bulletin – New Motor Vehicle Registrations.*

industry would respond to moral suasion although, in this case, his optimism was not misplaced and considerable progress towards rationalisation was achieved after the measures were announced.

By the end of 1989, five low-volume models including the Mitsubishi Colt and the GMH Camira had been dropped from production and the minimum acceptable production volume was raised to 30,000. As a result, producers of the remaining low-volume models such as the Toyota Corolla and the Nissan Pintara undertook to raise the output of those vehicles through a combination of model-sharing and export programs. This reduced the number of models produced in Australia to eight, although only two of these, the GMH–Toyota Commodore/Lexcen and the Ford Falcon/Fairlane/LTD, were produced in annual volumes above 40,000 (Table 6.2). The other six models were produced in volumes well below what

Table 6.2 *Volume performance by passenger motor vehicle model line and plan producer, 1989*

Sales volumes	Model lines	Plan producer
0–19,999	Colt	Mitsubishi
20,000–29,999	Corolla/Nova	Toyota/Holden
	Pintara/Corsair/Skyline	Nissan/Ford
	Pulsar/Astra	Nissan/Holden
30,000–39,999	Camry/Apollo	Toyota/Holden
	Laser/Capri	Ford
	Magna	Mitsubishi
40,000+	Commodore/Lexcen	Holden/Toyota
	Falcon/Fairlane/LTD	Ford

Source: PAXUS Australia Pty Ltd, *Bulletin – New Motor Vehicle Registrations.*

industry analysts believed was the minimum acceptable for profitable production in Australia. This figure improved considerably in 1990 when four of the eight models manufactured locally were produced in annual volumes above 40,000.[59]

In addition to rationalising model production, the Button plan also sought to improve capacity utilisation in Australia's assembly plants which was well below the world standard of 200,000 to 250,000 vehicles per year. In 1987 Ford and Nissan commenced a product-sharing arrangement which increased capacity utilisation at several facilities. A year later, in July 1988, General Motors-Holden's Motor Company (Holden's) and AMI Toyota began the first stage of a joint venture project that was aimed at eventually sharing all models and production facilities of both companies. This resulted in a reorganisation of both companies' assembly operations which meant that plants in Elizabeth, Port Melbourne and Dandenong would each be devoted to the production of a single model line.[60] But neither of these arrangements led immediately to any plant closures. As a result, in 1990, four of Australia's seven assembly plants still produced volumes less than 40,000 – well below Australia's major competitors. Only the Ford plant at Broadmeadows in Victoria produced an annual volume above 100,000.[61] Therefore, we can conclude that the Button plan was gradually achieving its objective in reducing the number of companies, but if the drive for efficiency were to continue factories would have to be closed.

The thorn in the side of the Button plan was the components sector which was plagued by work stoppages and poor delivery performance. Many car manufacturers had adopted innovative stock control systems such as 'just-in-time' which reduced inventories and led to improved product quality and productivity. However, a brief work stoppage or late delivery in the components sector could close down an entire car manufacturing plant. Partly as a warning to the components sector, Button exempted Nissan Australia from the local content requirement when one of its suppliers could not meet its schedules in January 1988.[62] Product quality of components was another serious problem. In late 1987, the chairman of the Automotive Industry Authority, Bill Scales, claimed that of the 35 components manufacturers which produced 70 per cent by value of the sector's output, ten or eleven were 'nowhere near the required standard'.[63]

The snail-like progress in the components sector led Button to abolish the local content scheme in April 1988 as part of the changes designed to bring more competitive pressure to bear on the industry. Beginning in January 1989, plan producers were able to import 15 per cent of their components duty-free and, export credits aside, additional components could be imported at the prevailing tariff rate for passenger vehicles.[64] Since then, there is evidence that component suppliers have responded to the pressure of the tariff-only regime by rationalising their facilities and phasing out production of their least efficient products. However, in 1990, the car manufacturers were still critical of the overall performance of the components sector, especially in the area of price.[65]

A global survey of the automotive manufacturing industry undertaken by the Massachusetts Institute of Technology (MIT) concluded that the most efficient assembly plants were those with high levels of automation and effective management practices. Not surprisingly, the survey found that Australia ranked poorly in both areas. Assembly plants in Australia were among the least automated in the world, probably because they were relatively low-volume plants and therefore could not justify the expenditure required to increase automation.[66] The MIT study also found that Australian car manufacturing ranked lowest in the world in the three principal areas of effective management: a factory system which emphasised the reduction of waste, a work system based on labour flexibility and, most importantly, a human resources management system which motivated the entire workforce. This was borne out by figures which showed Australian car companies had the highest number of faults per vehicle, invested the lowest number of training hours per new employee, placed little emphasis on employee participation and, in 1987, had the highest labour turnover rates of more than 80 plants surveyed worldwide. The high labour turnover added $850 to the price of locally manufactured vehicles through the costs incurred by recruitment, training and the loss of skills and experience.[67]

Since the MIT study was completed, there has been progress in many of these areas. The quality of Australian-built cars has improved during the life of the plan but, in 1990, the Automotive Industry Authority still measured a considerable gap between the quality of locally produced and imported cars, a gap which the AIA believes could take four years to close.[68] What is particularly alarming is the quality of Ford's highly touted Capri sports car, designed for export to the US market. Although figures indicating average faults per vehicle for the Capri are buried in the statistics for the Ford Laser, Capris which have been sold in Australia have proven to have a high incidence of faults including leaky convertible roofs. In addition, the revelation that metric speedometers were installed in the first shipment of Capris bound for the United States (where imperial measures are used), a discovery which was not made until the Capris had been loaded on board ship, demonstrates an alarming inattentiveness during the manufacturing process.

In 1991, the AIA reported that there had been considerable improvement in the attitude of the plan producers and unions to the implementation of workplace reforms.[69] In particular, it noted that labour turnover had decreased dramatically (although it was hard to disentangle this result from the effects of the recession), that industrial disputes had decreased, and that award restructuring was in progress. The unions were singled out for special praise in their efforts to involve rank and file members more fully in the restructuring process. No doubt the vehicle unions had learned from the experience of the steel plan that without shop-floor support for the car plan, the restructuring process was bound to be impeded by low morale and industrial disputes. To this end, in 1990 the Federation of Vehicle Industry Unions (representing 15 unions across the industry) established a series of nine working parties to study the state of the industry and make recommendations to changes in union policy which would facilitate the development of an internationally competitive industry. The areas considered by the working parties were: industrial relations, work organisation, occupational health and safety, tooling and R&D, quality, labour turnover and retrenchment, industrial democracy, training and technological change.[70]

THE DEBATE OVER FUTURE ASSISTANCE

The debate over post-1992 assistance to the automotive industry sector was characterised by the now familiar tensions between the 'economic rationalists' and those who favoured a more gradual and interventionist approach to industry restructuring through sectoral corporatism. Tensions also emerged between Button and Treasurer Paul Keating in April 1990 over the determination of post-1992 assistance for the car industry. Keating wanted to refer the issue to the Industry Commission, which had been recently transferred to his portfolio, whereas Button favoured a less formal and quicker process of industry consultations. Button's desire to bypass the usual procedure of an IC inquiry provoked Keating into accusing him of attempting to concoct 'private deals' with his 'clients' in the industry.[71] This accusation was unfair; Button's desire to by-pass the lengthy IC inquiry process was based on the urgent need for the plan producers to know future assistance arrangements in order to make long-term investment decisions.[72] Button was supported by the car companies, the unions and even some vehicle importers, and the issue was quickly resolved with a compromise which resulted in an immediate and speedy IC inquiry to recommend future assistance.[73]

Submissions to the Industry Commission inquiry revealed that some companies had adapted better than others to the political realities of the 1990s. GMH and Mitsubishi proposed that tariff reductions should continue downwards to reach approximately 27 per cent by the year 2000. By contrast, Ford recommended that tariffs be phased to 30 per cent by 1997 but also proposed additional restrictions on importers, the overall effect of which would be to increase not reduce protection for the local manufacturers. Naturally, the Industry Commission was incredulous.[74]

Among the most enlightened submissions to the Industry Commission was that made by the Federation of Vehicle Industry Unions. The FVIU proposed tariff reductions to 25 per cent by 1996/97 and urged manufacturers to negotiate partnership agreements with government (similar to those for the information and telecommunications industries) for plans to produce new niche market vehicles with good export prospects such as four-wheel drives or luxury sports cars. Under the FVIU's proposal, manufacturers who did not want to negotiate partnership agreements would progressively lose their 15 per cent by-law entitlements for imported components.[75]

During the course of the Industry Commission inquiry, the industry participants argued that macro-economic factors such as fluctuating exchange rates, high interest rates and inflation levels, and micro-economic inefficiencies in the labour market, telecommunications, and road, rail and sea transport 'dwarfed the impact of assistance arrangements'.[76] Their concern was that further tariff cuts at the sectoral level without accompanying improvements in the macro- and micro-economic settings would eventually ruin the car industry. This view along with claims that the industry needed further assistance to get its house in order, that it deserved exceptional treatment because of its other economic linkages, and that other countries protect their domestic car industries, were all rejected by the Industry Commission.[77]

In its *Draft Report* released in September 1990, the Industry Commission commented favourably on the Button plan, noting that:

> In comparison to previous assistance packages, the Button Plan has had important positive features, although it has continued to make available very high assistance to the automotive industry . . . The basic framework and direction of the plan has been adhered to. For the first time in twenty years there have been ongoing reductions in assistance to the industry. And finally, and perhaps most importantly, the termination of import quotas and the local content scheme has removed the mechanisms which for many years had automatically increased assistance to the industry whenever its competitiveness declined.[78]

Given the achievements of the plan to that point, the IC argued that 'there was no compelling reason why the automotive industry should continue to receive high assistance'. Nevertheless, it recognised that the Garnaut proposal of zero tariffs for the car industry by the year 2000 would 'impose undue adjustment pressures on the industry'.[79] Accordingly, the IC recommended continued phased tariff reductions on imported vehicles to 15 per cent by 1996 with no further reductions until 2000, the removal of the 15 per cent by-law concession on components by 1996, and the retention of the Export Facilitation Scheme except for exports to New Zealand.

The post-1992 assistance arrangements were announced in the March 1991 Industry Statement. The government adopted the IC's recommendation of a 15 per cent endpoint for tariffs on cars and components, but slowed the speed of those reductions so that they would be made over eight years (to the year 2000) rather than the four-year period advised by the IC.[80] In order to maintain the pressure for rationalisation, the Minimum Volume Requirement would remain in place until 1996. The Export Facilitation Scheme (EFS) was retained (except for exports to New Zealand) to the chagrin of economic purists who denounced it as an export subsidy by any other name. The government was willing to shoulder this criticism because the EFS reflected the government's desire to help Australian manufacturers adapt to the globalisation of the industry and lift exports overall. Until recently, Australia had exported a very small proportion of cars, representing only 1.6 per cent of total CBU sales in 1989 and destined mostly for New Zealand.[81] This has changed in the 1990s with all producers making efforts to expand export programs. Most notably, Ford launched its new Capri for export to the United States, Germany and Japan as well as New Zealand, and Mitsubishi decided to make its Adelaide plant the sole producer of station wagons for its global production network.[82]

BUTTON VINDICATED

There is no doubt that the Button plan has been successful in meeting its original objectives. Protection has been lowered significantly; in the fifteen-year period from 1985 to 2000, real tariffs will have been slashed from nearly 100 per cent to 15 per cent. Quality has improved, industry efficiency has increased, and the prices of both locally produced cars and imports have fallen in real terms.[83]

Perhaps the most promising change produced by the Button plan has been the switch in orientation towards exports both of cars and components which have risen to a third of all Australian manufacturing exports in 1991. Heading component exports is the Holden Engine Company's (HEC) export of engines from its Fisherman's Bend plant which in 1990 contributed more than half of the $360 million total. This will increase further as HEC's four-cylinder engines are fitted to Vauxhalls and Opels to be sold throughout Europe. The total value of automotive exports rose dramatically from $370 million in 1986 to nearly $1 billion in 1990,[84] and by an additional 15 per cent to more than $1 billion in 1991. Such trends have been endorsed with enthusiasm by chief executive of the Federal Chamber of Automotive Industries, Ian Grigg: 'what we're seeing now is the payoff from the Button Plan. We've managed to convince our industry to be export aware'.[85] Thus, despite the recession in 1991 and 1992 there are positive signs that Australian car makers are developing an export orientation with special niches in world markets.[86]

A further plus for the plan is that through all the restructuring and job shedding, employment disruptions have been minimised. But there are difficult times ahead and, as tariffs continue to drop, competitive pressure will continue to mount on the industry. Toyota has already axed 500 jobs through a voluntary redundancy program in 1990, and in November 1990 Ford revealed that up to 25 per cent of its workforce would be cut.[87] Further rationalisation and job losses are inevitable.

Finally, the bottom line is profitability and on this measure the results to date have been grim. In 1990 the five plan producers recorded an aggregate loss of $224 million. Although this loss was attributed to overproduction in 1989/90 and the subsequent recession which triggered heavy price discounting, it should be noted that aggregate profitability has been achieved in only two of the first six years of the Button plan.[88] According to the AIA, profitability was unlikely to improve while the industry retained its present structure of four manufacturing groups and seven assembly plants. Nevertheless, until Nissan finally threw in the towel in February 1992 (discussed below), the car makers seemed determined to remain in Australia for reasons of corporate pride, especially among the Japanese who would consider it a loss of face to pull out of manufacturing in Australia.[89] In some cases, the transnationals' Australian operations are part of a long-term strategy to use Australia as a production base for future exports to the Pacific Rim and Southeast Asia. Perhaps the greatest commercial reason behind the transnational car companies' determination to remain in the market has been the export facilitation scheme which allows the Australian subsidiaries to import duty-free components and cars from their parent companies. In 1989, for instance, through exports of aluminium castings and cars manufactured at its Adelaide plant, Mitsubishi earned enough export credits to import duty-free its entire model range apart from the Magna which it produces locally.[90]

There was a remarkable turn around in July 1991, however, when Toyota announced plans for a $430 million greenfield plant at Altona in Melbourne's western suburbs adjacent to its existing engine plant.[91] This new plant will be geared to annual production of at least 100,000 units and use the latest Japanese techniques for production and quality control. It also incorporates an innovative 'partnership deal' to streamline industrial relations. Toyota insisted on work practices that will enable the proposed plant to be globally competitive and provide for a high level of training and multi-skilling in return for high wages and job security. Senator Button had held extensive negotiations with Toyota regarding Australia's ability to provide such conditions, while the details were worked out with a union team headed by ACTU President, Martin Ferguson.[92] The Toyota decision to invest in a giant new production plant is final proof of Button's original corrective approach of weaning car makers from protection using a consultative process and gradual but persistent pressure through reducing tariffs. The Toyota plant will entail a qualitative leap in Australian production technology and work processes.

Further hard evidence that the plan is working was Nissan's announcement on 3 February 1992 that it would close down its car production by October. This came as little surprise because Nissan had slumped from fourth position to become the smallest producer of the five Australian manufacturers with only 10 per cent of the market. The company had lost money for each of the last ten years: despite a large capital investment of $500 million to improve its market share, it had accumulated losses of more than $500 million. Among the causes of its demise as an Australian car maker – Nissan will continue as a smaller components manufacturer making aluminium castings for export to Japan – Nissan executives blamed the government's tariff reduction policy.[93] Button himself was quite sanguine about Nissan's demise: 'I believe we have got a better industry now in spite of what happened at Nissan'.[94]

Most significant of all was the decision of General Motors-Holden and Toyota announced in March 1992 to merge fully their passenger car manufacturing operations in Australia.[95] Such a merger had been on the agenda of both companies since 1984, and was strongly favoured by Button as a means of achieving the Car Plan's goal of having only three Australian car makers. A joint holding company had been set up in 1988, but working out the details of a joint venture agreement that was acceptable to both companies proved to be a lengthy task involving issues of capital investment, asset valuation, integration of manufacturing plant, use of export credits and the disposition of GM's tax liabilities in the wake of its 1987 financial restructuring. The Australian partnership between these two giants is based on the Toyota–GM merger in the United States and is designed to achieve economies of scale in manufacturing, product development and the sharing of export credits to bring in models not produced locally. The commercial vehicle operations of the two companies are not part of the deal, nor is the Holden Engine Company. Nevertheless, the full integration of passenger vehicle production has created an Australian manufacturing giant with assets of about $1.4 billion. With justification, Senator Button welcomed the merger as 'an historic decision' and 'an important step in the restructuring of the Australian car industry'.

Despite the pain of nearly two thousand direct job losses and more to come in related industries, Nissan's demise and the restructuring of GM and Toyota mark an important stage in the quest for a healthier Australian car industry, and the achievement of Button's original goal of having only three car makers in Australia. The prospects are now good for the competitive manufacture of motor vehicles finally to come of age in Australia.

NOTES

1. Peter Stubbs, *The Australian Motor Industry: A Study in Protection and Growth*, Cheshire, Melbourne, 1972, pp. 6–15.
2. The Lyons measures provoked an angry response from the US government which withdrew most-favoured-nation trading status from Australia until the quotas on American chassis were lifted. J. G. Crawford, *Australian Trade Policy, 1942–1966*, Australian National University Press, Canberra, 1968, pp. 393–4.
3. Quoted in Stubbs, *Australian Motor Industry*, p. 19.
4. 'The Motor Vehicle Industry', A study prepared for the Committee to Advise on Policies for Manufacturing Industry, September 1975, p. 408.
5. Australia, House of Representatives, *Debates*, 22 March 1945. Speech by the Minister for Post-war Reconstruction, J. J. Dedman, on the bill to repeal the 1940 legislation which had given ACI the exclusive right to manufacture cars in Australia.
6. Stubbs, *Australian Motor Industry*, pp. 26–7.
7. Figures based on statistics in Tariff Board, *Report on the Automobile Industry*, June 1957, p. 59.
8. Department of Industry, Technology and Commerce, *The Automotive Components Manufacturing Industry in Australia*, Australian Government Publishing Service, Canberra, 1981, p. 7.
9. The origin of the local content plans is obscure. Most analysts see them as a direct outcome of the upsurge in component imports following the abolition of import licensing. However, based on oral evidence from a senior public servant, Stubbs argues that they were developed as early as 1960 in response to a proposal from one of the American multinationals to incorporate its Australian operations into a system of worldwide sourcing. See Stubbs, *Australian Motor Industry*, p. 79.
10. Initially, the scheme was relatively straightforward with three different plans designed for manufacturers and assemblers. Plan A granted by-law concessions (i.e. duty-free entry to components usually subject to a 35 per cent tariff rate) to high-volume producers such as Ford and GMH who undertook to increase the local content of specific models to 95 per cent over five years. Plan B1 gave by-law concessions on components to low-volume producers who undertook to manufacture

vehicles with 55 per cent local content while Plan B2 offered the least assistance to assemblers of CKD (completely knocked down) imports. Statement by Minister for Trade and Industry, John McEwen and Minister for Customs and Excise, Senator Henty, press statement 460, 1 May 1964, reprinted in 'The Motor Vehicle Industry'.

11. By 1971, any model manufactured or assembled in Australia could be entered into one of five plans ranging from 45 to 95 per cent local content.
12. John Warhurst, *Jobs or Dogma: The Industries Assistance Commission and Australian Politics*, University of Queensland Press, St Lucia,1982, p. 184.
13. IAC, *Passenger Motor Vehicles, Etc.*, 10 July 1974, Australian Government Publishing Service, Canberra, 1974, Appendix 4.
14. Cairns quoted in L. Glezer, *Tariff Politics: Australian Policy-making, 1960–1980*, Melbourne University Press, Melbourne, 1982, p. 162. For a full discussion of the bureaucratic wranglings and political deliberations, see Warhurst, *Jobs or Dogma*, Ch. 10.
15. IAC, *Passenger Motor Vehicles, Etc.*, 1974, Appendix 1.
16. ibid., pp. 158–72.
17. Glezer, *Tariff Politics*, pp. 163–4.
18. Plan participants which did not fulfil the 85 per cent local content requirement paid a 25 per cent tariff on imported components plus a penalty rate determined at the industry minister's discretion.
19. Glezer, *Tariff Politics*, p. 166 and Warhurst, *Jobs or Dogma*, pp. 206–8.
20. Whitlam, Press Statement 366, 14 November 1974, quoted in 'The Motor Vehicle Industry'.
21. The Study Group on Structural Adjustment, Crawford Report, 1979, Ch. 11, p. 18.
22. Minister for Industry and Commerce, Sir Phillip Lynch, quoted on 18 July 1980 in *Commonwealth Record*, Vol. 5, No. 28, p. 1049.
23. Statement by Deputy Prime Minister and Treasurer, Dr J. F. Cairns, 28 January 1975 reprinted in 'The Motor Vehicle Industry', pp. 485–6.
24. The White Paper, 1977, p. 25.
25. Crawford Report, Ch. 11, p. 20.
26. For a critique of the world car strategy, see David Friedman, 'Beyond the age of Ford: the strategic basis of the Japanese success in automobiles', in *American Industry in International Competition: Government Policies and Corporate Strategies*, eds John Zysman & Laura Tyson, Cornell University Press, Ithaca, 1983, pp. 350–90.
27. *National Times*, 27 December 1981.
28. Statement by Lynch and Business and Consumer Affairs Minister, John Moore, 13 January 1981 in *Commonwealth Record*, Vol. 6, No. 2, pp. 26–7.
29. IAC, *Passenger Motor Vehicles and Components – Post-1984 Assistance Arrangements*, Report 267, 24 June 1981, Australian Government Publishing Service, Canberra, 1981.
30. Report of the Car Industry Council, 14 December 1983, pp. 4–5.

31. Statement by Lynch, 21 December 1981 in *Commonwealth Record,* Vol. 6, No. 49, pp. 1701–3.
32. *National Times,* 27 December 1981.
33. The changes to the Export Facilitation Scheme provoked a backlash from the Federation of Automotive Parts Manufacturers (FAPM) which claimed that if the ceiling on the scheme was raised to 15 per cent, their annual sales would be cut by over 50 per cent and thousands of jobs would be lost. On the other hand, GMH's managing director, Charles Chapman, declared that if the ceiling remained pegged at 7.5 per cent, his company would be 'dead'. The rest of the industry was divided, with Mitsubishi, Toyota and the unions supporting the FAPM, Nissan desiring a 10 per cent ceiling and Ford willing to live with the 15 per cent scheme. *Sydney Morning Herald,* 1 August 1983.
34. The AMC and its sectoral councils had not yet been established.
35. Statement by Button, 6 October 1983 in *Commonwealth Record,* Vol. 8, No. 40, pp. 1677–8.
36. Statement by Button, 20 May 1983 in *Commonwealth Record,* Vol. 8, No. 20, p. 652.
37. 1983 Car Council Report, 14 December 1983, pp. 29–30.
38. ibid., p. 36.
39. ibid., pp. 29–30.
40. Interview with Button, 27 July 1991.
41. AIA, *Report on the State of the Automotive Industry, 1990,* Australian Government Publishing Service, Canberra, 1991, p. 8.
42. Department of Industry and Commerce, Motor Vehicle Policy Statement, News Release 37/84, 29 May 1984.
43. In order to provide some immediate stability in the car market, the tariff rate on light commercial vehicles and four-wheel drives was lifted to 57.5 per cent in line with the tariff on other types of passenger motor vehicles.
44. The AIA expressed reservations about the effectiveness of the LATA scheme which paid an additional benefit above unemployment benefits to those who undertook full-time vocational courses to upgrade their skills. In the period from May 1984 to June 1986, 2,415 workers retrenched from the car industry were eligible for the scheme; however, only 426 of them actually commenced job retraining. AIA, *Report on the State of the Automotive Industry 1987,* Australian Government Publishing Service, Canberra, 1988, pp. 38–9.
45. *Sydney Morning Herald,* 30 May 1984; *Australian,* 30 May 1984.
46. 1983 Car Council Report, p. 37.
47. Gary Sampson & Graeme Woodbridge, 'An analysis of the post-1984 arrangements for motor vehicles', *Economic Papers,* Vol. 3, No. 4, p. 57; Industry Commission, *Draft Report on the Automotive Industry,* September 1990, p. 83.
48. Bureau of Industry Economics, 'Prospects for the Australian Passenger Motor Vehicle Industry under the Government's Post-1984 Assistance Plan', November 1985.

49. In 1989 and 1990, imports accounted for 29.8 and 33.7 per cent respectively of the small car market. By contrast, Australian-built products dominated the medium and large car market. AIA, *State of the Industry 1990*, p. 18.
50. For a fine discussion of why US manufacturers cling to Fordism see Friedman, 'Beyond the age of Ford'.
51. *Award Restructuring in the Australian Vehicle Manufacturing Industry*, Report of the Tripartite Study Mission to Japan, United States of America, Federal Republic of Germany and Sweden, September/October 1988, Australian Government Publishing Service, Canberra, 1989.
52. AIA, *State of the Automotive Industry 1989*, Australian Government Publishing Service, Canberra, 1990, p. 15.
53. AIA, *State of the Automotive Industry 1986*, Australian Government Publishing Service, Canberra, 1987, p. 3.
54. Minister for Industry, Technology and Commerce, News Release, 13 April 1988.
55. AIA, *State of the Automotive Industry 1989*, pp. 15–16.
56. AIA, *State of the Automotive Industry 1986*, p. 44.
57. AIA, *State of the Automotive Industry 1989*, p. 21.
58. IAC, *Annual Report*, 1986–87, pp. 105–6.
59. AIA, *State of the Automotive Industry 1990*, p. 49.
60. AIA, *State of the Automotive Industry 1988*, Australian Government Publishing Service, Canberra, 1989, p. 55.
61. AIA, *State of the Automotive Industry 1990*, p. 50.
62. AIA, *State of the Automotive Industry 1987*, pp. 65–6 and the *Australian*, 20 January 1988.
63. *Australian Financial Review*, 24 November 1987.
64. Minister for Industry, Technology and Commerce, Press Release, 13 April 1988.
65. AIA, *State of the Automotive Industry 1990*, p. 57.
66. AIA, *State of the Automotive Industry 1989*, pp. 35–36.
67. ibid, pp. 29–32 and 76–7; Automotive Industry Council, *Labour Turnover and Absenteeism: Costs and Causes in the Australian Automotive Industry*, Australian Manufacturing Council, Melbourne, 1990.
68. AIA, *State of the Automotive Industry 1990*, pp. 38–9.
69. ibid., p. 68.
70. The Final Consolidated Report of the Federation of Vehicle Industry Unions, 9 Working Parties, February 1991.
71. Echoing the Treasurer's sentiments, the *Australian* suggested that Button had fallen prey to the Stockholm Syndrome in which hostages become sympathetic to their captors' aims. *Australian*, 15 August 1990.
72. *Australian Financial Review*, 24 April 1990.
73. Button's remarks were publicly supported by Nissan managing director, Ivan Deveson; Ford managing director, Jac Nasser; the Vehicle

Builders Employees' Federation; and the managing director of BMW's import operation. *Australian Financial Review*, 11 May, 15 May, 22 June and 14 August 1990.

74. Behind Ford's demands were veiled threats made during the March 1990 federal election campaign when Ford's new general manager, Jac Nasser, intimated that Ford would cease manufacturing in Australia if tariff levels did not remain high. In late 1989, however, Nasser's predecessor, Bill Dix, had stated that Ford could live with a 25 per cent tariff in the 1990s. See Ford Motor Company of Australia Ltd, Submission 64 to the Industry Commission Inquiry, 23 August 1990; Industry Commission, *Draft Report on the Automotive Industry*, September 1990, pp. 85–6; *Sunday Herald*, 19 March 1990 and *Australian Financial Review*, 14 August and 3 October 1990.
75. Federation of Vehicle Industry Unions, Submission 52 to the Industry Commission Inquiry, 17 August 1990.
76. Industry Commission, *1990 Draft Report*, p. 3.
77. ibid., pp. 62–5.
78. ibid., pp. 122–3.
79. ibid., p. xiv.
80. Statement by Senator John N. Button, *Building a Competitive Australia* (March Industry Statement), 12 March 1991, Australian Government Publishing Service, Canberra, 1991.
81. AIA, *State of the Automotive Industry 1989*, p. 53.
82. Angus MacKenzie, 'Automotive exports racing ahead', *Australian Business*, 3 July 1991, pp. 30–1; and Federated Chamber of Automotive Industries, Press Release, Canberra, June 1991.
83. AIA, *State of the Automotive Industry 1990*, p. 28.
84. March Industry Statement, section 3, p. 5.
85. Quoted in Mackenzie, 'Automotive exports racing ahead', p. 30.
86. Michael Lynch, 'Car industry's export drive gets up speed', *Australian Financial Review*, 8 January 1992.
87. *Australian Financial Review*, 5 November 1990.
88. AIA, *State of the Industry 1990*, p. 34.
89. Walter Uhlenbruch, *Australian Motor Vehicles and Parts: A Study of an Industry Shaped by Government*, Committee for Economic Development of Australia, Melbourne, 1987.
90. Michael Lynch, 'The power behind motoring quintet', *Australian Financial Review*, 8 June 1990.
91. *Age*, 27 July 1991, and anticipating report *Australian Financial Review*, 24 July 1991.
92. Button interview, 29 July 1991.
93. *Australian Financial Review*, 4 February 1992.
94. Quoted in *Australian Financial Review*, 5 February 1992.
95. Details and subsequent quote are from Michael Lynch, 'GM–Toyota give birth to local giant', *Australian Financial Review*, 18 March 1992.

CHAPTER 7

The Textiles, Clothing and Footwear Industries

> They passed with the tall, cold boss, talking in high, affected voices. The women by their machines looked after them with great distaste. Nothing illustrated so well the great gulf that lay between two classes. Here they were, dirty, sweaty, chained to a cantankerous machine, gazed at as if they were creatures from another planet. Then, when the whistle blew, they'd rush to the washroom, try and scrub off the grease with cold water in the cracked hand basins, comb their hair, put their lipstick on, and rush home to children and husbands, tea to be cooked, kids to be bathed.
>
> Dorothy Hewett, Bobbin Up (1959).

PROFILE OF THE TCF SECTOR

Ever since the advent of textiles, clothing and footwear (TCF) industries in Australia in the mid-nineteenth century, the sector has been an important source of employment. In 1988, TCF companies employed approximately 115,000 factory workers, over 10 per cent of the manufacturing workforce. Over two-thirds of these workers were engaged in clothing and footwear production as pattern cutters, sewing machinists or in knitting mills. The remainder worked in textile production, from raw material processing such as cotton ginning and wool topmaking to dye-matching, weaving, fabric printing and rope-making.[1] These employment figures do not include outworkers, mostly unskilled migrant women who do piece-work in their homes, working long hours for very low pay. The Clothing and Allied Trades Union (CATU) estimates that there are up to 60,000 outworkers but these numbers are very hard to verify. Language difficulties, employer threats and, in the case of illegal immigrants, fear of being exposed and deported have all ensured that the outworkers remain largely an underground economy. As a result, although outworkers have been covered by an industrial award since late 1987, few have come forward to claim better wages and conditions.[2]

Traditionally, the textile, clothing and footwear workforce has been dominated by low-paid female work. This is partly because the unskilled nature of the work has allowed women, whose working patterns were determined largely by family and economic circumstance, to move easily in and out of the factory workforce. In 1988, 40 per cent of textile workers and 76 per cent of the clothing and footwear factory workforce were women.[3] TCF production has always been labour intensive and, in order to maintain profitability, factory owners have needed to keep wages low. Even today, TCF workers are among the most poorly paid in the manufacturing workforce. Average weekly gross earnings for male TCF workers in 1989 were $399, almost $50 less than the average for all manufacturing employees. Women in the TCF industries fare even worse. In May 1989, their average weekly earnings were $330 which puts them at the bottom of the industrial wage scale.[4]

The TCF sector is highly fragmented, comprising a few very large corporations and many more small family-owned businesses. The industry has been dominated by a number of large conglomerates including Pacific Dunlop, the Brenmoss Group, JGL Investments, Sportscraft, General Investments Australia, Textiles Industries of Australia and the troubled Linter Group which was broken up in January 1990.[5] Three of the TCF empires - Pacific Dunlop, Brenmoss and Bonds - have completely integrated lines from spinning through to clothing production. Others, such as Sportscraft, also have retail divisions. In addition to these major players, there are hundreds of small single-establishment enterprises. Throughout the 1980s there were on average over 2,500 separate factories; in 1988, that number had reached 3,063.[6]

The diffuse nature of the industry is reflected in the plethora of industry associations and groups which represent and lobby on behalf of the TCF interests. Generally, industry associations which represent the interests of a specific sector, such as the Carpet Institute of Australia, have a relatively high degree of internal cohesion and consensus. Similar interest-specific associations have included the associations for Footwear Manufacturers, Garment Manufacturers, Non-leather Footwear Manufacturers, Quilted Products Manufacturers, Wool Textile Manufacturers and Vinyl Garment Manufacturers. Manufacturers were also represented by broader industry councils such as the Confederation of Apparel Manufacturers, the Knitting Industries Council, the Fashion Industries of Australia, and the Textile Council of Australia. By virtue of their long experience in representing an industry in decline, these councils were highly effective lobbyists whose reputations as powerful pressure groups were increasingly enhanced as successive governments raised the barriers to imports. However, in view of the Hawke government's determination to reduce protection to manufacturing industry, in 1984 these four organisations were amalgamated into a peak industry association, the Textiles, Clothing and Footwear Council of Australia (TCFCA) which could present a strong and united front to the forthcoming Industries Assistance Commission inquiry into the TCF industries.

The Textiles, Clothing and Footwear Council of Australia has over 600 members representing designers, retailers, and manufacturers.[7] By contrast, there are also TCF industry associations which conflict with the manufacturers and unions. Groups such as the Apparel Importers Association, the Australian Retailers Association (now defunct) and the National Footwear Retailers Association have been keen to see tariff barriers dropped. The economic importance of this TCF service sector, already considerable, is growing. By the mid-1980s, the value added by TCF distribution (wholesaling, retailing, and importing) was greater than the value added by TCF manufacturing. The same was true in terms of employment figures.[8] Moreover, their case for tariff reductions has been strengthened by the Hawke government's commitment to the GATT Uruguay Round of multilateral trade negotiations and, in particular, by Australia's leadership of the Cairns Group which seeks fair trade in agriculture.

The TCF unions, the Amalgamated Footwear and Textile Workers Union of Australia (AFTWUA) and the Clothing and Allied Trades Union (CATU), do not fall easily into either the protectionist or free-trader camp. Although the unions' leadership is largely sympathetic to the Labor government's socio-economic aims, the immediate economic interest of TCF workers is bound up with their employers. Thus, in order to preserve their jobs, TCF unionists have tended to side with TCF capital in demanding import protection and production subsidies.

PROTECTION FOR THE TCF INDUSTRIES

In the past seventy years, over 500 government reports have been issued on the question of assistance to Australia's textiles, clothing and footwear industries.[9] Until the 1970s these reports invariably recommended increasing levels and varieties of assistance, culminating in the introduction of global quotas on most TCF imports in 1975. As a result, the TCF industries became one of the most highly protected sectors of the manufacturing economy. The cost of such protection was enormous: in 1986 the Finance Department estimated that protective arrangements for the TCF industries were equivalent to a 40 per cent consumption tax on clothing and were costing every household in Australia between $10 and $13 per week.[10]

From federation in 1901 until the end of the Second World War, the TCF industries were protected primarily by tariffs. After the war, import licensing arrangements, implemented in order to ease the foreign exchange crisis, effectively increased protection for Australian manufacturers. In 1960, import licensing was abolished and the tariff re-emerged as the key protective device for local industry. Manufacturers initially feared the consequences of ending import licensing but their concerns were at least partly allayed when the trade and industry minister, John McEwen, himself an ardent protectionist, ensured that the TCF sector continued to flourish through a combination of temporary assistance measures and increasing tariff levels. As a result of these policies, between 1968 and 1974 the average effective rate of assistance for the clothing and footwear industries was more than twice that for the manufacturing sector as whole.[11]

Despite these high levels of assistance, in the early 1970s the local market share for Australian TCF products began to be significantly eroded by imports. This was due in part to the improving price competitiveness of TCF exports from the low-wage Asian nations, although changing domestic conditions also played a considerable part in hastening the decline of the domestic industry. The revaluation of the Australian dollar followed by a 25 per cent across-the-board tariff cut in July 1973, significant wage increases for female workers as a result of Whitlam's equal pay legislation, and the removal of quotas on imported knitwear and woven shirts all served to unravel the cocoon of protection for the TCF industries.[12]

The first obvious consequence of these changing economic conditions was a sharp decline in employment in the Australian textile and clothing industry. In the textile sector alone, almost 9,000 jobs were shed in the twelve months preceding September 1975.[13] In the year from March 1974 to March 1975, employment in the TCF manufacturing sector overall fell by almost 25 per cent, or 34,000 jobs.[14] No government could ignore the extent of such job losses. A high proportion of the workers were women, many of whom were married and had restricted geographic mobility. Furthermore, many TCF workers were migrants who encountered difficulties in finding employment in positions which required a high degree of English language competence. On the whole, TCF workers were relatively unskilled and unschooled, which was a further limit to their employment mobility. Finally, the TCF industries were regionally concentrated; for instance, they accounted for 45 per cent of the workforce in Warrnambool and 70 per cent in Wangaratta.[15] This regional concentration and relative lack of mobility among TCF workers meant that job losses would have a considerable economic and social impact.

In addition to the social and economic consequences of declining production and job losses, there were potential political costs. The regional concentration of the TCF industries, together with the fact that many of these were located in marginal seats, meant that a TCF policy could make or break a government. Thus, Labor and Liberal governments alike were anxious to cushion the sector in order to prevent job losses and thus minimise political liabilities.[16] In 1974, in response to the sharp increase in TCF imports, the Whitlam government negotiated voluntary restraints with major textile exporting nations under the Multi-Fibre Arrangement (MFA), a derogation of the GATT, which established guidelines for bilateral agreements to restrict trade in textiles and apparel. But, unlike the North American and European nations, Australia lacked the size and political clout to negotiate effective restraint agreements which, in any case, proved to be antagonistic to Australia's trade relations with many Asian countries.[17] As a result, in early 1975, the voluntary restraint agreements were replaced with a system of tariff quotas which restricted imports by quota holders at the normal rates of duty and allowed imports above quota subject to an additional penalty duty rate.

In addition to increased protection for the TCF industries, the Whitlam government also introduced two programs to ease the hardship caused by his government's 25 per cent tariff cut. The schemes for Structural Adjustment Assistance and Special Assistance to Non-Metropolitan Areas provided compensation, subsidies and employment maintenance to assist employees, firms and regions affected by the cuts. An indication of the extent of the TCF sector's troubles was that half the payments made by these schemes went to those involved in TCF industries.[18]

A SECTOR IN DECLINE: THE POLITICS OF SURVIVAL

As early as the 1950s, the TCF sectors in industrialised nations were beginning to feel the pressure of import competition, first from Japan and later from developing nations such as Taiwan and South Korea. Unable to lower labour costs to match those in the developing countries, governments in Australasia, North America, Scandinavia, the United Kingdom and Western Europe were forced to take political action to protect and, in some cases, restructure their TCF industries. With few exceptions, however, incentives to restructure were underpinned (and undermined) by new arrangements such as industry subsidies and voluntary export restraint agreements with supplier nations.[19]

The nature of assistance given to declining TCF sectors in developed nations mirrors that given to the steel and automotive industries. Thus, governments in the United States and United Kingdom responded to the crisis in their domestic TCF industries through defensive policies to protect the status quo while Japan and Canada tried to effect policies of positive adjustment to contract the sector. However, in all four cases the policies had little success in returning these industries to profitability, a fact which underlies the problematic nature of the TCF sector.

Typically, the US government moved to protect its declining TCF sector rather than facilitate the orderly contraction of production and employment. There is a long history of protection of the American TCF sector beginning in 1937 when textile imports from Japan were first limited by an export restraint agreement. Since then a fibre-textile-apparel coalition led by the cotton textile industry with considerable support from the unions has been instrumental in winning congressional support for significant increases in protection for the US textile and clothing industries. Despite the government's effort to maintain employment and prevent the closure of mills, some structural adjustment has occurred as the textile industry has become more concentrated in order to realise economies of scale. Footwear manufacturers, who have less political salience and clout, have been far less successful in gaining government support for increased protection.[20]

In the United Kingdom, successive governments have also adopted defensive policies to prevent job losses in the textile and clothing industry. Since the end of the Second World War, domestic production has been protected by tariff and non-tariff barriers against imports which are blamed for market erosion. These restrictions culminated in the government's decision to become a signatory to the Multi-Fibre Arrangement (MFA) in 1974. Unlike the United States, the British government has also intervened selectively to encourage rationalisation in the textile sector. Such intervention, however, has had little impact and was undermined by subsequent programs to prevent redundancies, especially in depressed regions where years before the government had actively sought investment in the textile industry.[21]

In Canada, government policy towards the TCF industries has been a mixture of defensive assistance and positive adjustment strategies. On one hand, the Trudeau government recognised the need for structural adjustment in the TCF industries and to that end adopted sectoral policies for textiles in 1971 and footwear and tanning in 1974. Underpinning such policies were a number of programs to encourage these industries to become internationally competitive and export-oriented. In addition, labour adjustment schemes which offered compensation through early retirement programs or, alternatively, skills retraining and relocation assistance were implemented. In 1981, the various *ad hoc* schemes which provided assistance for restructuring were scrapped and replaced with the Canadian Industrial Renewal Board, a single 'one-stop shop' that provided assistance to textile and clothing firms wanting to modernise and restructure.[22]

Political considerations have also been a key element in determining the federal government's TCF policy and have resulted in protectionist measures which stand in stark contradiction to the sectoral policies designed to restructure the industry. Ontario and Quebec together accounted for 90 per cent of employment in textile and clothing industries in 1976; Quebec alone accounted for 59 per cent of such employment, and, in electoral terms, 71 out of 75 federal ridings in Quebec were home to textile and/or clothing factories.[23] It is an axiom of Canadian politics that no party can win government without Quebec; thus, the federal government's desire to avoid provoking separatist sentiments has also figured in its protective policies towards the TCF sector. Much of the incentive for industries to restructure has therefore been undermined by the use of tariff and non-tariff barriers similar to those in the United States and Great Britain. In 1974, Canada, like the United States, the United Kingdom and Australia, joined the Multi-Fibre Arrangement and has been a signatory to successive MFAs through the 1980s.

Even the Japanese government, which is renowned for its state-directed policies to achieve the rationalisation and contraction of declining sectors, has not been immune from the political imperative to limit adjustment in the textile sector. The textile industry, Japan's oldest industry, is dominated by thousands of small firms generally owned by farmers who form the backbone of the ruling Liberal Democratic Party. In 1973, when Japan become a net importer of textiles, the government attempted to direct restructuring by the vertical integration of small firms to increase the value-added of their products. The policy instruments used to encourage this were low-interest loans, tax incentives with an accelerated depreciation scheme, and employment subsidies to companies which hired workers who had been retrenched as a result of vertical integration. The success of these programs has been limited and profitability in the textile sector remains lower than in other manufacturing industries. One reason for this may be special fiscal measures which prevent the bankruptcy of small textile firms during recessions.[24]

AUSTRALIAN TCF POLICY UNDER FRASER

The Fraser government's policy towards the TCF sector can be typified as defensive, similar to that of the US and British governments in the 1970s. In Australia, the imposition of tariff quotas on many TCF imports in 1975 had been insufficient to halt the flood of imports and the decline of the local industries. Thus, in 1977 the Fraser government imposed global quotas on a broad range of TCF imports while it considered how to deal with the industries in the medium term. Unlike tariff quotas, global import quotas set an absolute limit on the quantity of goods that a quota holder can import in a given period. Such assistance ran counter to the Industries Assistance Commission policy which aimed to reduce protection across the economy, especially for highly protected, uneconomic industries. In a draft report on the TCF industries in August 1977, the IAC concluded that, as a consequence of past assistance policies, the Australian TCF industries had 'developed as inward-looking, tariff dependent and fragmented industries which are ill-equipped to accommodate the major domestic and international changes that have occurred in recent years and seem likely to continue in the future'.[25] In the IAC's opinion, neither employment considerations nor regional benefit was a sufficient trade-off for the costs of TCF protection to the community as a whole and it recommended the phasing out of all quotas and the reduction of assistance to the average rate for all manufacturing.

Prime Minister Malcolm Fraser rejected the IAC's recommendations. His government was politically committed to an industrial policy which would maintain jobs and investor confidence. This was to be achieved in part through the development and application of sectoral policies designed to preserve a smaller, more efficient industry within declining sectors such as textiles, clothing and footwear, whitegoods and passenger motor vehicles.[26] In November 1977, as part of this overall strategy, the Fraser government announced a three-year assistance program to stabilise production and employment in the TCF sector. Global import quotas and bounties for yarn production were extended and tariff levels were adjusted, usually upward. In July 1979 the scheme was extended for another year while the government considered future assistance arrangements to take the TCF industries into the 1980s.

Measured against the government's objectives, the 1977 stabilisation plan was an unqualified success. Tariff and quota protection had ensured a stable investment environment, encouraged some rationalisation and maintained employment. The IAC, however, was not satisfied with the scope or speed of rationalisation in the TCF sector and, in a 1980 report, repeated its previous recommendation to drop tariff levels and phase out quotas.[27]

The TCF manufacturers lobbied strongly against the IAC report. With years of experience in defending a heavily protected sector, the TCF industry associations worked together as a highly organised and skilful pressure group. Rather than self-interested wailing about declining profits, sell-outs and business foreclosures, they spoke of the impact of thousands of job losses.[28] This was calculated to appeal to public sympathy and political vulnerability. Various TCF industry councils and federations also waged an intense private campaign at Parliament House which included circulating a detailed breakdown by electorate of the number of people who would be adversely affected by tariff reductions.[29]

The lobbying paid off and once again the Fraser government

rejected the IAC's recommendations to cut protection. However, in considering a plan for future assistance to the TCF industries, the cabinet did recognise the need for greater and faster structural adjustment in the sector. Accordingly, the new seven-year plan devised by industry minister, Phillip Lynch, was designed so that the benefits of growth in the local market would go to importers. It was hoped that this pressure would serve as 'a stimulus to local industry to concentrate its activities on the more efficient areas of local production'.[30]

Although the Lynch plan was designed to encourage structural adjustment within the TCF sector, the plan was more carrot than stick. Global quotas were retained on most apparel and footwear; certain fabric and textile products were protected by tariff quotas; yarn production and fabric printing were supported by bounties; a government subsidy was paid as a percentage of production costs; and complex policy by-laws allowed duty-free entry for some fabrics.[31] One of the paradoxes of assistance under the Lynch plan was that quotas were based on volume rather than value. This gave importers an incentive to bring in expensive goods at the top end of the market, leaving Australian manufacturers to focus their production in cheap, standardised products, areas in which they were least competitive by world standards.[32] The plan certainly achieved its objective in attracting new investment in plant and equipment[33] but investment and productivity in the TCF sector rose far more slowly than that in the manufacturing sector overall.[34]

NO MORE MAGIC PUDDING: THE 1986 IAC REPORT

In October 1984, the Hawke Labor government's industry minister, Senator John Button, referred the textiles, clothing and footwear industries to the IAC which was to recommend new assistance arrangements to take effect after the Lynch plan expired in December 1988. While the Hawke government was clear in its intention to reduce protection of the TCF industries, the terms of reference implied that the government would not welcome any proposal for tariff reductions tailored purely on textbook economics; the IAC's recommendations would have to reflect the government's desire to minimise the human hardship caused by tariff reductions and industry restructuring.[35] Under the Lynch plan, TCF factory jobs had been lost at an alarming rate: between November 1978 and

November 1985, total employment across the economy had risen by 14 per cent whereas employment in the TCF industries had fallen by 13 per cent.[36] Clearly, a Labor government could not afford to promote continuing heavy job losses without some form of compensation.

Since the 1970s, the IAC had come under increasing attack for its hardline attitude to tariff reductions. This time, in an effort to produce a politically palatable report, the Commission proposed several scenarios for future assistance to the TCF industries. Broadly speaking, the various options would result in the reduction of protection to maximum tariff rates of 75 per cent, 50 per cent or 25 per cent. While supporting the retention of yarn bounties, the IAC argued against any labour adjustment or industry assistance to temper the restructuring process.

Industry reaction to these proposals revealed the extent of the manufacturers' dependence on barrier protection. The Textiles, Clothing and Footwear Council (TCFCA) told the IAC that even if the *existing* assistance arrangements were continued, market shares for the local production of knitted garments, hosiery, cardigans and pullovers, trousers and jeans, footwear, leather tanning and fur dressing would continue to decline. The implication of these claims was that if present market shares were to be maintained, protection would have to be increased. In the TCFCA's opinion, a 75 per cent tariff was the absolute 'minimum sustainable by industry'.[37]

The defensive nature of their position was echoed in the submissions advising measures to help industry and the labour force adjust to lower protection levels. The vague and generalised nature of these proposals stood in stark contrast to the highly detailed submissions concerning protection levels. The IAC noted with perceptible annoyance that their proposals were typically self-seeking: 'labour-intensive firms sought labour subsidies; capital-intensive firms sought capital subsidies; potential exporters sought export subsidies; potential importers sought import subsidies'.[38] This was not a complete surprise given that the TCF industries had never before been asked to consider positive, rather than defensive, forms of assistance, but it also suggested that the TCF industries did not believe that the government had the political will to kick out the crutch of protection. Their disbelief was justified by past experience; even the tariff-cutting Whitlam government had granted special treatment to them.

In its final report, tabled in May 1986, the IAC outlined four possible proposals to achieve tariff reductions. Its preferred option was a program to phase out tariff-quota assistance by reducing a common out-of-quota rate from 134 per cent to 50 per cent evenly over seven years. By January 1996 the result would be the end of quota assistance and a maximum tariff of 50 per cent. The second option would have reduced protection more quickly and dramatically by dropping the maximum tariff to 25 per cent by 1996 from an an initial out-of-quota rate of 110 per cent. The third option, essentially a variation of the 'preferred option', would have reduced the maximum tariff to 25 per cent from a common out-of-quota rate of 134 per cent. The fourth option, which the IAC rejected out of hand, would have reduced tariff assistance to 75 per cent by 1996. The IAC preferred the 50 per cent option because, in its opinion, it would strike an appropriate political balance between limiting the hardships of adjustment and improving the efficiency and competitiveness of the TCF industries. However, the IAC rejected any notion of subsidies, positive adjustment assistance measures or a watchdog advisory committee to monitor the effects of tariff reductions. Instead, the Commission preferred to allow the free market to exact its toll and suggested that this would go a long way in signalling that Canberra was no longer 'the Magic Pudding'.[39]

By the TCFCA's previous estimations, the IAC's preferred option would destroy the TCF industry in Australia and, naturally, there was an immediate backlash against the recommendations. TCFCA president, George Innes, deplored the IAC's 'incredible misunderstanding of the difficulties and realities faced by labour-intensive industries in meeting import competition from low-wage countries'.[40] Many of the major manufacturers threatened to move offshore if the tariff cuts were effected. Coats Patons yarn-spinners threatened to close seven of its eleven plants if tariffs were reduced to 50 per cent. Joseph Brender, owner of one of Australia's biggest textile empires, said that if the 50 per cent option was adopted he would close down his Wangaratta textile mills leaving 800 jobless.[41] There were a few manufacturers who welcomed the IAC's recommendations but such companies were a tiny minority.[42]

The manufacturers' protests were echoed by the unions whose membership levels had been falling since the inception of the Lynch plan. The Tasmanian state secretary of the AFTWUA, Des Capstick, said that none of the IAC's options was acceptable.[43] The president-elect of the Victorian branch of the AFTWUA, Nick Paola, voiced an opinion shared by many that high protection for TCF industries in other countries such as the United States justified high protection in Australia.[44]

Invariably any structural adjustment which occurred as a result of tariff reductions was bound to result in the contraction of production, plant closures and job losses. Predicting job losses, however, was a moot point. The IAC suggested that 19,000 manufacturing jobs would be lost under the preferred option but stressed that these would be offset by new employment opportunities in retailing. The TCFCA and the unions, which took a rather dim view of the IAC's calculations and its optimism about new jobs, suggested that the number of jobs at stake was closer to 60,000.[45] For state governments in Tasmania and Victoria, the exact figures were irrelevant but the political implications were enormous. In Tasmania, tariff reductions threatened not only jobs but entire towns; Devonport, for instance, depended wholly on the textile industry. In Hobart, state government minister, Ray Groom, claimed that even the IAC's 'soft option' of a 75 per cent tariff would cause Devonport's collapse.[46] Although the Victorian economy was larger and more diversified, it too would suffer greatly from any contraction in TCF production. Victoria alone accounted for 55 per cent of all TCF employment. Half of that, or about 50,000 jobs, were in Melbourne; elsewhere, in towns such as Geelong, Warrnambool and Wangaratta, TCF factories were major employers. The Victorian government joined the backlash against the IAC recommendations and state industry minister, Robert Fordham, criticised the IAC for failing to address the social and economic impact of plant closures and job losses as a result of tariff reductions.[47]

Senator Button was sympathetic to the grievances of the manufacturers, unions and state governments. He too was unhappy with many aspects of the IAC report, particularly its failure to recommend positive incentives to encourage restructuring. Button believed that short-term assistance for industrial and labour adjustment was vital, especially because the TCF tariff reductions, unlike those made in the steel and passenger vehicle sector, would inevitably result in thousands of retrenchments.[48] Despite the deficiencies in the IAC report, however, there was no question that industry reforms would go ahead. The government's industry policy was committed to fostering the development of internationally competitive, export-oriented, innovative industries which could survive and prosper without protection and other forms of assistance. Tariffs would be reduced: the questions were how fast? by how much? and with what assistance measures?

THE TCF PLAN: NEGOTIATIONS AND ESTABLISHMENT

In their work on sectoral policy networks, Atkinson and Coleman have argued that corporatist networks frequently develop in sectors 'faced with the problem of stemming serious decline'. They argue that typically the state's involvement in the sector has been fragmented, with a host of different agencies dealing with various aspects of the sector including industry regulation, protection measures, trade promotion and employee training. By contrast, the industry, long experienced in aggressively defending its interests, has a highly sophisticated associational system which can deal effectively with other groups, particularly labour. Thus, 'the state, lacking the organisational capacity to resolve the social conflicts and the hardships involved in decline, delegates to organised interests the problem of formulating a long-term policy solution to these problems'. As an example of this, they cite the Swedish shipyard case in which industry associations, labour organisations and financial firms cooperated to create a new industrial strategy funded by the state.[49]

The negotiations leading up to the textiles, clothing and footwear plan and the administration of the plan itself provide an Australian approximation to the emergence of a corporatist network in a troubled industry sector. On one hand, there was a host of state agencies dealing with the TCF sector, with the added complications and fracturing of the federal system which leads to multiple agencies pursuing multiple goals at two levels of government. On the other hand, the peak industry association, the TCFCA, incorporated in 1984 with the express purpose of lobbying to defend its interests, had a long history of defending the TCF industries' interests, usually with the active support of the unions.

However, the TCF plan diverges from the case of the Swedish shipyard because, initially, the Australian TCF industry was not a willing and enthusiastic party to industrial restructuring. The industry's concerted opposition to tariff reductions posed a considerable obstacle to organising a corporatist network to achieve industry restructuring. Moreover, the establishment of a viable industry plan was made doubly difficult because of outspoken opposition to the IAC report from within the governing Labor Party. The National Conference of the party, meeting in Hobart in July 1986, called on the Hawke government to reject the report.[50] Delegates who supported this move were motivated by two considerations: a humanitarian concern for the unemployment effects of tariff reductions, and concern for the threat to Labor's political credibility if massive job losses did occur.[51] Left faction leader and chairman of the caucus industrial committee, Gerry Hand, said bluntly: 'Textile, clothing and footwear workers are Labor's industrial base. They did not elect a Labor government to see themselves thrown to the wolves'.[52]

Hand's position was typical of the traditional position of the Labor Party, its trade union base and the industry, and stood in stark contrast to the economic rationalists, both outside and within the government, who believed that tariff reductions and industry restructuring should happen quickly and with a minimum of government intervention. This view was typified by the head of the National Farmers Federation and new right spokesman, Ian McLachlan, who supported the adoption of a 25 per cent maximum tariff rate, the toughest of the IAC options.[53] Within the government, the Department of the Prime Minister and Cabinet (DPM&C) also took a tough line on tariff reductions, actively seeking a 30 per cent maximum tariff rate for the TCF industries.[54] By contrast, Button and the Department of Industry, Technology and Commerce supported the IAC's preferred option of 50 per cent with generous programs to assist labour adjustment.[55] Whether DPM&C believed the 30 per cent tariff was politically attainable is another issue. Certainly it represented the government's commitment to bringing about significant tariff reductions, and it was an important signal of Australia's intentions to lower trade barriers to its trade partners in the Asia–Pacific region. In addition, it gave Senator Button some ammunition and leverage in negotiating with the industry and unions to produce the TCF plan.

In order to produce a plan that was broadly acceptable to the participants, Button engaged in intensive private consultations with the TCF Industry Council, an industry advisory group headed by the General Manager of the Linter Group, John W. Blood. The Council appointed five working parties to study and report on issues such as potential employment effects of reduced protection. The

TCF Industry Council included representatives from the TCF trade unions, industry associations such as the TCFCA, private companies, retailers, and a senior public servant from the Department of Industry, Technology and Commerce.[56]

The discussions within the TCF Industry Council and its working parties were often difficult. Although the council members agreed in principle on the extent of the industry's problems, there was little consensus on the solutions. The interests of retailers and importers were usually at odds with the desire of unions and industry to retain very high rates of protection. In particular, the manufacturers continued to demonstrate unwillingness to participate in the process, provoking Button to complain about their lack of interest at a TCF industry dinner.[57] Some firms within the industry were also critical of the attitude taken by the peak TCF industry association, the TCF Council of Australia (TCFCA). In a letter to the *Australian Financial Review*, David P. Jones, the managing director of Fletcher Jones, argued that the TCFCA's 'gloom-and-doom advocacy leavened with large dollops of status quo-ism has not been highly effective'.[58] Unlike similar industry councils for the steel and automobile sectors, which had issued reports on future assistance for their industries, the TCF Industry Council did not issue a final report on post-1988 assistance. Instead, the result of the Council's deliberations was conveyed in a private letter from Council chairman John Blood to Button.[59]

Button also engaged in public consultations and factory visits which were frequently stormy. When Button visited Wangaratta, home to thousands of TCF workers, townspeople wore black armbands and left a cardboard coffin outside his motel room.[60] In Sydney and Melbourne, thousands of TCF workers marched in mass demonstrations against tariff reductions. There was a desperate edge to the protests which reflected an immediate concern for loss of livelihood, but also an undercurrent of xenophobia and anger against cheap Asian imports with which Australian industry could not possibly compete. One placard featured a very stout TCF employee saying: 'Asians don't make knickers big enough for me'.[61]

During the course of the consultations, two principal objectives emerged. The first was to reach a mutually acceptable tariff level which would be high enough to prevent the complete eradication of the Australian TCF industry, but low enough to encourage manufacturers to rethink and overhaul their production entirely.

The second was to formulate a package of assistance measures to encourage industry restructuring and to aid labour retraining and readjustment, again striking the balance between short-term government intervention and long-term dependency.

During the negotiations, the president of the Clothing and Allied Trade Unions, Fred Peterson, spearheaded an agreement among the unions, the TCFCA and the ALP to lobby for a heavily modified version of the IAC's preferred option, including an out-of-quota tariff rate of 75 per cent and positive industry and labour adjustment assistance.[62] This decision paved the way for compromise and, ultimately, the establishment of the TCF plan which Button announced in November 1986. The 'stick' in the new plan, which commenced in March 1989, was a reduction in protection through the eventual abolition of quotas (except on some fabrics) and phased tariff reductions to 60 per cent for clothing, 50 per cent for footwear and 45 per cent for fabric by March 1996. In addition, yarn bounty payments were to be rationalised and phased to 30 per cent by 1996.[63] However, in the May 1988 Economic Statement, even before the plan commenced, Button announced that protection for the TCF industries would be scaled down further and faster. Under the revised arrangements, the TCF plan was fast-tracked to end in June 1995, eight months earlier than scheduled, and the new endpoints for tariffs on clothing, footwear and non-quota textiles were each reduced by 5 per cent to 55, 45 and 40 per cent respectively.[64]

The 'carrots' included a labour adjustment scheme and an industry development package. The labour adjustment scheme was far more generous than similar programs which had been devised for workers retrenched from the steel and automotive industries. The adjustment package recognised and took into account the special requirements of TCF workers, many of whom were married migrant women with poor English language skills. Adjustment assistance included income support for language and job retraining; employment assistance in a full-time job *outside* the TCF industries; and, in recognition of the regional concentration of the TCF industries, enhanced relocation allowances including short-term rental assistance.[65] The core of the new plan was the Industries Development Strategy designed to provide incentives for companies to add value by further processing of raw materials in Australia; improve industry efficiency by providing assistance to companies for re-equipment and business planning; upgrade the industries' infrastructure by improving skills, design, and research and development; and increase the industries' export orientation. The total cost of the Industries Development Strategy would be $120 million over the seven year plan.[66]

A statutory corporation, the Textiles, Clothing and Footwear Development Authority (TCFDA), was established to develop, implement and administer the operation of the plan. The TCFDA was responsible for implementing the various programs offered under the Industries Development Strategy and conducting a mid-term review of the plan before 1992. It was also empowered to recommend the suspension of any feature of the plan for up to one year if TCF aggregate production seemed likely to fall by 15 per cent overall (or 10 per cent for textiles and 20 per cent for clothing or footwear). This safeguard was designed by Button to win support for the plan from the ALP Left faction, Labor members from marginal TCF seats, and industry and unions.[67] Throughout the negotiations with industry, Button was also engaged in the delicate political manoeuvrings required to forge and maintain a coaliton of support within the ranks of the Labor Party and government. With so much at stake electorally and for the unions, many key figures including the prime minister were uneasy about forcing change and inclined to favour the softest option.

Some detractors viewed the plan as a political compromise designed with an eye to an upcoming election in which several government seats, including Prime Minister Hawke's electorate of Wills, were directly vulnerable to major changes in the government's TCF policy.[68] And without doubt, political saliency was a key consideration of the Hawke government throughout the formulation and implementation of the TCF plan. More significant, however, was the novel development in the relationship between industry, trade unions and the state entailed in this and other comparable sectoral plans for steel, motor cars and heavy engineering. There is no doubt that the industry plans have been vital in engendering political support for sharply reduced protection in exchange for compensatory adjustment assistance. Nevertheless, a sectoral plan in itself is no guarantee that an industry will successfully restructure to meet the challenge of international competition.

THE TCF PLAN IN ACTION

In the early stages of the plan, protection remained very high. In fact, because of the nature of quota allocation, the effective rate of assistance for clothing and shoes was actually increased in the first year of the plan.[69] In 1989–90, the effective rate of assistance to textiles was 78 per cent and for clothing and shoes, 183 per cent.[70] Although there were a higher than normal number of factory closures, liquidations, receiverships, and retrenchments in 1989–90, the TCF Development Authority claimed that this was due largely to unfavourable economic conditions and a decline in real terms in consumer demand for clothing and footwear, a view vigorously disputed by the the manufacturers through the TCFCA.[71] Despite the TCFCA's claims that the plan had begun to bite in 1990, the TCF Development Authority expected that the real adjustment pressures occurring as a result of tariff reductions would not begin to bear on the industry until late 1991.[72]

There have been a few success stories: the retail chain, Country Road, has opened several stores in the United States, and Textile Industries of Australia performed well in the North American market with its Sheridan sheet range. On the down side, Australia has lost two of its best-known clothing manufacturers, Driza-Bone and Speedo, to British interests. Even more discouraging and ominous than these losses, however, has been the apparent lack of industry interest in the Industries Development Strategy, the core of the government's positive adjustment assistance for the TCF industry.

The Industries Development Strategy has four major components: the Raw Materials Processing Program, the Industries Efficiency Program, the Industries Infrastructure Program, and the Export Development Program. The Raw Materials Processing Program was designed to increase export earnings by encouraging more domestic processing of locally produced wool, cotton, sheepskins and bovine hides, most of which are currently exported in raw or semi-processed state. The TCFDA estimated that Australia could earn $2 billion annually by the year 2000 through the export of woollen and cotton yarns and fabric.[73] To that end, the Australian Industry Development Corporation (AIDC) was granted $27 million to finance the cost of borrowing in order to provide equity investment in raw material processing projects. However, there has been no funding yet approved under the program[74] and the opportunities for further raw material processing remain unexploited.

The Industry Efficiencies Program (IEP) is designed to encourage management and entrepreneurial skills, investment and increased efficiency, export orientation and import replacement and is targeted 'to a limited number of firms with demonstrated high potential to lift their competitiveness to a world class level'.[75] While the IEP has attracted more interest than the Raw Materials Processing Program, its success has been mixed. Of 62 companies that have applied for assistance for export-oriented and import-replacement projects, 42 were rejected. Applicants have been rejected for a number of reasons including failure to supply a satisfactory business plan or audited financial statements, or failure to identify clear targets.[76] The most publicised result of the IEP to date is the purchase of the Australian-owned, synthetic yarn producer, Fibremakers, by the American transnational, E.I. Du Pont de Nemours, in June 1990. This purchase was made possible by the Capitalisation Grants Scheme which enables yarn producers to apply for a one-off grant in lieu of continued bounty payment. Under the scheme, Dupont (Australia) Ltd received nearly $60 million ($36 million after tax) to restructure and invest in the synthetic yarn industry. In return, Du Pont entered into a formal five-year agreement with the government to invest more than $50 million in new technology, skills and product improvement.[77] The proposed restructuring would involve workforce reductions of up to 40 per cent and, in November 1990, Dupont confirmed that retrenchments would begin in 1991.[78]

The third program within the Industries Development Strategy is the Industries Infrastructure Program which provides support to upgrade industry skills and training at both the factory floor and management levels. This program has resulted in considerable research into skills analysis and efficiency indicators. In addition, a Joint Working Party of employers and unions has commenced work on developing new industry award structures.[79]

Finally, the Export Development Program (EDP) financed a TCF unit within the Australian Trade Commission (AUSTRADE) to facilitate TCF exports. This program has also been a mixed success. AUSTRADE has undertaken considerable market research to identify and develop export strategies for the textile and tanning industries and, to a lesser extent, due to their limited export opportunities, for the clothing and footwear industries. However, like the other industry development programs, the EDP is well under budget and program delivery through AUSTRADE has been hampered by a high rate of staff turnover, low morale, and bureaucratic problems within the Trade Commission.

Like their counterparts in the car industry, workers retrenched from the TCF industries have shown very little interest in the government programs to assist labour adjustment assistance offered under the industry plan. The assistance, especially tailored to the needs of TCF workers, includes wage subidies for re-employment outside the TCF sector, income support for language and skills training, and relocation assistance to offset the costs of moving to another area to work outside the TCF sector. They are administered by the Department of Employment, Education and Training through the Office of Labour Market Adjustment. However, of 4,500 TCF retrenchments notified to the Commonwealth Employment Service (CES) in 1989–90, only 280 persons availed themselves of the programs.[80] The low participation rate reflects the fact that many TCF employees are married women with restricted mobility. In addition, the statistics do not account for those retrenched from the TCF industries who remain unemployed for a period and then re-enter the workforce through other CES programs. However, there is also an apparent problem with information and program delivery; the unions complain that both employers and, surprisingly, CES regional offices are often ignorant of the labour adjustment programs.[81]

While it is too early to draw firm conclusions about the potential for structural adjustment within the TCF sector, the first few years of the TCF plan were characterised by a degree of suspicion and rancour among the key players. Part of the problem lay with the TCF Development Authority, the body set up to administer and monitor the progress of the plan. Unlike the Automotive Industry Authority, which developed an excellent relationship with plan producers based on professionalism and confidentiality, the TCFDA has been viewed with a degree of distrust by the manufacturers. In particular, the peak TCF industry association, the TCFCA, found the TCF Development Authority secretive about the various assistance programs and uncooperative in providing guidelines for potential program applicants. On the other hand, many manufacturers were reluctant to provide details about their profitability, investment plans, and similar information which was required by the TCFDA in order to determine a company's eligibility for positive assistance. And, acknowledging its past failure to pursue points of contention with the TCF Development Authority, the TCFCA must also accept responsibility for the rocky start to the TCF plan.[82]

The atmosphere of distrust and scepticism was heightened by the March 1991 Industry Statement in which Senator Button announced major changes to the TCF plan. The government had been disappointed with the progress of the plan, noting in particular that protection remained too high to encourage restructuring in the least efficient areas of the industry and that the sector continued to manifest an overwhelmingly inward orientation. Button was exasperated with the continuing protectionist mind-set of both TCF manufacturers and unions that seemed to be mutually reinforcing. Moreover, some more progressive union officials who were dissatisfied with the lack of progress in industry restructuring were not averse to unilateral government action. Therefore, dispensing with the tripartite discussions which had characterised the Hawke government's approach to industry policy-making, Button decided to revoke the safeguard mechanism and accelerate and extend the tariff reductions so that by the year 2000, the TCF industries would be protected by a tariff-only regime with maximum duty rates of 25 per cent.[83] Although this perpetuated the disparity between protection levels for the TCF industries and the manufacturing sector overall (with the notable exception of the passenger motor vehicle industry), protection for the TCF industries will have been dramatically reduced from the astronomically high levels of the 1980s.

The March Industry Statement was not all pain for the TCF industries. Most importantly, the announcement of assistance levels to the year 2000 gave the industry a reasonably predictable long-term environment in which to make investment decisions. Moreover, in recognition of the poor take-up rate of labour adjustment assistance, the government planned to review those arrangements with a view to making them more attractive to displaced workers. Finally, to encourage exports, the government introduced an Import Credit Scheme which allowed firms which added value to TCF exports (excluding wool, wool tops and cotton ginning) to reduce their tariff duty payments on TCF imports. The credits are transferable so that TCF exporters can sell their import credits to other companies.[84]

While the TCFCA and the main body of unions were unhappy with the government's unilateral action to pre-empt the plan by speeding up the tariff reductions, their criticisms were muted and some at least of the younger officials were privately supportive. Since then, however, the TCF industries have fared badly with continuing recession exacerbating the contraction forced by reducing protection. Membership pressure in the new amalgamated union, the TCF Unions Federation, has forced the leadership to change its tune on tariff cuts. After five years of support for the Labor government's corrective policies, Secretary Anna Booth announced in January 1992 that the unions could no longer support the government's plan, having been reduced to a 'complete state of moral disrepair and collapse'.[85] The situation is indeed grim even for many workers who have not lost their jobs: for example, all Fletcher Jones employees at its Warnambool, Mt Gambier and Brunswick factories have been working 'short weeks' almost equivalent to part time jobs, and there is no job security. With the financial failure of the Linter group and its purchase by the US Sara Lee conglomerate, the union has been frozen out of negotiations with the new owners of the biggest company in the industry.

The TCF Plan has been the least successful, very largely because the TCF industries are the least promising of Australia's manufacturing industries. According to the angry polemics of the TCF companies and unions, their survival in Australia is in jeopardy. According to the executive director of the TCFCA employer organisation, the government is indifferent to its plight: 'The message to industry from the March Statement was basically that we the government, are not interested in you'. He claims this is causing companies to run down their Australian production and move offshore. Industry Minister Button has admitted publicly that the industry is still 'pretty sick', but he remains optimistic that a more streamlined and efficient industry has a future in Australia, particularly in secondary processing, high fashion and major firms in the clothing sector if they develop better relations with retailers based on quick-response production.[86]

Button and the Labor government have kept their nerve in pushing for restructuring through phased reduction of tariff protection despite the political risks. The Wills by-election in April 1992 was a test of the government's resolve. The loss of this blue-ribbon Labor seat, previously held by Prime Minister Hawke, to a left-independent candidate was a sharp reminder to both major parties of the political backlash that tariff reduction plus economic recession can produce. Labor has only maintained its corrective course by insisting that it will retain residual protection whereas the Liberal opposition will abolish tariffs completely.

NOTES

1. These figures do not include outworkers or single establishment enterprises employing fewer than four persons. At the end of the June 1988 quarter, there were 35,400 textile workers, and 75,200 clothing and footwear workers. Australian Bureau of Statistics, *Manufacturing Industry Details of Operations, Australia 1987–88,* Cat. 8203.0.
2. *Age,* 8 February 1989.
3. Australian Bureau of Statistics, *Manufacturing Industry Details of Operations, Australia 1987–88,* Cat. 8203.0.
4. Australian Bureau of Statistics, *Distribution and Composition of Employee Earnings and Hours, Australia,* May 1989, preliminary catalogue 6305.0. These figures represent average weekly earnings excluding overtime pay for full-time non-managerial employees.
5. *Menswear Magazine,* August 1988, p. 8.
6. This figure includes 2,332 clothing and footwear factories and 731 textile factories. Australian Bureau of Statistics, *Manufacturing Industry Details of Operations,* Australia 1987–88, Table 1.
7. The Textiles, Clothing & Footwear Council of Australia Ltd, *Annual Report,* 1988–89.
8. Industries Assistance Commission (IAC), *The Textile, Clothing and Footwear Industries,* May 1986, Appendix H.
9. IAC, *Annual Report 1987,* p. 113.
10. *Age,* 5 November 1986.
11. IAC, *Assistance to Manufacturing Industries in Australia: 1968–69 to 1973–74,* Australian Government Publishing Service, Canberra, 1976, Table 5.2.
12. Textile & Apparel Industry Council, *The Australian Textile and Apparel Industries,* A Report by the Textile & Apparel Industry Council, Australian Government Publishing Service, Canberra, 1980, p. 2.
13. Amalgamated Footwear & Textile Workers' Union of Australia (AFTWUA), Branch Membership Reports, 1973–1990.
14. ibid. These job losses occurred during a period of high unemployment across the economy, however, the sharp decline in the TCF sector was the continuation of a long-term trend which had begun in the 1960s.
15. 'Employment and Social Considerations,' Post-1988 Working Party of the TCF Industry Council, Discussion paper 5, October 1985, pp. 1–2.
16. John Warhurst, *Jobs or Dogma? The Industries Assistance Commission and Australian Politics,* University of Queensland Press, St Lucia, 1982.
17. Interview with Peter Kreitals, Executive Director of the Textiles, Clothing & Footwear Council of Australia, 11 June 1991.
18. 'Employment and Social Considerations', p. 2.
19. OECD (Organisation for Economic Cooperation & Development), *Structural Problems of the Textile and Clothing Industry,* Paris, 1977.

20. Michael Trebilcock, *The Political Economy of Economic Adjustment: the Case of Declining Sectors,* University of Toronto Press, Toronto, 1986, pp. 149–58.
21. ibid., pp. 192–8.
22. For a fine study of Canada's textile policy from a Marxist perspective see Rianne Mahon, *The Politics of Industrial Restructuring: Canadian Textiles,* University of Toronto Press, Toronto, 1984.
23. Trebilcock, *The Political Economy of Economic Adjustment,* p. 75.
24. ibid., pp. 233–6.
25. IAC, *Draft Report on Textiles, Clothing and Footwear,* August, 1977, Part A, p. 1.
26. *White Paper on Manufacturing Industry,* May 1977, Parliamentary Paper 116/1977, pp. 24–6.
27. IAC, *Report on the Textile, Clothing and Footwear Industries,* Report 240, Australian Government Publishing Service, Canberra, 1980.
28. One example of literature from this effective campaign was a glossy brochure published by the peak industry association, the Textiles, Clothing & Footwear Council of Australia, entitled '120,000 Jobs on the Line: Why Australia Must Maintain its Textile, Clothing and Footwear Industries', Melbourne, 1980.
29. *Australian Financial Review,* 9 July 1986.
30. Textiles, Clothing & Footwear Advisory Committee (TCFAC), *Fifth Report,* May 1983, Australian Government Publishing Service, Canberra, 1983.
31. Details of the plan are contained in a statement by Phillip Lynch & R. V. Garland, 15 August 1980, *Commonwealth Record,* Vol. 5, No. 32. To provide advice on adjustments to quota levels, the Textiles, Clothing & Footwear Advisory Committee (TCFAC) was established comprising an independent chairman and senior officials from the Departments of Industry & Commerce and Business & Consumer Affairs. The TCFAC was required to monitor market conditions and employment levels and recommend to the departmental ministers any appropriate changes in quota levels.
32. Interview with David McCarthy, Chief Executive of the Textiles, Clothing & Footwear Development Authority, Melbourne, 7 November 1990.
33. TCFAC, *Eighth Report,* December 1984, Australian Government Publishing Service, Canberra, 1984.
34. IAC, *The Textile, Clothing and Footwear Industries,* Report 386, 19 May 1986, Appendix H.
35. ibid, Appendix A.
36. IAC, *The Textile, Clothing and Footwear Industries,* Report 386, 19 May 1986, Appendix H.
37. ibid., Appendix V and volume 1, p. xvi.
38. ibid., volume 1, p. xviii.

39. ibid., volume 1, p. xxiii.
40. *Australian Financial Review*, 12 June 1986
41. *Australian Financial Review*, 26 June 1986, 9 and 16 July 1986. After the TCF plan was in place, some manufacturers began to act on their earlier threats. In particular, several Sydney manufacturers of men's shirts and suits moved their operations offshore to low wage Fiji.
42. During the IAC inquiry, Fletcher Jones had embarrassed the other manufacturers by backing the 50 per cent option. Levi-Strauss, which had a well-established market niche and plenty of support from its US parent, was also happy to live with the tariff cuts.
43. Launceston *Examiner*, 8 August 1986.
44. *Age*, 13 September 1986.
45. *Age*, 18 June 1986.
46. Launceston *Examiner*, 17 October 1986.
47. *Age*, 18 June 1986.
48. *Australian Financial Review*, 16 July 1986.
49. Michael M. Atkinson & William D. Coleman, 'Strong States and weak States: sectoral policy networks in advanced capitalist economies,' *British Journal of Political Science*, Vol. 19, No. 1, 1989, p. 64.
50. ALP, 37th Biennial National Conference, 7–11 July 1986, *Proceedings*, pp. 170–92. The resolution to oppose the IAC report was supported by both right-wing and left-wing union leaders. It was proposed by New South Wales state secretary of the Amalgamated Metal Workers Union John MacBean, and by his Victorian counterpart John Halfpenny.
51. Unions, like the manufacturers, were quick to warn Labor parliamentarians with TCF industries in their electorates of the potential electoral consequences of factory closures and retrenchments. Interview with Brian Broomhall, Assistant National Secretary of the Amalgamated Footwear & Textile Workers Union of Australia, Melbourne, 8 November 1990.
52. *Age*, 20 October 1986.
53. *Australian*, 18 July 1986.
54. *National Times on Sunday*, 19 October 1986.
55. *Australian Financial Review*, 23 September 1986 and *Age*, 13 October 1986.
56. Australian Manufacturing Council (AMC), *Annual Report, 1986–87*, Australian Government Publishing Service, Canberra, 1987, pp. 40–41.
57. *Age*, 16 October 1986.
58. *Australian Financial Review*, 20 October 1986.
59. Brian Broomhall recalled that many of the Industry Council participants including the unions did not want to be associated with comments made by Blood, hence the absence of a published report. Broomhall Interview, 8 November 1990.
60. *Weekend Australian*, 15–16 November 1986.

61. *National Times on Sunday*, 29 October 1986.
62. *Examiner*, 8 August 1986.
63. 'Revitalising Australia's Textile, Clothing and Footwear Industries', News Release 166/86 by the Minister for Industry, Technology & Commerce, 28 November, 1986.
64. Statement to Parliament by the Minister for Industry, Technology & Commerce, 25 May 1988.
65. ibid.
66. Textiles, Clothing & Footwear Development Authority (TCFDA), *Annual Report 1988–89*, Australian Government Publishing Service, Canberra, 1989, pp. 16–31.
67. McCarthy Interview, 7 November 1990.
68. *Australian Financial Review*, 27 November 1987.
69. This apparent anomaly will cease in 1992 when base quota is abolished and all quota is put out to tender.
70. IAC, *Annual Report 1989–90*, Australian Government Publishing Service, Canberra, 1990, pp. 176–7.
71. Kreitals interview, 11 June 1991.
72. TCFDA, *State of the Industry Report 1990*, Australian Government Publishing Service, Canberra, 1990, pp. 2–3.
73. TCFDA, *Annual Report 1988–89*, p. 17.
74. TCFDA, *Annual Report 1989–90*, p. 4.
75. Minister for Industry, Technology & Commerce, 'Revitalising Australia's Textile, Clothing and Footwear Industries,' News Release 166/86, 28 November 1986. This is commonly known as 'picking winners' although critics note than it frequently results in 'backing losers'.
76. TCFDA, *Annual Report 1989–90*, p. 6.
77. *Australian Financial Review*, 21 June 1990 and *Age*, 21 June 1990.
78. *Age*, 8 November 1990.
79. TCFDA, *Annual Report 1989–90*, pp. 8–10.
80. ibid., p. 17.
81. Broomhall interview.
82. Kreitals interview.
83. Statement by Senator John N. Button, in *Building a Competitive Australia*, 12 March 1991 (Canberra, 1991).
84. The Import Credit Scheme is operated on the same principle as the Export Facilitation Scheme for the car industry; its nomenclature was chosen to fend off criticism that the TCF import credits are an export subsidy by another name.
85. Quoted by Sue Neales, 'Clothing industry model no longer suits', *Australian Financial Review*, 9 January 1992.
86. Sue Neales, 'TCF Sector facing a threadbare future', *Australian Financial Review*, 9 January 1992.

CHAPTER 8

Beyond the Protective State

Entering the last decade of the twentieth century, Australians were engaged in a national debate over an appropriate industry policy, the terms of which indicated just how far informed public opinion had moved beyond protectionism. In favour of deregulation were most economists and senior bureaucrats in influential public bodies such as the Industry Commission and the central agencies (the Departments of Treasury, Finance, and Prime Minister and Cabinet). In fact, 'economic rationalism' now pervades the senior Commonwealth public service.[1] The direction of public debate and political purpose in Australia has shifted decisively in favour of a 'level playing field' with leading ministers and shadow ministers on both sides of politics favouring deregulation and market solutions. This new orthodoxy was encapsulated in the influential Garnaut Report, commissioned by the Hawke government from an eminent free-market economist and presented in 1989. Garnaut argued that the only appropriate industry policy for Australia was free trade and recommended the phasing out of all tariffs by the year 2000.[2]

Alternative views supporting a more extensive role for government were also put forward but lacked coherency or crucial political support. The trade union leadership and its sympathisers at first advanced, rather wishfully, an idealised Swedish model of democratic corporatism in the 1987 document *Australia Reconstructed*.[3] The ACTU subsequently put forward a more pragmatic policy document that was broadly supportive of a somewhat more interventionist approach to industry strategy. In similar vein, the Australian Manufacturing Council weighed in with a moderate case for some state intervention in the market and the selective facilitation of industry in a major report released in 1990.[4] The alternative to the free market being proposed was not a return to traditional protectionism but limited government intervention of various kinds.

The final decision taken by cabinet and announced by Prime Minister Hawke in March 1991, however, came down on the side of the political 'dries' and economic rationalists. The Hawke government reaffirmed its commitment to tariff reduction, adopting the goal of moving by steps to 5 per cent nominal rates by the turn of the century and accelerating the special rates of reduction for the intractable textiles, clothing and footwear industries. There was virtually nothing in the March 1991 industry policy statement to console the so-called 'new Keynesians' and 'new protectionists' who favour greater state intervention and support.

At the end of 1991, with Australia in deep recession, the Labor government was again forced to review its policy direction. By this time, tariff reductions combined with the overall retraction of the economy were producing extensive job losses, particularly in the textiles, clothing and footwear industries. The Hawke government without Keating, who withdrew to the back bench after his first unsuccessful bid for the leadership, was lack-lustre and indecisive against an opposition buoyed up by the public response to its ambitious 'Fightback' package released in November.[5] Keating mounted a second challenge in December 1991 and this time was successful. On becoming prime minister, he reshuffled the government's front bench, appointing John Dawkins as Treasurer, and led a team of senior ministers in a round of consultations with state, business and union leaders in preparation for a major economic statement.

By now there was a broad support for stimulating the economy, with industry leaders and banks calling for up to $2 billion additional government spending. Keating's 'One Nation' statement delivered in February 1992 did precisely that, boosting government investment in major infrastructure projects and encouraging private investment by accelerated depreciation allowances.[6] While such stimulation was something of a departure from the government's austere course during the previous few years, its stance on phasing out protection remained unchanged. According to the 'One Nation' statement, the continuing reduction in tariff protection and non-tariff barriers was one of the most important that the government had taken in internationalising the Australian economy and would be adhered to. Nevertheless, in a desperate but futile bid to hold the seat of Wills, Keating championed the advantages of a minimal tariff over the Opposition's policy of total abolition.

The divide between the two major parties has been sharpest in the area of industrial relations where, despite its deregulatory stance on exchange rates and dismantling of protection for industry, the Labor government remained committed to centralised national wage-fixing. That was for obvious political reasons: the Labor Party's general need to preserve its power base in the trade unions and, more particularly, to protect the Accord. The Accord was central to much of Labor's economic policy since it enabled the government to restrain wages without massive industrial backlash. Senior Labor ministers negotiated periodic national wages deals with the ACTU which restricted wage increases partly in return for 'social wage' trade-offs such as universal health care and superannuation benefits. Until 1991, these government–union agreements were endorsed and readily implemented by the Industrial Relations Commission (IRC) through the centralised wage-fixing system.

The IRC had been restructured by the Hawke government in 1988, but not fundamentally changed as an independent statutory body. It worked in tandem with the Accord process both in curbing wage increases and promoting enhanced labour productivity through the so-called 'Structural Efficiency Principle' adopted in the 1988 National Wage Case.[7] Although the IRC was becoming increasingly anomalous for a deregulated Australia and a considerable constraint on flexible adjustment, the Hawke government remained committed to this bulwark of traditional Australian political economy because it had little choice politically, and had no alternative social policy for ensuring broad distributional equity that wage fixing traditionally took care of.

By 1990, however, the pressures from strong unions to break out of the Accord strait-jacket, which had delivered real wage cuts, were accommodated in the revised Accord Mark VI by including a component of modified enterprise bargaining. As well as enabling stronger unions to win better increases within a revised Accord, the Labor government's partial acceptance of enterprise bargaining was likely to neutralise the Liberal opposition's strident criticism of continued centralised wage fixing.

The government's opportunism in abandoning in part the substance of centralised wage-fixing while wanting to retain its traditional form was rejected by the IRC in the crucial April 1991 National Wage Case. The IRC based its decision on a range of reasons including its assessment of the immaturity of the parties in

Australia for more decentralised wage settlements, lack of agreement, particularly from the employers' side, on what would be entailed in enterprise bargaining, and a concern for the likely durability of such a system. 'Fundamental deficiencies in the system would, in all probability,' the IRC warned, 'cause industrial disputation and excessive wage outcomes, leading to the system's collapse.'[8] Critics of the IRC's decision interpreted it as having been at least partly motivated by institutional self-interest: if the IRC sanctioned the move towards enterprise bargaining, its own role would be diminished to that of ratifying specific agreements and maintaining some minimal wage standard rather than determining national wage levels across the board.

In turn, the government and ACTU repudiated the IRC decision and undertook to go ahead and implement the Accord Mark VI. Keating, then Treasurer, stated unequivocally: 'I disagree with the decision and I disagree most strongly with the conservatism of the commission that has clung to the pre-eminent role of the national wage case awarding increases and postponing the introduction of a more flexible system of enterprise bargaining.'[9] ACTU Secretary Bill Kelty used more colourful language, likening Australia's centralised system to that of Cuba, and the Commission chairman, Justice Barry Maddern, to Fidel Castro. Kelty asserted that the ACTU had 'accepted, unlike the commission, that it is important to devolve responsibility in wages to a far greater extent to unions and workers'.[10] The federal Labor government and unions proceeded to reach Accord Mark VI type agreements outside the National Wage Case principles for Commonwealth public servants, the building industry and the waterfront, and put them to the IRC for formal ratification. The IRC had put itself into an untenable position of having to back down or be bypassed by a determined government, with one senior minister, Ralph Willis, threatening 'a much reduced role for the commission' if it did not fall into line.[11]

Not surprisingly, the IRC reopened the issue of enterprise bargaining to argument and, in a national wage decision handed down at the end of October 1991, reversed its earlier decision. This time it sanctioned a new enterprise bargaining principle which allowed further wage rises to be negotiated between unions and employers in return for improved productivity at the enterprise level. The IRC set out a list of criteria that had to be met before enterprise agreements could be ratified under the Industrial Relations Act, including the stipulation that there be no reductions in workers' ordinary-time earnings or departures from IRC standard hours and leave entitlements. ACTU spokesman Bill Kelty welcomed the decision as being 'one of integrity which provides a truly flexible wages system, placing more onus on the parties but with the commission exercising general guidelines'.[12]

If the IRC was bullied into changing its mind by a determined Labor government, it can derive little comfort from the other side of politics because national wage-fixing has been targeted by the Liberal coalition for deregulation should it win office at the next general election. Given its anomalous character in an otherwise deregulated national economy, centralised fixing of national wages seems unlikely to survive through the 1990s regardless of which party is in office. If there is a change of government, wage fixing, compulsory unionism and closed shops are likely to become the battleground of national industry policy for the mid-1990s as a reformist Liberal coalition government, unsympathetic to labour unions, forces the pace on deregulating wages.

Another major area of Australian political economy which is coming under increasing critical scrutiny from both sides of politics is the public ownership and provision of infrastructure and services. Traditionally, the state in Australia served as 'a vast public utility' providing a plethora of services to citizens and businesses. This system of public enterprise was variously described as 'state socialism' and 'socialism without doctrine' when the extent and scale of such public enterprise seemed to distinguish Australia and New Zealand from other capitalist countries earlier this century. As banking, airlines and telecommunications were added to railways, roads, electricity and water, the scope and size of the public sector grew as Australia became less distinctive in the post-war era of big government. But the new orthodoxies of economic rationalism and managerialism favour the privatisation or, if that is not feasible, the corporatisation of public suppliers of services so that they approximate private corporate practice.

Under the Labor government, this process has been rather sporadic and *ad hoc* because of the Labor movement's traditional commitment to public enterprise and the entrenched power of public sector unions. Even so, the Hawke and Keating governments have made considerable inroads into the substance, as well as the symbolic heartland, of Australian public enterprise. Most notably, the Commonwealth

Bank, the flagship of successful government enterprise, was partly privatised in 1991 as the *quid pro quo* for rescuing the Victorian State Bank from bankruptcy - a lesser evil for the left-dominated but hard-pressed Victorian Labor government. In the key growth area of telecommunications, the established monopolies of Telecom and OTC are to be checked by licensing a private competitor.

In this vein, micro-economic reform of public infrastructure and services became the catchcry of the Labor government and its critics in 1990–91. Having exaggerated the significance of micro-economic reform - that is, making the rambling public utility, transport and infrastructure services that are riddled with inefficiencies and restrictive work practices more efficient, and streamlining regulatory regimes of the Commonwealth and the states - the Hawke government was pressed to deliver. But reforming the myriad of government enterprises and services has proved much more difficult than scaling down tariffs. This has been due in part to Labor's statist traditions, its party base in trade unionism and, increasingly, in the public sector unions, and the need to preserve the Accord.

Besides these constraints from within its own jurisdiction and party base, however, the federal Labor government has also come up against the fact of Australia's federal system which reserves large fields of jurisdiction to the states. In the provision of public services and infrastructure, the states remain bigger players than the Commonwealth. Hence, the Hawke government's push for micro-economic reform in 1990 led, naturally enough, to an ambitious attempt at 'Closer Partnership with the States'. Hawke's 'New Federalism' was launched in July 1990 to improve the efficiency of Australia's federal system by streamlining intergovernmental relations and removing overlap and duplication in the provision of public services.[13] The first of a series of Special Premiers Conferences was held in Brisbane in late 1990 and a framework agreed upon for reviewing major policy areas and regulatory regimes, trading enterprises including the provision of public infrastructure, and most notably electricity and rail, the environment and industrial relations. The communiqué from that conference emphasised that the strong motivation for the exercise was economically based: creating 'a more efficient public sector' in order to 'make Australia's economy more competitive and flexible'.[14]

Improving national efficiency and international competitiveness, which was essentially the Commonwealth's purpose, drove Hawke's

New Federalism. This was apparent in the agenda of joint Commonwealth and state working parties and committees, and in the rhetoric of the communiqués and working documents. A second Special Premiers Conference in July 1991 concluded agreement on a range of reforms, mainly in the micro-economic areas of national standards and rationalisation of public services provided by the states. These included agreements on the following: mutual recognition of regulations and standards governing both traded goods and occupations; a national scheme for heavy vehicle registration and road-use charges to be overseen by a National Road Transport Commission; establishment of a National Rail Corporation as a commercial body owned jointly by the Commonwealth and the states (except Queensland and South Australia which nevertheless supported the proposal); coordination of the electricity industry in the eastern and southern states through a National Grid Management Council; establishing a framework and standard indicators for national performance monitoring of Government Trading Enterprises; and working towards an intergovernmental agreement on the environment including the possible establishment of a national Environment Protection Agency to help secure effective arrangements for setting of standards and implementation.[15] This conference also endorsed the commitment to a national system of food standards administered by the National Food Authority that had been agreed to in the earlier conference and was to commence operation in August.[16]

Despite such notable achievements, Hawke's New Federalism was derailed by Keating's leadership challenge. Having failed to oust Hawke in his first attempt, Keating waited on the back bench for a second chance to pounce. This was provided by growing disquiet among ministers and the federal Labor caucus over proposals to untie policy conditions attaching to major Commonwealth grants and return some share of income taxing power to the states. In a spirited National Press Club address, Keating blasted such undertakings which the prime minister had given to win state cooperation and criticised the bureaucratic and secretive nature of the process.[17] Hawke was pressured to back down on his undertakings to the premiers, and they in turn announced a collective boycott of the November Special Premiers Conference. Instead, the premiers held a states-only conference in November but, despite putting on a brave face, failed to get the process back on the rails. Within a month,

Keating's second challenge was successful as Hawke's cabinet minus Keating floundered in the wave of public enthusiasm which greeted release of the Liberals' 'Fightback' package. Keating's accession to the prime ministership pushed New Federalism off the federal government's agenda, although state premiers remain anxious to keep it alive.

To sum up then, the current debate on, and plausible political options for, national industry policy in Australia have moved beyond the protective state. Tariffs, the mainstay of protectionism, are being systematically reduced and will be virtually abolished for all but a few sectors by the turn of the century. National wage-fixing, the supplementary pillar of Australia's protective political economy, is under threat. At the very least, it will be moderated by enterprise bargaining if Labor remains in federal office, but, more likely, under a Liberal coalition government will be demolished. The state as a vast public utility providing services and infrastructure is being cut back and streamlined by privatisation and corporatisation according to the new orthodoxies of economic rationalism and managerialism. Through New Federalism initiatives, there are efforts, albeit presently stalled, to extend the process of micro-economic reform to the states.

While much has changed in the 1980s in going beyond protection, the role of state action and the precise shape of industry policy in the 1990s will depend on the contingencies of political and economic developments, as was the case in the 1980s. We have identified two broad options represented by the major political parties: on the one hand, a further levelling of the playing field and greater reliance on market mechanisms advocated by the Liberals, with the proviso that pressures of government invariably force some moderation of programs devised in opposition; and, on the other hand, somewhat greater reliance upon government intervention through sectoral industry plans and part retention of centralised wage-fixing. While the differences between the two sides should not be overstated, especially given the bipartisan agreement on reducing tariff protection and restricting the role of government overall, the differences are nevertheless greater than in the decades of grand political consensus when protectionism was a settled national policy.

Nor can we be certain that the political system, together with the established state institutions and bureaucracy, will be capable of devising an appropriate state role and industry policy for Australia in the future, regardless of which party is in office. Neither party has an adequate strategy for domestic compensation on the scale that will likely be required with a more open national economy and a volatile and perhaps more restrictive world economy. The inevitable by-product of carrying forward the restructuring of Australian manufacturing to produce more competitive and export-oriented industries will be continuing job losses in sectors such as textiles, clothing and footwear and regional decline in areas dependent on protected industries. This is already becoming apparent. Areas worst hit by the current recession are those which have had the most highly protected industries, such as the Victorian regional cities of Geelong, Ballarat and Warrnambool, as well as the inner industrial areas of most capital cities, but especially Melbourne and Adelaide. Detailed studies by the Office of Local Government and DEET show that regions that have relied heavily on protection are the least likely to bounce back from recession without direct government aid.[18]

Moreover, a likely consequence of running an open and export-oriented manufacturing sector, given the volatility of world markets and the speed of technological innovation, will be periodic industrial dislocation. The obvious need, therefore, which has not yet been seriously addressed in Australia, is for a complementary politics of domestic compensation. Without some national system for compensating losers and facilitating structural adjustment, either the politics of deregulation will be challenged as they were in the Wills by-election or the consequences will become quite tragic for many Australians.

One thing is certain from our study: if Australia fails to develop a new national political economy with institutions and policies capable of balancing the gains from a more open economy with the losses that impact unevenly on people and regions, it will constitute a failure of political will and creativity in policy development and institutional design, and not of basic governability. This is a key point and an appropriate one on which to conclude this book. Our purpose in the book has been to explain how Australians first created and then, in the 1980s, began deliberately and systematically to demolish their protective state. Our study shows the real autonomy and strength of the state in forging and then undoing major national policies of protectionism. The challenge facing Australia in the 1990s is to develop a suitable role for the state and national policies which are appropriate for our new political economy beyond protection.

NOTES

1. Michael Pusey, *Economic Rationalism in Canberra: a Nation-building State Changes its Mind,* Cambridge University Press, Sydney, 1991.
2. Ross Garnaut, *Australia and Northeast Asian Ascendancy: Report to the Prime Minister and the Minister for Foreign Affairs,* Australian Government Publishing Service, Canberra, 1989.
3. ACTU/TDU, *Australia Reconstructed ACTU/TDU Mission to Western Europe,* Australian Government Publishing Service, Canberra, 1987. It should be noted that Sweden has now decided to join the European Community and this, combined with efforts to throw off its present economic malaise, will erode the distinctive Swedish model that has been so much admired by the left in other countries. See Don Rawson, 'Swedish wage policy and Australia: three years after "Australia Reconstructed"', *Australian Journal of Political Science* 26, 1991, pp. 95–110.
4. Australian Manufacturing Council, *The Global Challenge: Australian Manufacturing in the 1990s, Final Report of the Study by Pappas, Carter, Evans & Koop/Telesis,* Australian Manufacturing Council, Melbourne, 1990.
5. *Fightback: the way to rebuild and reward Australia,* Liberal Party of Australia, Canberra, 1991.
6. *One Nation,* Statement by the Prime Minister, the Hon. P. J. Keating, Australian Government Publishing Service, Canberra, 1992.
7. Australian Industrial Relations Commission, *National Wage Case,* August 1988, Print H 4000, pp. 5–6.
8. Australian Industrial Relations Commission, *National Wage Case,* April 1991, Print J 7400, p. 39.
9. Quoted *Australian,* 17 April 1991, p. 4.
10. Quoted *Australian Financial Review,* 24 April, 1991, p. 14.
11. Quoted *Canberra Times,* 20 May 1991, p. 3.
12. *Australian Financial Review,* 31 October 1991.
13. Robert J. Hawke, 'Towards a Closer Partnership', Speech to the National Press Club, Canberra, 19 July 1990.
14. Communiqué, Special Premiers Conference, Brisbane, 30–31 October 1990, Towards a Closer Partnership.
15. Special Premiers Conference, Communiqué, Sydney, 30 July 1991.
16. Special Items in the October 1990 Special Premiers Conference Communiqué, Attachment 4 [2 December 1991].
17. Paul Keating, 'The Commonwealth and the States and the November Special Premiers Conference', National Press Club address, Canberra, 22 October 1991.
18. Reported in the *Australian,* 21 January 1992.

Index